REAL
FOOD

FOR A CHANGE

REAL
FOOD
FOR A CHANGE

WAYNE ROBERTS, ROD MACRAE
AND LORI STAHLBRAND

RANDOM HOUSE OF CANADA

Canadian Cataloguing in Publication Data

Roberts, Wayne, 1944-
 Real food for a change

ISBN 0-679-30973-X

1. Food. 2. Nutrition. I. MacRae, Roderick, John. II. Stahlbrand, Lori.
III. Title.

TX353.R627 1999   641.3   C98-932545-8

Cover and interior design: Eva Kiss

Printed and bound in Canada.

10 9 8 7 6 5 4 3 2 1

Dedicated to our parents

Dave and Dorothy Roberts
Herb and Mary MacRae
Gordon and Mary Stahlbrand

CONTENTS

ACKNOWLEDGEMENTS

A lot of people got us through this project, giving us constant reminders of a central theme in this book: the dynamic relationship between Real Food and Real Friends. Many people introduced us to new ways of thinking about food: Debbie Field, Stuart Hill, Brewster Kneen and the members of the Toronto Food Policy Council, among others. Cover designer and layout artist Eva Kiss stuck by us through thick and thin, pinch-hitting with child care, helping us edit, dropping by with steaming coffee at just the right moment. Wally Seccombe showed support early on, providing the money to get us started. Herb and Mary MacRae, Anne MacRae and Steve Estey, Jennifer Welsh and Julie Couch also confirmed our faith in the Entrepreneurial Bank of FFA—friends, family and associates—in the early stages when we thought we'd have to self-publish.

Just as we ran through the loans, friend and business writer Jim Harris opened the door to his literary agents, Robert Mackwood and Perry Goldsmith of Contemporary Communications. They connected us with Sarah Davies at Random House of Canada, who championed the book, and then guided the manuscript through to completion with care and passion. As luck would have it, Random House is not only the country's most successful publisher, but is also brimming with Real Food enthusiasts. It has been a treat to lose our prejudices about mainstream publishers and to work with the wonderful team that Random House offers.

Random House solved our problems of paying printers and distributors, but gave us a tight deadline. We couldn't have burned the midnight oil without the friends and family members who came to our aid: Sandi Stahlbrand and Richard Ellis, Eva Leach, Jane Upham, Penelope Laycock, Marilyn Whidden, and the parents at Beaches Alternative School, who helped with child care; Michael Berger, who kept the Coalition for a Green Economic Recovery going while Wayne was out of commission, and offered his cottage for isolated writing away from the blistering heat of Toronto; our chiropractor, Johanna Carlo, who kept us from keeling over; the folks at Mersini, our favourite café on Toronto's Beaches strip, who kept us plied with hot drinks and home cooking during the endless hours of meetings and writing that took place there; Wayne's daughter Jaime, who helped organize boxes of loose clippings into files we could use; and Lori and Wayne's six-year-old daughter Anika, who showed patience far beyond her years, but has determined that she doesn't want to be a writer when she grows up, because "there are too many deadlines."

Life doesn't stop for a book. Rod got married, bought a house, nurtured one child and fathered another, knowing he had loving support and appreciation for delayed gratification on the home front from Kate and Lena. His extended family, co-workers at the Food Policy Council, friends and golfing mates still call, glad to know the book didn't do him in, and waiting for a dinner invitation.

Unfortunately, death doesn't stop for a book either. Wayne's father died of prostate cancer in June of 1998. John Ford, Liz Jansen, Heino Nielsen, Shannon Thompson and others came through with emotional support and practical help during an incredibly difficult time.

The emphasis we give in this book to family meals and warm sociability around food comes from the privilege we enjoyed, growing up in homes where meals were special times. Lori's parents in Montreal started following many of the healthy eating practices we discuss way back in the 1950s. Rod's parents in Nova Scotia had careers in the field of food and agriculture, and inspired him to follow in their footsteps. Wayne's parents in Toronto, lifelong happy warriors for social justice, made daily meals a time of great fun and political conversation. It is an honour to be able to dedicate this book to them.

INTRODUCTION

REAL FOOD:
THE MISSING INGREDIENT

Since you're reading this book, you must already have a sense that something is missing from your food. It's not in any of North America's major food groups—sugar, salt, grease and caffeine. It's not in the pill-popper guides to supernutrients. It's not in the miracle diets that promise to take off thirty pounds in thirty days. We call this missing ingredient Real Food. This book will show you how to find it and enjoy it.

At its most basic, Real Food is fresh, local food grown without toxic chemicals and processed without harmful additives. But it's more than just what you put in your mouth. It's about health at a fundamental level: health that stems from quality food low in cholesterol and high in complex carbohydrates to be sure, but also health that comes from simpler lifestyles and richer relationships that let food keep body and soul together. It's an innovative approach to buying, cooking and savouring food, an approach that can be the basis for a new life ethic.

The concept of Real Food also involves an awareness of the personal, social and economic consequences of food choices. The link between what you eat and your personal health is pretty straightforward; but what you buy and eat has just as much impact on the health of your community, and even of the planet. It plays a role in determining what stress you're under, what taxes you pay and what future your children will have. Real Food is the link between your food and four key elements: health, joy, justice and nature.

Real Food is a hot topic, because everyone knows something scary is happening to our food supply. Most people have heard snippets about the six thousand versions of chemicals sprayed on food, the drugs and hormones fed to livestock, the seeds being concocted in corporate labs. Most people know someone who has been sick from salmonella poisoning or hamburger disease, or who has developed a sensitivity or allergy to a common food. If worry led you to pick up this book, we'll do our best to make sure that positive energy keeps you from putting it down.

This book pulls together the alarming details of what goes into most of the food we eat, and exposes government and industry silence on this critical information that the public has a right to know. This book also offers solutions—fresh, practical, step-by-step and positive solutions that individuals, neighbours and community groups can act on in the here and now. We'll show you how to use the power of positive eating to create a Real Food Revolution. It's simpler and more satisfying than you may think.

THE ELEMENTS OF REAL FOOD

Health

The first dimension of Real Food is health. Real Food is for people who want to find health at the kitchen table, not on the operating table. The proposition to let "food be your medicine and medicine your food" goes back to ancient Greece. Hippocrates, the founder of Western medicine, put it at the centre of his teaching. His wisdom has been confirmed many times over. Before this century, once-common diseases such as scurvy, pellagra and rickets were cured as soon as nutritional deficiencies were understood and remedied. We now know that many of the "diseases of civilization" that plague us—cancer, heart disease and diabetes among them—can result from bad diets.[1] The U.S. Surgeon General's landmark 1988 *Report on Nutrition and Health* concluded that up to 71 per cent of deaths, including one-third of cancer deaths, are related to diet.[2] Elaborating on the cancer connection, the World Cancer Research Fund recently concluded that "at least 20 percent of lung cancers, 33 percent of breast cancers, and 66 percent of colon cancers are preventable by appropriate diets, together with the associated factors of regular physical activity and maintenance of healthy body weight."[3] Even when germs are the immediate cause of a disease, we are more susceptible when our immune systems are weakened by malnutrition or overburdened with food contaminants. It's as simple as the colds you get when you're run down, as tragic as the rate of tuberculosis among the homeless.

In the popular mind, especially among older generations, sickness and disease come from the inadequacy of the body. That's why we go to the doctor to get our parts fixed. It is also why the medical profession generally pays better than farming and food preparation, and why health care consumes a whopping 10 percent of Canada's GNP, not counting pills and drugs. The medical establishment buys into the myth that elevates doctors above nature and food. Until a decade ago it was almost unheard of for doctors to receive much training in nutrition; it was regarded as amateur and inconsequential stuff, safely left to public health staff. The quality of hospital food speaks for itself. In addition, hospital incinerators are a leading industrial source of deadly dioxin pollution, which contaminates the entire food chain.[4] This is an industry that gets to create its own customers.

This medicalized mind-set also determines public policy, which rarely treats food as key to maintaining health. No jurisdiction in North America spends more than 1 percent of its health budget on food-based disease prevention.[5] It's acceptable for governments to finance doctors, drugs and hospitals, but not food. This is why medicare is a sick care system, not a health care system.

The health benefits of food are not championed by the mainstream food industry either. One would think it would be out there competing for its share of public health dollars, but major players in the prepared food industry made their fortunes in tobacco, booze and pop. Kraft, for instance, is owned by tobacco giant Philip Morris. Likewise, supermarket owners work both sides of the ill-health aisle: on one side are foods with fibre and key nutrients removed so that the food can stay on the shelf longer; on the other side are laxatives and antacids.

Real Food, by contrast, puts the healthfulness of food at the centre of personal and public health policy.

Joy

The second element of Real Food is joy. Think of how a sense
of celebration can turn even the simplest meal into a feast.
Any camper who's revelled in the taste of beans and potatoes
baked over a smoky fire knows that taste owes as much to circum-
stances and camaraderie as to fancy ingredients and method of
cooking.

It takes time to enjoy food. Joyful eating is not a luxury but
a necessity. Chewing and swallowing slowly, pausing to savour, to
chat, to laugh, to compliment the cook, is critical to effective
digestion. That's the effortless way to watch calories. Slow eating
gives the brain's hunger thermostat the delay it needs so it can turn
off at the proper time. But making the time for enjoyment is a challenge. Time is the one thing we never seem to have enough of.
Unless we make time work for us instead of against us, we'll never
get past the microwaveable instant entrée for dinner or the fat- and
sugar-laden cereal bar for breakfast, gobbled down in the car on the
way to work.

As a flavour enhancer, joy is a powerful equalizer. It costs nothing,
is not in short supply and cannot be monopolized. And company
adds to the joy of a meal. The word *company*, like *companion*,
comes from the Latin word for sharing bread. This reflected
a shrewd understanding of what economists now call "social
capital." Social capital is not something that can be seen or quanti-
fied, but it makes a lot of things go round. It is the invisible but
powerful force that makes things happen just because people are
people. Social capital is neighbours taking out the garbage or shovelling the sidewalk for an infirm senior so he doesn't have to be put
in an institution. It's moms pitching in so an emergency doesn't
become a crisis. It's community potlucks where local businesses
get hatched. Social capital is the democratic version of "it's not
what you know, it's who you know." Social capital opens doors
wherever trust, cooperation and connection count. But it doesn't
just drop from the sky; it's offered on a platter. Breaking bread is
how most groups develop their social capital. So kids who pick up
their social skills at the dinner table instead of on the street have
been given a bigger head start than those who spent a month at a
fancy computer camp.

Putting joy at the centre of meals pays tribute to the fact that food—like love, sex, friendship, spirituality and art—is about human relationships, and is defiled when commercial calculations take over. Yet we've allowed food production, distribution, preparation and consumption to be treated as entirely commercial propositions. Real Food reclaims the social dimension of food, whence comes its joy.

Justice

The third dimension of Real Food, justice, is harder to grasp. Justice has a natural connection with food, but because of the way things are classified, the connection is not always obvious. Food preparation and celebration aren't classified as cultural activities, so efforts to maintain food culture get none of the government support enjoyed by, for example, folk-dance troupes. Home cooking isn't classified as a basic skill, so free government training programs are provided for people who want to learn about computers, not cooking. Healthy food isn't classified as part of the health sector, so naturopaths who specialize in nutritional therapies aren't covered by medicare. Fishing and hunting aren't classified as food gathering, even though they account for as much as one-seventh of the protein intake in some areas of Canada, so they're handled by government tourism and recreation departments.[6] Farming isn't classified as a solar industry, so farmers aren't invited to environmental trade shows. If the link between food and justice isn't transparent, it may be due to our bizarre and ill-conceived classification systems.

Food goes with justice because food grows on common ground. No matter how people are divided by race, class, creed or country, we all eat for a living. In a world short of common denominators, the basic stuff of food is non-denominational; it's based on universal biological, social and spiritual needs. Food that is produced without justice affects us all. Clouds of pesticides rain down on the just and unjust, rich and poor, rural and urban alike. Kids from well-to-do families are as likely to be bouncing off the walls from caffeine and additive jags as kids from low-income families. And everybody pays, if only through taxpayer-funded medicare programs, for the illnesses that befall us when food is not given its due.

A rising tide raises all boats, and so it is with the rising tide of food justice. The need for food is inelastic, as the economists say, meaning there's only so much anyone can eat. If you eat too much, it's yourself, not the poor, you punish. Likewise, there's no reason why anyone would get less pleasure from a meal just because others were also enjoying their meal. The bottom line is that food justice is in everyone's interest, even to everyone's advantage.

There is no reason for food justice to be scarce. Food is not scarce. The idea of scarcity has been manufactured. If the truth be known, the problem plaguing most farmers is superabundance and glut. There's so much food on the market that they can't get paid enough for what they grow to make a living. Across North America, mountains of food are stockpiled; other mountains of food are just plain wasted. It's estimated that 40 percent of the food we produce is lost to waste.[7] Fields' worth of vegetables are left to rot each year, not because there's anything wrong with them, but because they aren't the perfect, identical size demanded by agribusiness. Still other mountains of food, commonly referred to as weeds, are destroyed with toxic chemicals because people don't recognize their nutritional value.

Despite efforts to scare the daylights out of us with predictions of dire shortages, food producers face a crisis caused by surplus. A food system that's in a crisis of overproduction while millions starve and close to a billion are malnourished—now that's worth being scared about![8] There is no need for more food production to meet the needs of the hungry. What we need is a more just way, with proper income and social benefits, to spread the food around.

Food without the bitter aftertaste left by exploitation is coming within reach. Ethical consumers are goosing the market, demanding products that incorporate justice for other humans and species. It's kids' stuff really, as shown by the child-enforced boycott of tuna caught in nets with dolphins. Even adults who lack their children's sense of the magic of the natural order are up to the challenge, as shown by the boom in coffee and tea from organic co-ops.

This ethical surge is powerful because food gets personal. It has a family tree and can be traced back to the people who grew, harvested, packed or served it. That's not as true for steel, plastic or cardboard, which fit into an impersonal production system. Food choices also lend themselves to personal ethics, because there's more room for individual choice than in, say, transportation or energy. For most people it's pretty hard to opt out of buying a car, because transportation planners have built cities and suburbs around the needs of cars, not pedestrians, bikers or public-transit users. Similarly, local by-laws make it almost impossible to opt out of the energy or sewage grid and build a self-sufficient, sustainable home. In these areas the deck is stacked against personal choice. Ethical food is one area where the average person can still have clout. And it works because of the old adage "what goes around comes around."

Here's how it can work. Sally, a rural teacher, decides to help the families of some of her students by getting most of her food from the local farmers' market. All of a sudden, her money, which used to leak out of the local economy, starts to circulate there. It creates what economists call the "multiplier effect." The local farmers whose produce Sally purchased stay in business, pay their school taxes and help keep Sally in her job. The ricochet romance has only begun. Local produce comes to market in a light pick-up, not a trac-tor trailer. The air is cleaner, and the tax bill for highway repairs is cut. Farmers at the local market breathe a sigh of relief. They get to keep a bigger slice of Sally's food dollar than they would ever get from the supermarket brokers, so they no longer require off-farm jobs to make ends meet. They quit, creating job openings for some of the parents of Sally's other students, who had been struggling with unemployment. Their children are now coming to school much happier, better fed and keen to learn. Now that more towns-people are earning and spending money, more people are shopping at the farmers' market. And they want variety. So the farmers begin to cater to local demand and start growing a score of crops, rather than endless fields of soy beans. Switching to a variety of crops allows farmers to experiment with organic farming practices, meth-ods that are incompatible with monoculture. They plant onions with their carrots, sidestepping the need for pesticides. They plant lettuce after beans, eliminating the need for chemical fertilizers, since beans draw down nitrogen (the main component of these fer-tilizers) from the air. Having cut their input costs for chemicals, the farmers are really in the money. One makes a free loan of a few acres of land to a local antihunger group, which offers low-income families the chance to grow their own food and bring their kids to the country for the day. Instead of paying more taxes to cover increased social assistance, the farmer bags a tax deduction for the charitable donation. More farmers hop on the bandwagon. And around and around we go.

Sound simple? Amazingly, it is. It doesn't require an army of bureaucrats. It doesn't require a major investment of cash. And it feeds into a second rising trend in the justice movement: self-reliance. With a little help from their friends and innovative social agencies, people are practising the generosity of the dinner table— help yourselves. Self-reliance can be a major tool of personal and community development. Community gardens and kitchens offer a quality of food and dignity of person that food banks can never match. Local food preparation and catering offer rewarding careers that the McJob economy can't beat. This is why Real Food can alleviate problems that charity and food banks compound.

Nature

There is one type of justice that we often ignore: respect for nature. In our glass-and-concrete world, we've moved so far away from our natural roots that many schoolchildren, when asked where milk comes from, answer "a carton." The connection with the cow has been almost forgotten. But Real Food grows with the flow of nature, and understanding how nature works is integral to finding balance in our food and in our lives. Many of us have a sense that something is wrong when our food is removed from nature. Cheese is not supposed to be bright orange. Bread is not supposed to be pasty white. But knowing how to bring nature back to our food is often a challenge.

In everyday conversation "nature" usually refers to the country-side, implying that nature, like farming, stops at the city limits. People will refer to some societies as being closer to nature than ours, as if we don't breathe, drink and eat nature, bring it into the innermost parts of our lives as much as they did in the Stone Age. When people acknowledge similarities with nature, it's when someone is stubborn as a mule, stupid as an ox, disgusting as a rat, greedy as a pig. About the only positive reference is to party animals.

These common attitudes account for a lot of upside-down think-ing about food. Food, the part of nature we get in touch with several times a day, invites us not just to think outside the box, as the business consultants like to say, but to think outside our skin. We'll get a grip on food when we recognize its role in meeting our basic animal needs, which are not only physical but cultural and spiritual. That in turn will put us in touch with the planet as an extension of ourselves, not just as a storehouse of resources to be exploited.

Economists, and especially food economists, also see nature's call as something to be wiped out. Our basic system for measuring economic transactions, the Gross National Product, doesn't even take account of nature. There's no place to depreciate an asset when topsoil or farmers are lost to the land, or when farms are paved over. There's no account to credit when tomatoes are grown in the backyard or when pesticide use is reduced, because no cash register rings up any sales. Infant formula, junk food, cavities and pavement, on the other hand, all contribute to economic growth. The GNP registers sales, not worth. Like Oscar Wilde's cynic, the GNP knows the price of everything and the value of nothing. With the books cooked like this, it's no surprise that economists are the only professionals who are well paid for being consistently wrong. This might also explain why media pundits can get away with ridiculous debates about economics versus the environment, as if there could be any kind of economy without the environment.

As a result of upside-down economics we have come to accept that food production is about conquering and dominating the natural environment, rather than working with it. The very words *pest* and *weed* suggest how oblivious this mind-set is to the complex interplay of all life forces in nature, which rely on balance, not domination, for stability and dynamism. Even the brand names of commonly used pesticides—Killex and Ambush are two good examples—suggest the conquering, not stewardship, model of land management.

The application of chemical sprays to farm fields was an early sign of a food system at war with nature. Genetic engineering (GE) escalates the war. Scientists working in this field think they know better than nature, and can come up with combinations of plants and animals that stupid old nature never got around to in over 4 billion years of evolution. They're putting fish genes in tomatoes and sugar beets, scorpion toxin in rice and tobacco.[9] Genetic engineering, by its very nature (or lack thereof), has nothing to do with life forces and natural cycles. That's the reason why many GE foods don't *go* bad on the shelf: they just *stay* bad.

After chemical fertilizers, sprays and genetic engineering take the country out of food, the transport, packaging and retail industries take food out of the country. The makings of the average meal eaten in North America have travelled 1,500 miles before they're gobbled down in seconds flat.[10] Food spends more time in the back of a truck or warehouse than in the intestinal tract. These trucks burn gas, a fossil fuel that contributes to global warming. With the spectre of global climate change becoming more real each time there is another "natural" disaster, the distance between us and our food makes no sense.

REAL FOOD
WITH THE WHOLE WORKS

Connecting the food you eat with health, joy, justice and nature is what Real Food is all about. Making these links undercuts one of the central myths in our current food system—the myth of consumer sovereignty, that the food on our supermarket shelves is there because we chose it. Never has a sovereign had fewer rights. Consumers have no right to know if the seeds that grew into their food came from biotech labs, no right to know what their food has been sprayed with, no right to know if their meat, milk and eggs are adulterated with hormones and drugs, no right to know if their fish comes from factory ships. Not much sovereign choice there.

Real Food offers that choice. And the best thing about Real Food is that it's eminently doable. Farmers are already growing it economically. Distributors are learning to distribute it efficiently. It's fun to cook. Eaters are delighted. The economy benefits. The environment starts to heal. Almost everybody wins. Real Food will be the easiest revolution in history. And also the most difficult. It depends on individuals, not on leaders, parties and organizations speaking and acting on their behalf. *You* have to make the choice and the commitment; no one can make it for you. Choice and commitment take courage, confidence and vision. If you're up to the hard part, we'll try to show you why Real Food is easier done than said.

In Chapter 1, we'll tell you why the most important move you can make is to go organic. We'll talk about what organically produced food is, why you should eat it and where you can find it. From there we'll tackle the very real question of cost. We'll show you how you can make the switch to organic food without blowing your food budget. We'll also show you how new low-cost lifestyle options can be based around food. Whether you want to fine-tune your eating habits or make wholesale change, Chapter 2 is brimming with tips and strategies to help you get the most from your food. And just to prove that this is not pie in the sky, we'll introduce you to people who are applying these strategies all over Canada.

When you're ready to start shopping for Real Food, we'll show you how in Chapter 3. When eaters and producers collaborate, they have the power to change the food system. We'll show you how you can use your buying power to ensure that the Real Food you want will be at your local store. We'll talk about the power of the boycott/buycott strategy. We'll also introduce you to some of the new food entrepreneurs who are part of the Real Food Revolution. In Chapter 4 we'll explain how the food system is one of the biggest sources of the gases that are causing global climate change, and we'll show you some practical ways that your buying, eating and cooking strategies can help reduce global warming. Finally, we'll help you set the table for the future with some fresh ideas for longer-term projects that can create sweeping improvements in all our lives.

CHAPTER I

EAT ORGANIC

EAT ORGANIC

Going organic is one of the best all-round decisions you'll ever make. It's a wise investment in long-term securities: your health and the health of the planet. And it's not too much to say that it will flavour your entire outlook on life. Food, after all, meets more than biological needs. In the right settings it nourishes all our senses, serves up a range of physical, cultural and spiritual delights, fills us with sociability, romance, grace and celebration. So switching to organic is more than buying a cleaner fuel for your body; as you grow with your decision, it's only natural that organic approaches will help you savour the greater gifts of food.

In this chapter we'll introduce you to the working principles of organic. We start with a description of the top ten reasons to make the change. This will also serve as a primer on the major problems in today's industrialized and conventional food system. After that, we tour the country for profiles of organic "bioneers"—growers and processors who show what can be done with intelligence and integrity. We end the chapter with some hands-on advice for first-time organic shoppers, including those who want to dip their toes in the water before making the full leap. By the time you're reading that, we hope you'll want to know how you can afford to buy organic all the time, a topic that will be addressed in Chapter 2. Leave your cost concerns aside until then. For now, just consider the merits of the case, the ten reasons why organic will lead to positive and authentic differences in your life.

TEN REASONS TO EAT ORGANIC

1. Organic food is anxiety-light.

With organic, you'll learn to stop worrying and love food. It's a sad commentary that the biggest selling point for organic food today is that it won't harm you. Consumers are realizing that this claim can't be matched by the conventional food industry, where a chemical stew is applied to almost every food that's grown.[1]

Organic is insurance that food is as pure and safe as can be. Most people are surprised that governments don't guarantee that. To be blunt, that's the least of it. The government doesn't even have a policy to let the buyer beware. There's no requirement that food be labelled with information about any of the seeds, fertilizers, chemicals, drugs or hormones that went into it. The only labels you'll find are on packaged foods, and they only list some of the chemicals added during processing. In the conventional food industry you make most of your purchases on blind trust. Given what's being revealed in the media almost every day about government and food-industry ethics and practices, many people feel better setting their own health policy on what goes into their bodies. Organic food lets you do that.

Canada's food inspection system can't assure safety.[2] Quality control commonly means random and casual inspections, often relying on "sniff and poke" checks. To make matters worse, the government agency responsible for inspection is the same one that is supposed to be promoting export sales of Canadian food. It's a simple case of conflict of interest.

At any rate, food is not inspected for purity; it's assessed for risk. Risk assessment is a bureaucratic way of saying that the solution to pollution is dilution. Everyone knows there are skulls and crossbones on the containers of many farm chemicals; if they weren't poisons, they couldn't kill weeds and bugs. But as long as the residues left on the food are very tiny, the bureaucrats say that the risk is low. Who's going to be scared about one part per million? The same concentration of poisons fed to laboratory rats doesn't cause them any problems, they say, so humans shouldn't be harmed either. In other words, it shouldn't kill you because it doesn't kill rats. They find this claim so convincing and undebatable that they see no need for labels on food so that you could make up your own mind.

This approach to quality control is simply out of date. "Don't sweat the small stuff" does not apply to body chemistry. Ross Hume Hall, retired biochemistry professor at Hamilton's McMaster University, points out that eight parts per billion of vitamin B12 makes the difference between healthy vitality and illness. The human body is very sensitive to submicroscopic doses of any kind. If damage doesn't show up in rats, he argues, it's only because they don't live long enough to suffer from the slow build-up of toxins over decades. To make matters worse, governments estimate risks one at a time, as if people were only ever exposed to one toxin. The reality is that hundreds of chemicals are applied to food, and no one knows what happens when they're all mixed together in the body. Modern researchers have proven what's called the "synergistic effect," whereby the full damage of two or more chemicals is many times worse than the sum of the parts. Given this evidence, it's comforting to know that organic farmers follow a fail-safe principle: if it isn't used, it can't contaminate the food.

2. Organic food is delicious.

Organic passes the taste test of the world's most demanding chefs. Many are so keen that they've joined organizations such as Chefs Collaborative 2000 or Knives and Forks to encourage local growers who can keep them supplied with the best in the field. Something is cooking when chefs are so particular.

For some reason, this is a well-kept secret. Maybe people like to file good taste and good health in separate compartments, or think it's superficial to support organics on such shallow grounds. But taste is anything but shallow. It testifies to the complex and full-bodied natural fertilizers and composts that enrich the depths of organically managed soil.

Compost conditions and revitalizes soil with nutrients, and with worms and insects that break down minerals and debris in the soil so that plant roots can take them up. Some organic farmers add rock dust or seaweed to their soil to ensure the presence of rare trace minerals. A minority, followers of biodynamic beliefs, apply preparations including a diluted spray made from selenium and manure at specific times when the moon is said to create waves of energy in the soil, just as it creates ocean tides. Such tricks, which hearken back to the old days of farmers' almanacs, give bio-dynamic food its "out-of-this-world taste," says Bruce Blevins, one of the most respected vegetable growers in the United States.

The organic taboo against chemicals is meant to protect the beneficial underground critters that bring life to the soil. When they're exterminated by toxic sprays, the result is dead soil and erosion, both common to conventional farms. To compensate for depleted soil, conventional farmers shoot up their fields with chemical fertilizers, usually made from natural gas. Many scientists believe that the quick release of nitrogen from these fertilizers interferes with sugar formation in plants.[3] Some blame our overconsumption of sugar on the sweetness deficiency brought about by this interference with natural sugar formation. Organic fruits and vegetables, especially beets and carrots, have a richly sweet taste. Extra sweetness is also noticeable in dairy products from cows that feast on new springtime growth in organic meadows.

3. With organic, what you see is what you get.

Keeping up appearances is a full-time job in the conventional food industry, but appearances can be deceiving. The plump look of fruits and vegetables could come from excessive use of nitrogen fertilizers, which cause plants to shoot up quickly and suck up extra water. The plump look on meat might come from feeding salt to cattle before they're put on the auction bloc, causing them to bulk up with water. In both cases the nutritional value is watered down, sometimes by as much as 20 percent. To prevent the dry skin and wrinkles that come with old age, vegetables get a wax coating (often impregnated with fungicides) to seal in their water. Bananas, usually picked green, turn yellow thanks to ethylene gas applied in trucks and warehouses. Oranges from Florida, green when they're ripe on the tree, owe their orange colour to dye. The label indicating the use of dye is placed on the crate, which warehouse workers get to see but not shoppers. Plastic wrap keeps dirty paws from directly touching food, but the plastic that directly touches food may well contain toxic stabilizers that can leach into foods with a high fat content. These are looks that kill.

The food industry forces nature to imitate ads. Advertisers create their postcard images, then the food has to conform. Fruit and vegetables that aren't picture perfect won't be accepted for sale. As much as 20 percent of the harvest is left in the field to rot at a time when millions are using food banks and going without fresh fruit and vegetables.[4] Cosmetic expectations dictate excessive use of pesticides to prevent the smallest spot, which doesn't affect the taste or quality of the food. Creating and catering to false expectations of food fit for Barbie and Ken indicate an industry that has lost its moral compass.

Organic customers develop an eye that can see beauty that is more than skin deep. If apple juice looks cloudy, that's because it's apple juice, not apple water with all the fibre filtered out. If honey isn't transparent, that's because the original minerals are still there. People need to ask themselves if they'd rather have a spot on their apple or a spot on their lung. Organic enjoys a reputation unblemished by the use of artificial dyes or preservatives. It's one of the reasons why *organic* and *integrity* are virtual synonyms.

4. Organic food is more nutritious.

The hard science on this is just developing, but the evidence and logic are compelling. Nutrients in food come mainly from nutrients in the soil. If soil is treated like dirt—if nutrients are depleted by growing the same crop in the same soil year after year, for instance—then the cheque written against the bank of nutrients will eventually bounce.

Chemical companies claim that their chemical mix of nitrogen, potassium and phosphorus fertilizers is a quick fix for soils depleted by lack of rotation or compost. In fact, the chemical fix instigates growth so fast and furious that it sacrifices the slow and steady uptake of complex nutrients. As in any rush job, the details get left behind, which is what happens to micronutrients. It's thought that the growth spurt fuelled by synthetic fertilizers leaves calcium, magnesium and zinc—all crucial to heart, bone and mental health—in the dust.

To date, the strongest proof of the organic difference comes from animal studies. Test animals raised on organic crops are more fertile, a standard measure of overall health among animals.

Reproductive systems are supersensitive to seemingly minor dietary changes, so it's likely these findings will also hold for humans.

5. Organic food is properly processed.

In the industrial food system, the needs of centralized processors, not the health needs of eaters, dictate how food is processed. The most telling example is what has happened to oils and fats. The oils and fats most people eat today have been processed for ease of transport and long shelf-life. These include cooking oils, margarines and fats used in almost every processed food you can name. These "industrial fats" are produced in massive manufacturing facilities, using heat and chemical processes to extract the most oil from the oil-bearing plant. The industrial food system uses oils that are low in essential fatty acids, or EFAS, such as soy, corn and canola, because they go rancid less easily. The problem is that EFAS are essential for health, playing a role in the construction and maintenance of cells. The human body is incapable of producing these substances itself except in breast milk (a sure tip-off to their importance).

Organic oils are processed entirely differently. They are usually made in small batches, using cold-press methods that preserve EFAS such as linolenic and linoleic acid, which are particularly delicate and easily lost in industrial processing. Fish oils, pumpkin seeds and flax oil are good sources of EFAS.

Another feature of industrial processing is hydrogenation, whereby oils are hardened into solid form by adding hydrogen. Margarine and shortening are the two main products of this process. Hydrogenation is popular with the food industry because it makes oils easier and cheaper to transport. Because it extends shelf-life, it paved the way for prepared foods. Margarine allowed marketers to tout vegetable oils as the answer to widespread concern over the health impact of saturated fat, found mainly in meat and dairy products.

But hydrogenation and high-temperature refining have created a new health problem known as trans-fatty acids, or TFAS. As it turns out, these processes change the properties of fats and the way they act on the body. Two of the leading scientists in the field, Harvard's

Walter Willet and Bruce Holub from the University of Guelph, believe trans-fatty acids do a lot of harm. They say TFAS increase what's known as "bad" cholesterol and blood fat levels (both contributing factors to heart disease), disrupt the functions of essential fatty acids (which have a role in cancer prevention), reduce the activity of certain cells involved in immune function, and disrupt a range of reproductive activities in both men and women.[5]

The Canadian government has consistently refused to require labelling of trans-fatty acids because of strong opposition from the food industry.[6] Without labelling, the best way to avoid TFAS is to go organic. Organic oils are not hydrogenated. Organically processed foods rarely contain hydrogenated fats. Combined with the fact that many organic processors deliberately source oils high in EFAS, it's clear that going organic means much more than avoiding foods grown with pesticides.

6. Organic food offers real variety.

Superstores sell a dazzling array of exotic kiwi, papaya and shrimp, as well as tomatoes and strawberries any month of the year. But what is it to gain a cardboard tomato and lose a hundred varieties of home-grown apple? That's the direction superstores are taking with their top international hits.

If you want true variety, organic is the way to go. Variety is the spice of life on organic farms, and for very practical reasons. Variety can solve so many problems at once, and all without chemicals. For example, organic farmers are big on rotation. They don't do the same thing twice in the same place. Rotation is good for the soil and also discourages insects, which are often a lazy lot, unwilling to follow their favourite food to its new site. Companion planting—using combinations of plants that do the work of chemical fertilizers and pesticides—is another way to keep pests at bay and automatically double the variety on any patch of land.[7]

Variety also comes when organic farmers try to stagger production so that something new is always cropping up. Mustards and radishes spring up fast. Different varieties of fruits, greens and potatoes stretch out each season's greetings. Hardy bok choy, cabbage, Japanese eggplant and snow peas can take the fall cold. Many root vegetables can be overwintered. Cover them with a bale of straw to hold in the earth's heat and they can be picked fresh in January in many parts of the country. And unlike conventional farmers, who are limited to crops that can be mechanically seeded and harvested for mass marketing, organic farmers can custom grow whatever their soil, inclination, curiosity and knowledge can handle.

The-more-the-merrier approach also explains why organic farmers are so keen on traditional livestock and seeds, many on the brink of extinction because of pressures in conventional farming to boost yields and standardize product. Several older breeds of chicken produce distinctive egg and meat flavours, and it doesn't matter that they don't bulk up fast or adapt to barn confinement. Organic growers have also rediscovered and popularized older varieties of grains. These are closer to the seed stock of their wild relatives than the highly manipulated grains that are mass-produced today; so they're more able to fend for themselves against weeds, pests and drought, and are often more nutritious than grains bred for ease of commercial processing. Protecting genetic diversity is part of organic stewardship.[8]

When farming isn't based on sound stewardship for the long term, the land gives out. This isn't of concern to the superstores in this age of the global pillage; they simply head off for greener pastures on the other side of the world. That's why your iceberg lettuce might come all the way from California or Korea. The variety in organic farming means not only a wide range of food choices but something else the superstores can't offer: an opportunity to support something really different—sustainable agriculture.

7. Organic food offers a different shopping experience.
Most organic food is sold through "alternative" channels, such as health food stores, farmers' markets, roadside stands and home delivery of organic boxes. Line-ups are short, there's no elevator music, and no trashy snacks or tabloids at the checkout counter.

Some organic farmers have gone a step further, offering human contact and customer service. Besides home delivery, some have on-farm visits, play days for the kids and harvest hoedowns. You know your doctor, they say; why shouldn't you know your farmer, who's just as important to your health? Some people refer to this as putting the culture back into agriculture. Business strategists call it niche marketing or shortening the supply chain. Bridging the social distance between farmers and eaters puts human intangibles back into the food, without which something in food has withered.

8. Organic food won't turn you into a guinea pig.

Organic farmers carry out a lot of experiments to find out how their gardens grow, but the organic code prohibits experiments with unnatural seeds, chemicals, drugs, hormones or radiation. Therefore, eaters are never an object of these experiments. Alas, the same can't be said for the conventional food industry or its government regulators. They're now conducting two experiments that have been approved neither by voters nor by Parliament, and that consumers are made to participate in without their knowledge or consent.

The first experiment involves what's called biotechnology, or genetic engineering. By making changes to gene structure, lab workers can now create seeds and hormones that would never evolve in nature. Biotech tomato seeds are injected with fish genes to produce tomatoes that can take cold storage. Canola and soy are manipulated so they can withstand a drenching from toxic weed sprays. "Terminator seeds" are being developed, which die before reproducing—a nifty way of ensuring that farmers become repeat customers. At least eighteen genetically engineered foods are already on the market, and approvals for eighteen more have been granted.

The genes have been let out of the bottle, and the experiment is already heading out of control. As much as 60 percent of processed foods are liable to contain genetically engineered products.[9] But what if the bacteria inserted in many seeds to poison pests end up poisoning people too? In the United States, Monsanto's New Leaf Potato seed is actually registered as a pesticide, not a seed. What if gene structures of foods that some people are allergic to are inserted in foods that people with allergies buy unwittingly? And why is no one in government, the universities and medical circles demanding answers?

Other than buying organic, shoppers have no way of knowing if they are buying food grown from genetically engineered seeds. The Canadian government requires no separation or labelling of these products. This is in stark contrast with Europe, where consumers and governments insist on their right to know. In Britain, MPs won't allow biotech in the parliamentary dining room. Prince Charles reviles biotech foods as abominations of divine law. Shoppers call them mutant seeds and "Frankenseeds," and won't buy them. Out of respect for their customers, many British supermarkets won't stock them. Monsanto, the leading supplier of genetically altered seeds, has even apologized to the British public for not labelling its products. But not in Canada. Pity. However, if you don't want to become evidence in this particular experiment, you can buy organic, which guarantees that no genetically altered seeds were used to grow raw foods and that every effort was made to screen them out of processed foods.

Irradiation is the second experiment conducted on our food without our knowledge or consent. Bombarding fruit, vegetables and meat with rays from Cobalt-60 will delay spoilage and kill off salmonella and hamburger disease—or so the theory goes. Since nuclear radiation's glowing reputation scares people off, promoters call this process "cold pasteurization." The technology for nuking food is built, sold and regulated by the Canadian government, which also licenses it for use on spices, onions, potatoes and wheat products. Pressure is mounting to give the treatment to chicken, beef and strawberries.

Independent scientists are alarmed. Since nuclear blasts kill indiscriminately, vitamins and friendly bacteria are as likely to be destroyed as diseases, they say. Karen Graham, former chair of the Canadian Dietetic Association's special committee on irradiation, says that vitamins A, B, C, D, E and K are burnt to such an extent as to seriously reduce nutrient levels.[10] George Tritsch of Buffalo's Roswell Park Cancer Institute says irradiation can produce so much genetic damage and create so many carcinogens that cancer rates will inevitably increase. Dr. Samuel Epstein of the Chicago Medical School calls irradiation one of "the largest prospective toxicological experiments in human populations in the history of public health."[11]

The food zappers don't inspire with their knowledge of food issues. U.S. beef is irradiated with the force of 30 million X-rays, someone complained to Pat Hansen, leading chemist with Washington's pro-irradiation Food and Drug Administration. "You can do a lot of things to your food that you don't do to a living thing," Hansen replied.[12] If only food weren't a living thing, an industrialized food system would have such an easier time keeping food sterile. But since even spoilage and disease are part of the life cycle, it's smarter to look for solutions that support life, not to nuke it. That's why the organic code enforces high standards of animal welfare, and prohibits the factory barns and mass-production slaughterhouses where diseases fester and spread. It's also why many organic growers go to great pains to deliver food fresh, before spoilage becomes an issue. Since not all irradiated foods are labelled, the only way to make sure you're not conscripted in this experiment is to buy organic, a label that's only issued to nuclear-free operators.

The deployment of atomic power on the food supply is a reminder that the stock of weapons used in chemicalized agriculture mostly comes from the military machine. After World War II, nitrogen manufacturers had no market for explosives, chlorine manufacturers had no market for poison gas, tank makers had no market for tanks and nuclear manufacturers had fewer bombs to rush into production. Chemicalized agriculture became a make-work project for them. Nitrogen went into fertilizers, chlorine went into chemical sprays, tanks became tractors and the peaceful atom was used for sterilization equipment. The origins of chemicalized food in the military-industrial complex of the 1950s may explain the fondness for pesticide trade names such as Avenge and Machete, and standard references to pests as enemies that must be conquered and destroyed. The same mind-set may also explain the government's provision of information to citizens on a "need-to-know" basis, just like in the military. At any rate, a strange love for mad science experiments was carried over from war production to food production. In this perspective, going organic is a declaration that the war is over, that government propaganda, secrecy and denial of civil liberties are no longer needed, and that combat ethics must give way to ethics that respect life.

9. Organic food is better for your kids.

If you have children, or if you're pregnant, moving to organic is as important as any safety measure you take. Food testing by industry and government does not take children into account. Risk levels from exposure to toxic chemicals are set for adult bodies and eating patterns. But children are much more vulnerable than adults. Their acutely sensitive nervous systems are developing rapidly. Pound for pound, they eat four times more than adults. They drink twenty times more apple juice and eat seven times more vegetables.[13] None of this is taken into account when risk levels are set. It's child neglect, pure and simple.

Expectant parents need to be especially aware of the risks of genetic pollution from conventional food. It's now well documented that the by-products of atomic radiation and chlorinated chemicals—dioxins and furans are in the headlines most often—are absorbed by adults when they eat, stored in their fat and passed on during pregnancy. Though fear of cancer is uppermost in most people's minds, this threat to reproduction is more worrisome.[14]

When chlorinated chemicals break down, they can act as "hormone imposters" or "hormone disruptors." Chlorine is a lab-made product of the twentieth century, so our bodies have not evolved to treat it as a foreign invader. The rogue hormones infiltrate cells, are accepted as natural hormones, and start turning genetic information switches on and off. Their effect has been likened to the crashing of computer message centres by viruses.

The impact of these rogue hormones on wildlife is recognized by leading scientists and independent government agencies. The International Joint Commission on the Great Lakes, for instance, has called for a phase-out of chlorine in agricultural sprays and other products. Theo Colborn, the wildlife expert who marshalled evidence for the commissioners, believes humans now show the tell-tale signs of damage she first observed lower down the food chain. In *Our Stolen Future* she blames runaway rates of female breast cancer, male infertility, males with undescended testicles and children suffering from attention deficit disorder on rogue hormones. Because rogue hormones migrate to body fat, the basic material in sperm, placenta and breasts contains them in high concentrations.[15] When the threat of rogue hormones is understood, the only acceptable level of residues from chlorine-based chemical sprays is zero.

Avoiding foods that carry agents of reproductive pollution is the best way to protect future generations. That means avoiding foods grown on fields fertilized with sewage sludge, which commonly includes chlorine-based cleaners and solvents that have been flushed down the toilet. Safety also means avoiding foods with any residues from chemical sprays. Only organic producers follow a code that prohibits these products.

We are exposed constantly to radioactive and chlorine pollution in the air we breathe and the water we drink. But the major carrier of these pollutants is the food we eat, not air and water, although these get most of the attention.

10. Organic food leaves no bitter aftertaste.
Organic food isn't cheap, and for good reasons; chemicalized food is, and for bad ones. It will leave a bad taste in your mouth, body and heart that will linger a long time.

There are two short-term explanations for the difference in sticker prices between organic and chemicalized food. The first is the law of supply and demand. Demand for organic is brisk, up 15 percent a year for the past decade.[16] Chemicalized food markets, by contrast, are glutted, and the food is sold off, often below cost. This is why so many farmers are going bankrupt, despite high yields. New organic growers and processors also have to recover the costs of their steep learning curve. So part of what today's consumers are paying for is innovation. Neither of these factors will determine organic prices for long. As more farmers shift to organic the price gap will close.

The long-term forecast for organic and chemicalized price tags is another story. Organic farmers receive almost no subsidies, so consumers pay the full shot. Chemicalized farming is subsidized to the hilt, with taxpayers picking up a good part of the tab. Since there's no sign that governments will stop tilting the playing field any time soon, some price difference will be around for a while—or until you try some of the options we offer in Chapter 2.

There are two types of subsidies that favour chemicalized farming. One type covers direct costs of chemicals, energy, transport, crop insurance and so on. The Organization for Economic Cooperation and Development, a think-tank sponsored by Western governments, ranks Canadian subsidies as the highest in the industrialized world, averaging about $100,000 per farm job.[17] To give a small but grating example: conventional farmers pay no GST on polluting fertilizers, sprays or fuels; organic farmers pay the GST if they buy a how-to book on organics, and shell out payroll taxes if they hire people to do the work carried out by untaxed chemicals and fuels on other farms.

Conventional farms are eligible for a second set of subsidies that lead to big, if indirect, savings. These are sometimes called regulatory subsidies. They let conventional farms pollute for free, to "externalize" their costs, as the economists say, to the general public and future generations. The Great Lakes, for example, have been used as a free garbage dump for more than 28,000 tons of agricultural pesticides.[18] The resulting damage is partly responsible for the destruction of a world-class commercial freshwater fishery and an associated tourism industry. About 25 million people drink their water straight from the Great Lakes. It's no exaggeration to say that the Canadian economy loses more than $50 billion a year in missed tourism opportunities, lost jobs and increased medical costs as a result of food producers externalizing their clean-up costs. Bundle the two types of subsidies together, and the real cost of cheap food is almost double what's on the sticker price.

There is no such hidden price tag on organics. When you buy organic, you're paying the farmer to "internalize" the full costs of production, to sacrifice immediate gain for the greater good of the public and environment by handling waste on site. When you buy organic, you only pay once; you don't pay again, with ill health or with high taxes for environmental clean-ups. When you buy organic, you are making a sound and ethical investment in the future. There's no other food that can make that claim. In the profiles that follow, you'll get a close-up on the people and practices that your investment supports.

FRUITS AND VEGETABLES

Ken McMullen is a management consultant with dirt under his fingernails, an artist who works with plants, an avid environmentalist who leaves half his farm to wild creatures, and one of the country's most successful vegetable growers. His farm, a fifty-acre piece of paradise bordering the Long Point Biosphere on Lake Erie, is an organic combination of business, art, environment and healthy food.

With a sales style that makes soft sell seem like a K-Tel ad, the short, muscular farmer with a light-greying beard lets the flavour of his produce sell itself. Let your kids try the potatoes and carrots, he says, and see if they still have trouble eating their veggies. No fire and brimstone about the dangers of toxic sprays. "Avoiding chemical poisons is negative," he says. "No philosophy can be built around negatives." But behind the hippie-style exterior clicks a shrewd business mind.

Organic farmers rely on brains rather than chemical brawn, and they succeed because they use the whole brain. They integrate the so-called right and left sides—the gentle, accepting side that nurtures creativity and sees connections, and the hard, driving side that pursues efficiency and sees red and black ink on a ledger.

Like all organic farmers, McMullen treats his soil with tender loving care. He invests a lot of time preparing and applying composts that are full of beneficial insects and bacteria. These organisms gently churn the soil and create pathways for air and water, at the same time breaking down the nutrients in soil debris into forms that plants can absorb. One acre of topsoil that's not "broken," to borrow the phrase of farmers bent on conquering nature, includes some 3 billion bacteria and 25 million mites, ants and earthworms. Composting pays nature the highest form of compliment: imitation. For McMullen, organic farming is just that, learning to mimic natural cycles for human needs.

McMullen calls his compost heap one of his farm's six profit centres. He strives to avoid off-farm purchases of things he can do himself on-farm. This is the secret to the healthy bottom line in organics, why it is the only form of agriculture that can save the family farm from extinction. Conventional farmers have to spend money on chemical inputs. This raises their cost of doing business and means it takes longer before they start paying off their debts or paying themselves a salary. Organic farmers don't have these expenses. With their lower costs, organic farmers often make money from the get-go. Their profit ratio is high enough that they don't need to worry so much about volume. Keeping four dollars out of five is better than keeping six dollars out of ten. That grade-school math accounts for the time McMullen spends on compost. To pay for his time, he also sells the surplus to home gardeners.

Toxic sprays aren't an option for McMullen. They're expensive and they're counter-productive. Since only about 1 percent of sprays actually hit their target, 99 percent are overkill.[19] The excess kills worms that aerate soil, bees that pollinate plants, birds that eat bugs. It also pollutes nearby sources of water by seeping into creeks and groundwater. Chemicals would also poison relations with his customers, people McMullen describes as "friends who buy things from me." Friends don't let friends eat toxins.

So once again McMullen takes nature as his model. He strives for a live-and-let-live approach. This is why he has no weeds. "I call them volunteers," he says. They shade delicate plants from the blazing sun. Their long roots dig up trace minerals from the deeps. At the right time McMullen plucks them and drops them beside his plants, using them as mulch to shade the soil and prevent evaporation. So weeds save him the cost of mineralizing and irrigating his soil.

When dealing with weeds and insects, it's often wiser to retreat, or rather advance in another direction, than assault directly. We've tried direct assault for the past fifty years and we've only succeeded in hurting ourselves. Farmers still lose about 20 percent of their crop to weeds and insects, the same proportion they lost in the 1930s, before the era of petrochemical sprays.[20] As in arms races, escalation breeds counter-escalation, not superiority. Weeds and insects have simply evolved to get around the defences we throw in their way. The result is that nine hundred species of insects and pathogenic moulds and bacteria can now survive at least one pesticide, and eighty-four species of weeds can survive at least one herbicide.[21] We are poisoning our food and the general environment for no net gain.

Companion planting is one way to control pests without toxic chemicals. Farmers become matchmakers, pairing petunias with beans, marigolds with tomatoes, and so on. Besides avoiding chemicals, each addition of a species to a patch of soil increases the productivity of that patch of land, probably because each species takes up and gives back different nutrients. So, a farmer who "intercrops" carrots and onions will have more to sell than the farmer who grows carrots or onions alone. Diversity is the way to get more out of life. This was known to Native farmers long before Europeans settled in Canada. The Huron and Iroquois grew the "three sisters": corn, beans and squash. Beans used the corn stalk to support their growth and fed nitrogen to the soil, which the corn desperately needed. Squash leaves spread over the ground, protecting it from weeds, erosion and evaporation. McMullen has adapted this classic combination to his farm.

Another natural process that can be used as an ally is what's called "biological pest control." Buying a cat to keep mice out of the barn is biological pest control. So is building a perch for barn owls who eat mice off the field. So is keeping old wooden fence posts where bluebirds can nest and eat their fill of insects from the apple orchard. McMullen's farm borders the major bird expressway in Canada. He leaves half his land wild so birds can use it as a pit stop on their spring and fall migrations. The grateful birds eat the insects off his fields.

McMullen also spends a lot of time researching and collecting heritage seeds, by and large hardier, tastier and more nutritious than modern seeds bred for the fashions of the processing industry. One of twenty-two tomato varieties he grows is the ancient "apple of love," the original tomato taken from Peru by Spanish conquerors in the seventeenth century. He's gained access to the seed collection of the French master painter Claude Monet, and his fields are galleries of the colours that made impressionism famous. Monet's flowers attract bees that pollinate the fields, and they are later sold to provide a feast for the eyes of McMullen's food customers.

The diversity of McMullen's farm is much like a good investment portfolio, making money from a variety of sources. To recover the costs of research and of travel to collect seeds, he sells small packets of seeds to gardening enthusiasts. He also sells surplus seedlings, and he teaches organic gardening to home growers. The lands he leaves wild yield wild grape and ginger, which he sells as preserves. In the fall he holds canning and preserving workshops,

which also allow him to sell tomatoes by the bushel basket instead
of by the pint. After the harvest rush he can experiment with value-
added products: herb salts, chive vinegars, plum and ginger jams, all
ideal for Christmas gift baskets.

McMullen goes the distance to cultivate close relations with his
customers. He practises what is known as CSA, which stands for
Community Supported or Community Shared Agriculture. CSA
reorganizes the retail landscape as much as organic production
methods reorganize the farm landscape. Though there are many
variations, the basic idea is to cut out the middleman and put farmers and eaters in direct contact. The lion's share of the food dollar
that used to go to the middleman is split two ways, between the
farmer and the eater. So the farmer gets a premium price and the
eater gets top-quality product and service for supermarket prices.
McMullen faxes his offerings for the week to his hundred customers, they fax back their custom order, he picks it and delivers it
the next day. The telecommunications revolution doesn't only
favour the virtual communities of the anonymous global village.

McMullen insists on CSA relationships for a number of reasons.
He doesn't want to short-change all his work by putting a prema-
turely cut harvest in a truck, warehouse or store for a week before
it's sold. Tomatoes gain 80 percent of their vitamin C from the time
they turn pink to the time they turn ripe red, and they lose these
nutrients almost as quickly once they've been picked. So he wants
a system with a one-day turnaround. Most of all, McMullen says,
he needs steady customers he knows and counts as friends on those
steaming hot days when nothing else but their needs could get him
off the hammock and into the field. Some things money can't buy.
Shrewd as McMullen's business strategies are, they rely on direct
human contact and warmth to bring organic home.

POTATOES

Pirmin Kummer has something to tell the giant companies pushing
a new breed of genetically engineered potato: rotate. That's how he
manages a premium crop of spuds grown without pesticides on his
two-hundred-acre farm near Port Elgin, New Brunswick.[22]

Kummer faces the same problem as all potato growers across the continent: the bright orange Colorado Potato Beetle, which can devastate an entire crop within days. By planting his potatoes in different fields every two years, Kummer outsmarts them. The beetle is a couch potato. If the crop is moved, it won't keep up and it starves.

But there's more to Kummer's bag of tricks than rotation. To minimize handling and the infections that can come with it, he plants potatoes whole rather than cut into chunks. He walks his fields every day during critical periods with a vacuum cleaner and sucks up any beetles the day they show. He cures potatoes under the open sun, which dries and disinfects them. Drier potatoes are less likely to get mould and blight when they're stored. Finally, he wraps his potatoes in a bag, affixes his label, "Grown Without Pesticides Added," and sells them for a premium price at roadside stands, farmers' markets and local groceries.

The top-selling vegetable in Canada can't get no respect. Most potatoes end up in french fries and potato chips. This has given the potato beetle its chance to take over the continent by keeping step with the spread of factory-farmed potatoes for factory processors of fries and chips. Processors insist on late-harvesting potatoes, just one among many potato varieties. Late potatoes are long, slice well and turn a nice golden colour when boiled in fat or oil; other potatoes turn brown. The problem is that these late bloomers leave fields exposed for much of the summer, resulting in major losses of topsoil to erosion. They're harvested too late to be cure-dried in the sun, and are stored damp, making them prone to mould and blight. To assure supply, processors also try to lock farmers into long-term contracts for their entire crop, a practice that leads farmers to grow the same variety of potatoes in the same place, year after year. Beetles love these contracts. They are permanent job security for bugs. To make matters worse, the beetles have adapted to escalating levels of chemical spraying. Any that survived a spraying passed on their traits to their offspring, and the survivors in each generation have become more resistant. Without meaning to, potato growers have become their own worst enemies, running a breeding program that created superbeetles that can outmanoeuvre their increasingly dull weapon.

Enter Monsanto. Once known for barbaric weapons of chemical warfare—Monsanto's Agent Orange was one of the horrific chemicals dropped on peasant villages in Vietnam during the 1960s—the company has since turned over a new leaf to become the world's most powerful "life sciences" conglomerate. Monsanto's New Leaf Potato is part of a new chapter in seed breeding. From the dawn of agriculture until the 1970s, breeders took the pick of the crop with a view to propagating seeds and plants that produced the reddest roses, biggest pumpkins, most cold-hearty wheats, longest potatoes and so on. But genetic engineering, Monsanto's specialty, is different. It doesn't just speed up natural selection or direct natural selection for human needs; it does what nature cannot do. It crosses the species barrier by splicing a gene sequence from one species into a gene from another to produce a seed that nature could never develop.

To concoct the New Leaf Potato, Monsanto lab workers spliced the genes of a soil bacterium called Bacillus thuringiensis, or B.t., into a potato seed. B.t. has long been the potato growers' helper. The bacteria live in the soil. When eaten by a beetle, they release a poison that paralyzes the beetle, causing its digestive system to shut down. The New Leaf Potato, approved by the U.S. government in 1995 and by Canada in 1996, comes with its own built-in B.t.[23]

Genetic engineers can splice genes, but they are potato heads when it comes to ecology or human health. New Leaf Potatoes won't solve the problems created by the demands of potato-chip and French-fry processors any more than toxic sprays did. All it takes is one promiscuous beetle with one chance trait that helps it resist one bacterium, and a new generation of immune beetles will evolve. There are already reports of beetles adapting to B.t. Many experts say that B.t. will be useless within a decade. This is the folly of genetic engineering, which has only one trick up its sleeve. By contrast, Pirmin Kummer has a bag of tricks. That means an exponentially higher number of chance traits have to coincide before beetles can win the genetic lottery against his methods.

The real hot potato, however, is the human health impact of genetically engineered potatoes. No one knows how the gene of a bacteria that poisons and suffocates a beetle will react in a human stomach over time. And no one has any inkling of how potatoes with natural poison in their genes will react in the human stomach when joined by the manufactured genes of other common food products.[24]

Only organic growers can guarantee the absence of genetically engineered plants. And only organic growers give the potato the respect it deserves for the central role it has played in Western history. Originally bred by Peruvian Indians thousands of years ago and domesticated as far north as Canada prior to European settlement, the potato changed the course of history when it was transplanted to Europe. Its storehouse of essential nutrients—one medium-sized potato helps fill daily needs for protein, vitamins B and C, as well as iron, phosphorus, magnesium and copper—greatly improved the health and energy levels of the poor. A potato can be taken right out of the ground and put on the stove—no processing or middleman necessary. It's an unfortunate irony that a crop that originally allowed the poor to eat well and gave farmers independence from processors has been turned into a French fry, the quintessential greasy processed food.

More than half of all potatoes grown in Canada end up in factory-processed foods. In some provinces the figure can be over 80 percent, according to Agriculture and Agrifood Canada. This means that processors often dictate how farmers grow those potatoes. Eating more unprocessed potatoes and discovering the hundreds of ways to prepare them is essential to the success of farmers such as Pirmin Kummer. When more growers can sell potatoes the way he does, success for organics will be in the bag.

GRAIN

Darryl Amey has made an organic machine that splits peas, hulls grains, bags beans and may hold the cure for allergies, cancer and rural depopulation. The tool shed behind his farmhouse in Radisson, Saskatchewan, houses his many inventions, all jimmied from motors, springs, pulleys and gears rescued from the scrap heap. "People think I invent things," Amey says, "but I just take existing technology and rearrange it." Amey is most proud of a Rube Goldberg contraption. Depending on the insert, it can clean, split and package sunflower seeds, peas and lentils, or clean, hull, grind and package wheat, buckwheat, barley and oats.

This machine is what made Amey's decision to take over the family homestead viable. He'd spent twenty years tramping the world as a freelance heavy-motor mechanic, topping the tour off with a round trip to Inuvik by motorcycle. "I didn't find anything out there any more interesting than right here," he says. So he decided to put down roots. His parents left him half a section. That left him with a decision: he could go to the bank to borrow money, buy another section and try to grow a big enough volume of wheat to make up for the low price per bushel; or he could go organic and use his mechanical skills to stay small, debt-free, close to his neighbours and customers, and happy in the slow lane. "I want to enjoy life by the moment," he says, "not be thinking all the time about what I haven't finished yet."

Amey's idea was to use his machining skills to add value rather than volume to his crops. By delivering fresh, ready-to-use flours and seeds to nearby co-ops and bakers, he nets about three times more per acre than a farmer who delivers rough product to a processor. That means he breaks even on a farm one-third the prescribed size. "If I can find a way to make a living feeding a hundred people instead of a thousand," he says, "there would be an opportunity for nine other people to do the same."

Amey's home-processing and delivery system goes against the historical grain of wheat, which has always been identified with the expansion of empires. The ancient Romans put wheat at the centre of their empire. Because it stored well, it was ideal for armies on the march across continents. Because it was a relatively cheap and plentiful source of essential nutrients, it kept the masses fed and passive. "Bread and circuses" was the key to civil peace in Roman times. Likewise, British manufacturers in the 1800s saw wheat as the key to industrial empire. They counted on their Canadian colony to provide cheap food to keep industrial workers alive even though they were paid miserable wages.[25]

The three U.S. multinationals—Cargill, Continental and Archer Daniels Midland—that dominate today's multibillion-dollar global grain trade aren't much different. They provide Canadian wheat to U.S. pasta makers, who then sell it back to us as spaghetti and macaroni. The Third World is another major market, where grain is fed to livestock for meat that only the rich can afford. These companies make their money on percentages of shipping and handling, not on food value or farm-based processing. The more they have the monopoly on separating the wheat from the chaff, the more farmers are separated from the dough.[26]

Health experts, however, are blowing the whistle on the global grain trade and its reliance on prolonged storage. Fungi and moulds do nicely on wheat grown with chemical fertilizers and stored over lengthy periods in grain elevators. They produce poisons called mycotoxins, which get into our bodies when we eat wheat products. Mycotoxins are heavily implicated in cancer and heart disease, says Dr. Antonio Constantini of the UN's World Health Organization. Traces of these mycotoxins have been found in 40 percent of samples taken at Canadian blood banks.[27] Wheat may also be partly responsible for runaway rates of food allergies and sensitivities among youth. Children are often sensitive to the high gluten content in wheat, and to heavy doses of yeast, wheat's sidekick in baking.

These health findings throw a spanner in the gears of the huge machinery behind today's global grain trade. If chemical fertilizers encourage moulds and fungi, then wheat should be fertilized with compost.[28] If grain elevators are breeding grounds for mycotoxins, then farmers should deliver fresh grain directly to customers. If eating too much wheat is creating sensitivities, then people should vary their diets and sample buckwheat, barley, rye, kamut, spelt, quinoa and teff, as well as wheat.

Variety has other benefits as well. Rye and buckwheat, for instance, are easier on the land than wheat. Traditional grains, closer to the wild originals, are hardier. Wheat farming is also largely responsible for the loss of western wetlands. Forty percent of natural marshes and sloughs have already been ploughed under. When wetlands disappear, so do the birds that use them as resting spots during their long migrations.

As farmers and consumers diversify what they grow and eat, they can save the prairie economy and society. The dependence of farmers on a single crop is called monoculture. Monoculture leaves farmers vulnerable to being caught in a classic squeeze. They buy all their supplies from, and sell all their harvest to, monopolies.

It doesn't take a financial genius to stick it to them at both ends, which is what conventional farm economics is all about. At the very least, diversification will likely increase the number of suppliers and buyers and create a little old-fashioned competition. If something like that doesn't happen, huge swaths of the west will become economically and socially unsustainable. Prices on glutted wheat markets are too low to support any but the biggest landholders with the largest volumes. There aren't enough people on those farms to support schools, hospitals and basic services in rural towns.

People like Amey offer hope. E.F. Schumacher, the guru of green economics who coined the slogan "Small is Beautiful," calls them "homecomers." Homecomers have the skills to build what Schumacher calls "appropriate technologies," human-scale machines that liberate humans from drudgery without enslaving them to centralized corporations. Technologies that are people- and health-friendly are both cost-effective and productive, Schumacher argues. They require "primarily an effort of the imagination and an abandonment of fear."[29] Darryl Amey is in his toolshed, tinkering with parts that can be moved by this spirit.

MILK

With milk, it's hard to know what will squeak by the government and what won't.

About thirty-five miles southeast of Ottawa, in the heart of Ontario's dairy country, the St. Albert Cooperative Cheese Manufacturing Association sells curds so piping hot they squeak. Customers line up to get them while they're being stirred in the vat, then gobble them up on the spot. In 1992, local health authorities moved to clamp down on the hot curds, claiming unrefrigerated milk products were a hazard. But no one wants hot curds that are cold, the co-op protested. Fortunately for the co-op, it's close to Quebec, where such French specialties are *de rigueur*. In a breakthrough for warm relations with Quebec tourists, health authorities backed off.[30]

The incident tells us something about the double standards

applied to milk safety and purity. The era of hand-milking the family cow on a three-legged stool is long gone. Milk production is thoroughly mechanized. Save for the cows, milk is a purely industrial product. Laws governing milk protect its industrialization more than its quality or safety. Milk is pasteurized at fairly high temperatures, probably destroying enzymes that aid digestion, so that it can be transported farther and stored longer. It's homogenized—shaken up to permanently disperse the fat—so we have no choice but to buy cream as a separate product rather than letting it rise to the top. And all milk is pooled together, so we can't identify where it came from. That eliminates the possibility of individual farmers developing a reputation for the unique tastes and qualities of their own milk. In effect, pooling gives control of the dairy industry to huge name-brand corporations selling a uniform product. The government and dairy industry work together to thwart organic producers, processors and distributors. Only Quebec and Ontario allow a few organic dairies to hold their milk back from the pool and sell it separately.

The latest development in milk production brings the government's central role in the milk industry back into the public spotlight. Recombinant Bovine Growth Hormone, or rBGH, extends milk industrialization to its illogical conclusion.[31] It's a genetically engineered drug made by inserting cow genes into bacteria, which causes cows to increase milk production. To cover up its role as a performance-enhancing drug, government and industry refer to BGH as BST, the innocuous-sounding Bovine Somatotropin. BGH is legal in the United States. Canadians are most likely to be exposed to it when they buy imported frozen pizzas and TV dinners. Thanks to an effective campaign by a coalition of farm, public health and consumer rights groups, the Canadian government refused to approve Monsanto's brand of BGH in early 1999.

The case against BGH is strong. The label on Monsanto's brand states that it can reduce rates of pregnancy in cows and increase rates of cystic ovaries, disorders of the uterus and mastitis. Indigestion, bloating and diarrhoea are other common reactions of cows to BGH. Most require treatment with antibiotics, which ends up in the milk. But the most ominous human health threat comes from another substance stimulated when BGH is injected. It's called

Insulin-like Growth Factor-1, or IGF-1, and it ends up in the milk. Several reports by independent experts link IGF-1 to breast and prostate cancer in humans.[32]

But the threat posed by BGH is by no means over. Rejection of Monsanto's application does not preclude the government from approving other brands or similar products. This puzzles Vic Daniel. He's a stockman from Kirkton, Ontario, and one of the most vocal critics of BGH. He wants to know how consideration of such a drug ever got so high on the government agenda. "How is it that a performance drug that doesn't perform, makes animals sick and may cause health problems in humans could still have a chance to be licensed in Canada?" he asks. "What problems does rBGH solve?"

Those aren't questions the government asks when considering animal drugs. Health Canada's Bureau of Veterinary Drugs reviews company data on a proposed drug. There's no need for the company to establish a problem that needs to be solved. There's not even a need to establish safety beyond a reasonable degree of doubt. On the contrary, the proposed drug is presumed innocent until proven guilty. If there are no studies proving ill effects—hard to obtain before the drug's been released—regulators can take this to mean that there's no problem. This approach is known as "the body bag school of evidence."

In the course of the BGH controversy, questions have also been asked about the government's reliance on company data, when companies have an obvious vested interest. Dr. Sol Gunner, former head of Health Canada's food directorate, has admitted publicly to being troubled by this.[33] Staff scientists were more troubled. Backed by their union, they charged their managers with pressuring them to approve BGH, despite major gaps in company data.[34] Although the union grievance was lost, reports of the whistle-blowing ran almost daily in the media, bringing attention to the deficiencies in Health Canada's regulatory system, and playing a key role in the government's decision to reject Monsanto's application. Still other questions have been asked about the right of companies to keep secret their studies on new drugs. Critics wonder whether protection of patent rights is more important than the public's right to know.

There are simple ways around this regulatory mess. The Toronto Food Policy Council (coordinated by one of this book's authors) has suggested that the first round of an animal drug review should centre on the following issues: What problems does a proposed drug solve? Do we have a quality problem, an efficiency problem, an availability problem? If so, what drug-free alternatives are available? How might these alternatives compare with drugs when it comes to ethics of animal treatment, environmental pollution, farm survival and public health? If a case could be made that a drug were the only or best remedy, then it would be appropriate to go to the expense of testing the drug and the risk of trying it. This is scientific policy based on what's known as the precautionary principle of "no regrets," where solutions with the least dangerous impact always get first consideration.

For anyone who believes in playing safe with milk, organic methods so outperform BGH on all counts as to rule out the need for any further consideration. The best that can be said for BGH is that it's a solution to a problem that doesn't exist. We do not have a milk shortage in Canada; we have an excess that no one, including governments, knows how to handle. We virtually give milk away to foreign countries—whatever is needed to keep the glut off the Canadian market so prices won't collapse. The Baskin-Robbins ice cream factory in China, for instance, uses cheap Canadian milk to make ice cream that it sells in Asia and the Caribbean. Nor is milk ever likely to be in short supply. The high fat levels in milk, and the high rates of intolerance and sensitivity associated with it, especially among peoples of Asian and African origin, likely mean that other drinks will increasingly replace it. The future of milk sales lies in niche markets.

Organic dairy farms do have lower milk yields, about 10 percent below the norm. That's deliberate. Less milking means less stress on the animals. Organic cows also get lots of time outdoors, munching on grass grown without the use of toxic chemicals. This is especially important with milk, because cows eat a lot of grass to produce relatively little milk; so toxins are bound to "bioaccumulate" or increase in proportion to the final product. (This is why there was such a furore around milk safety after nuclear tests in the 1950s and nuclear accidents at Three Mile Island and Chernobyl, and why

milk provides such a good read on levels of environmental pollution.) Organic farmers find that ethical treatment of animals pays off
in lower vet and drug bills. Even when forced to sell their milk into
generic pools, they can make enough to survive on at today's prices.

To thrive, organic dairies need government rules that will per-
mit them to sell milk directly to the public under their own farm
or regional name brands, and to process their own yogurt and
cheeses. Those tired of the taste of processed cheese slices could
try distinctive cheeses with flavours defined by the wild flowers
growing in the pastures of a particular region, as is common in
Europe. These are the kinds of products Health Canada could be
supporting instead of risky drugs, if they ever relent on the industrial model of milk production. For now, the kid-glove treatment
for drug companies contrasts with the crackdown imposed on
organic producers, and exposes a major barrier to healthful milk:
Health Canada itself.

BEEF

Taking a break from chores at his Tanglewood Ranch near
Didsbury, Alberta, the rolling foothills of the Rockies stretched
out behind him, Lloyd Quantz looks like he'd be more at home
on the set of *Bonanza* than bagging sprouts at a health food store.
Nobody would ever have guessed that one of Canada's most
respected cattlemen—formerly manager of the Canadian Charolais
Association, general manager of the biggest feedlot in the country, president of the Alberta Institute of Agrologists, founder of
AgriTrends Research, the most influential farm consultants in
the west, and dean at Olds College, the country's biggest agriculture school—would end up converting his million-dollar-a-year
ranch to organic. But he did. As a result, we can learn about alternatives in beef production from someone who knows the industry inside out.

Lucky for Quantz, he started with land that got it right the first
time. The sod at Tanglewood has never been broken. The original
native grasses, which evolved with the area's dry and brittle climate
over ten thousand years, are still intact. "I see cattle raising as

marketing my grass," he says. This is one case where livestock make the most efficient and environmentally friendly use of land. The wild grasses, unlike the hay, grains and beans planted on broken ground, survive without artificial fertilizers, chemicals and irrigation. Since they're perennials—plants that come up year after year without reseeding—Quantz has no need to burn up fuel ploughing and planting. Their roots run thick and deep, holding the soil against erosion. They dredge up rare trace minerals that cattle thrive on. "I've never had a deficiency problem with my animals," says Quantz. "Hay is for racehorses. This is great for cattle." Sometimes organic is as simple as knowing the value of what nature put in place, adjusting the farm to nature rather than nature to the farm.

Quantz raises Charolais cattle crossed with Angus steers. He spends nothing on artificial insemination, letting nature take its course. Oddly enough, this is an innovation in the cattle business. The meat-packing industry demands "straightline" breeding, breeding for characteristics that deliver a predictable and uniform meat product—master race cattle. "Nature has a better idea about diversity," Quantz figures. "Hybrid vigour is what makes for fertility, longevity and resistance to disease." The proof is in his vet and drug bills, which amount to next to nothing.

Quantz practises what's called paddocking or rotational grazing, the latest in organic feeding practices in North America, though considered old hat in New Zealand. Historians of the North American buffalo claim paddocking is close to the lifestyle of those roaming herds. Using portable fencing, Quantz keeps the whole herd in a ten- or fifteen-acre area for three days before moving them on to a new area. "It's a classic case of working with natural systems," he says. If cattle are given free range of the entire ranch, they're like kids in a candy store, he says. They chomp down fine grasses and turn up their noses at rough fescue. Over time, the fine grasses become overstressed. Paddocking pressures cattle to diversify their diet and graze on the fescue, which is rich in nutrients. This keeps the variety of grass species in balance, and gives the land a complete break from heavy stomping and time to absorb the rich manure after the cattle move to a new paddock.

Unlike most ranchers and government agencies, Quantz is keen on small farms. His own ranch is a quarter-section, a backyard garden by Prairie standards. He realized the economic virtue of small farms in the late 1980s when he led an Alberta commission investigating farm loans and witnessed the devastation caused by the agribusiness strategy of "get big or get out." Government agencies had encouraged farmers to speculate on bigger machines that could work bigger farms. To get cheap credit, all they had to do was put their farms up as collateral. But when all the farmers with bigger machines and spreads glutted the market with goods, prices collapsed. The farmers lost everything. If governments want to help, Quantz argues, they should support smaller farmers, who can keep their costs and debts low as a hedge against bad years, and set their minds on servicing small specialty markets where they can add some value to their raw resources, and so get paid for quality rather than quantity. "Farmers will be a lot stronger when they can look their customers in the eye," he says. Their output and gross revenues will be smaller, but their profit margins and net income will be higher. Not that this approach is well received by farm equipment and chemical manufacturers. They make money when farmers are spending on machines and chemicals, not when they're cultivating relationships with customers.

More farmers on smaller farms is the only way to save small rural communities, Quantz says, noting that nearby Didsbury is often nicknamed Deadsbury. "We can't have organic farmers without sustainable communities" where people can settle in for the long term, knowing there's a secure economic future for local butchers, bakers and candlestick makers. Organic farmers can only hold the course of land stewardship when they have deep and long-lasting commitments to people and places they'll be passing their land on to, he says. Without this inner core of identity, the market pressures to get through another season by using fertilizers, chemicals or other short cuts are too great.

As matters stand now, the absence of infrastructure for farmers and ranchers who want to get closer to their customers and communities is the major bottleneck in organic meat production, Quantz says. All roads lead to the giant meat-packing processors, who have the lock on access to the public through contracts with supermarkets. The processors don't like dealing with individual ranchers, organic or not—too many bookkeeping hassles, not enough control over delivery times, size and weight of cattle, and the uniformity of their grade and fat content. So they pay a premium, an offer ranchers can't refuse, for cattle hauled to feedlots, where they stay for two or three months prior to slaughter.

The feedlots are little more than sickbays, Quantz says, recalling the days when he ran one with 35,000 head of cattle. The cattle come in the door stressed from their truck drive and dumbfounded by their new surroundings. Their herd mentality and instincts are disoriented. They're fed a new high-protein diet that the bacteria in their stomach can't digest; many suffer abscessed livers as a result of this alien diet. They're rubbing shoulders with cattle suffering diseases to which they have no immunity. Up to a third are kept alive on antibiotics.

When they've reached the desired weight and fat content, the cattle are hauled to the auction yard, then again to the processor. They're made to stand for eight hours without food before being slaughtered. (The slaughtering is cleaner if they have an empty stomach.) The lack of digestive activity for this stretch of time encourages stomach bacteria associated with E coli 0157:H7, commonly known as hamburger disease and responsible for more than 40,000 cases of food-borne illness each year across North America, as well as several deaths.[35] E coli 0157:H7 is also associated with Hemolytic-Uremic Syndrome, or HUS. It is a life-threatening disease characterized by acute kidney failure, and is especially serious in young children. The meat from several cows may go into one hamburger patty, and the grinding machinery is used continuously without cleaning between lots, so one contaminated animal can infect thousands of hamburgers. It doesn't take much for disease to spread like proverbial wildfire in the processing plant, where thousands of cattle are slaughtered, butchered and ground up each day.[36]

The beef leaves the processor packed in styrofoam and plastic wrap, ready for sale at the supermarket. Consumers have odd food obsessions, Quantz says. They want their vegetables frozen when they should be eaten freshly picked; they want their meat freshly killed when it could well be kept longer or bought frozen. Beef needs to be aged if enzymes are to tenderize it naturally, without the addition of chemical tenderizers or flavour enhancers. Meat doesn't go bad for at least a week if it's kept cool and handled with extreme care for cleanliness, Quantz says. Most high-class steakhouses serve their meat naturally aged, just like their wine list.

If consumers accepted aged or frozen meat, they would provide the opportunity farmers need to bypass the feedlots, auction yards and supermarkets that detract from the value of what they've raised on the farm. Organic meat would require no premium in this decentralized system. As Quantz's experience shows, organic cattle ranching is relatively inexpensive; it's only the extra cost of segregating organic meat from a mass-production system that makes it expensive to buy. If the organic meat could be processed on-farm or at local butchers, then sold more directly to customers—perhaps, for nostalgia's sake, in brown waxed paper instead of styrofoam—both farmers and consumers would get good value.

Lloyd Quantz's perspective throws a bit of a monkey wrench in the standard stereotypes about organic. In most people's minds, the onus is on the farmer. Organic means that the farmer has produced quality without using chemicals or drugs. Quantz bats the organic challenge back to the consumers' court: as long as consumers demand plastic-wrapped, fresh-killed meat, this demand will work its way back through the system and lead to the feedlots from hell.

POULTRY

The Tilsley farm, nestled in the poetic beauty of Cape Breton's Margaree Valley, is a study of poultry in motion. Glen and Kimberly Tilsley raise about five hundred chickens in an innovative organic system known as "pasturing poultry."[37] It features mobile chicken coops, ten-foot-by-ten-foot wooden frames covered with chicken wire that sit directly on the ground. The coop protects the chickens from foxes and other predators while they cluck away inside, picking at weeds and insects. It's splendour in the grass for the chickens and a way for the Tilsleys to clean up their pasture. The light, portable coop is moved daily so the chickens can clean and renew a different section of pasture, removing weeds and pests and leaving a trail of nitrogen-rich fertilizer behind them. The birds are also fed grains, supplemented with fishmeal, brewers' yeast and lactobacillus culture, the disease-fighting bacteria found in yogurt. There's no need for antibiotics. Customers flock to the taste of range-fed chicken. The Tilsleys' market survey showed enough local demand for ten such operations.[38]

Eggs and white meat from chickens are regarded as health foods by many, a view that has not quite caught up to the realities of the poultry industry. In the factory barns that supply many supermarkets, chickens are packed cheek by jowl. Imagine living your entire life in a crowded elevator and you'll begin to get the picture. The birds are stressed by lack of fresh air and exercise. The intense crowding overpowers their ancestral sense of pecking order. As a result, their immune systems crash, leaving them vulnerable to disease. All it takes is for one to get sick and an epidemic can spread. That's why antibiotic drugs rule the roost in factory barns. The chickens are fed a steady diet of what are called "subtherapeutic levels" of antibiotics, doses below what's needed to overcome an acute disease. The drugs also work as a growth promoter, helping to fatten chickens for the kill inside of a month. Antibiotic feeds, available without prescription, are now standard for chickens, turkey, cattle, pigs and calves raised for veal. A third of all antibiotics used in Canada—22,000 tons a year—are fed to farm animals, which become the meat on our supermarket counters. Organic farmers forbid this practice.

Overuse of antibiotics is a well-recognized threat to humans.[39] Antibiotics are the golden egg of modern medicine, fighting infections and saving lives. But the less they're used, the better. That's because, sooner or later, a few mutant bacteria are bound to survive a dosage and pass on their successful traits to the next generation, encoding the higher resistance level in their genes. This process could eventually lead to the evolution of "superbugs" that can withstand all antibiotics. That's why we're always warned to avoid using antibiotics for everyday sniffles and common colds. To preserve their value for when we really need them, antibiotics must be used sparingly. We can choose not to use antibiotics wantonly on ourselves; but the Canadian Medical Association, in a 1998 report, has sounded the alarm that unless conventional farmers reduce their use as well, new infectious diseases will crop up that medical treatment won't be able to help.[40]

It's now known that superbugs from factory chickens can cross the road to the other side—to humans. "We have documented cases of bacterial resistance being transferred to humans," says Robert Hancock, professor of microbiology at the University of British Columbia. "We are on the verge of a significant health crisis in which the poor utilization of antibiotics with animals is a significant contributor."[41] In the United States, resistant strains of salmonella bacteria from chickens raised in factory farms cause four million illnesses and three thousand deaths a year. Drug abuse has come home to roost. This is why we're told to handle raw chicken with extreme care, scrub cutting boards with disinfectant and cook the meat well.

Alarm from health professionals has had no impact on politicians. The U.S. Food and Drug Administration tried to ban antibiotic use on animals in 1977 but failed. Since then, several other motions in the U.S. Congress have been defeated. Canada bans animal use of only one antibiotic: tetracycline. Instead of eliminating the dangerous and cruel livestock practices that lead to superbugs, there's a drive to use the Canadian government's nuclear technology to irradiate bacteria. This might solve the government's problem of finding a market for unsold nuclear equipment, but irradiation creates some sickening problems of its own, not the least of which is where to bury the waste of irradiated toxins that last millions of years.

Governments and factory farms are misusing one of the great medical advances of all time. Antibiotic drugs have saved many people's lives, but this invaluable resource is in peril. Organic methods are not only about taste, nutrition and avoiding senseless cruelty to animals; they have become fundamental to the preservation of human health.

FISH

Ray Rogers is a big, burly man with a warm but powerful voice, almost a stereotype of the hearty East Coast fisher. For twelve years he made his living with a thirty-five-foot boat off the shore of Little Harbour, Nova Scotia. Over those years he watched his catch decline and his community falter. Today Rogers is a professor of environmental studies at York University in Toronto. The collapse of the fishery still haunts him. Writing and teaching about what happened has become part of his life's work.[42]

Over coffee, Rogers recounts the life of the traditional East Coast inshore fisher. His day began at midnight, when he steamed out into the ocean looking for a good place to set trawls—a rocky bottom, away from the mud. When he found a good spot, he threw an anchor tied to a buoy over the stern, and then steamed away from the anchor, unravelling about two miles of hand-baited line as he went. "By the time the trawl is set, it's about four in the morning. You clean up your boat and lay down for an hour," says Rogers. "At daybreak you haul it back, take the fish off the hooks and steam back to the wharf. It's about four in the afternoon by the time you've unloaded your catch."

Rogers loved the life of the fisher, but that life is no more, for him or for thousands across Atlantic Canada. By the early 1990s most of the cod had disappeared and the federal government had taken the unprecedented step of declaring a moratorium in the cod fishery. Rogers says the roots of the collapse lie in the shift from the inshore fishery to the industrial offshore fishery.

The traditional inshore fishery worked with the rhythms of nature. Fishers didn't expect to be out on the sea twelve months a year. "I harvest my hay in May. I plant my garden in June. I fish in July and August. During the winter months I'm cutting wood. That was the life of the inshore fisher," says Rogers. And in the same way that organic farmers plant an assortment of crops, fishers thought about diversity. They netted herring and mackerel in the spring, long-lined in the summer and lobstered in the fall. Fishers lived an organic lifestyle in a naturally organic occupation.

But the industrialization of the fishing fleet changed all that. "I witnessed the disappearance of fish on a daily basis," says Rogers. "You'd steam out onto the ocean and come back with nothing." The thirty-five-foot dories equipped with a compass and a sounder were replaced by huge industrial ships laden with all the latest technology: radar, sonar, diesel engines, polypropylene rope, refrigeration.

The industrial ships first appeared after World War II, and grew in size and technological sophistication. William Warner, author of

"The Fish Killers," argues that the impetus for the factory ship came out of the decline of whaling.[43] That industry had already developed the technology for long expeditions at sea, and the offshore fishery quickly adapted these practices, then introduced technologies of its own. Before long, the ships had equipment for automated filleting, quick freezing and fishmeal processing, as well as ever more sophisticated electronic devices for locating the fish. Boats could stay out on the water longer because of their refrigeration units—catching, processing and freezing more than five hundred tons per day. Refrigeration also transformed the fishery at the distribution end; it meant that fish caught off Canada's shores could be sold all over the world.

Dragging became the fishing method of choice for the offshore fishery. The factory ships were equipped with steel doors that literally dragged across the ocean floor, scooping everything in their path into a giant net. "On a dragger," says Rogers, "you spend most of your time shovelling rocks and anything else you drag up off the ocean bottom." The quality of the fish declined dramatically with the draggers. "When you're dumping twenty or thirty thousand pounds of fish on the deck at a time, it can't all be looked after quickly enough. Some of it starts to rot," says Rogers. "And just think of the pressure on some poor cod or haddock at the bottom of that net. There's nothing left of it by the time you dump it out."

As a result, most fish caught in Atlantic Canada ended up as prison food or fast food. In fact, Mark Kurlansky, in his history of cod, argues that the development of the fast-food industry coincided with the "dragging-the-bottom-for-everything" approach to the fishery. The fishburger mongers of the world needed lots of fish for their industrial feeding machine, with little regard for quality. Dragging could deliver that.[44]

The development of new technologies masked the disappearance of the stocks. As the factory ships got better and better at finding scarcer and scarcer fish, their window into the fish ecosystem was skewed. That there were fewer fish in the sea was overlooked because the technology used to locate the fish that remained was becoming ever more efficient. The small inshore fishers who continued to fish in the traditional way had a clearer picture of what was happening; but their anecdotal evidence was disregarded. Meanwhile, while the commercial catch data indicated that everything was fine, research vessels were warning that disaster loomed. Finally, the federal government acknowledged this discrepancy and declared a moratorium in 1992.

What happened in Atlantic Canada is not unique. The B.C. salmon fishery is on the brink, and according to the United Nations, catches in thirteen of the world's seventeen oceans are in jeopardy.[45] The economic damage has been calculated. According to the Washington-based World Watch Institute, over 100,000 fishers around the world, mostly small ones like Rogers, have already lost their livelihoods. This number is expected to jump to 10 million in the next decade.[46] Small fishers make up 90 percent of those employed in the world's fishery. They will pay the price for the damage caused by the 10 percent who work on factory ships and hoard more than 50 percent of the catch. When the small local fishers are pushed out of business, a billion people worldwide who rely on local fish as their main source of protein will suffer. Ironically, this deadly process is being funded by government subsidies. The United Nations calculates that worldwide government investment in, and subsidization of, the factory fishery amounts to $54 billion each year, not to mention policies that directly or indirectly support overfishing and squeeze out the small local fishers.

Fish farming, or aquaculture, is being touted as the solution to the wild fish crisis. It's a rapidly expanding industry. Ninety percent of the salmon consumed in Canada today—and 40 percent worldwide—is farmed fish. Mussels, trout, shrimp and other species also come from these operations. But most fish farms are no different from other industrial farms; they operate on the same false premises we've already discussed. Fish are overcrowded in what amount to marine feedlots—tanks or pens on lake and sea coasts. In one operation in the Bay of Fundy, six thousand fish are forced into each pen, which is no larger than fifteen square yards. The conditions are ideal for disease to develop, and it has. Last year, hundreds of thousands of fish were killed in an epidemic of infectious salmon anaemia in New Brunswick. The same disease has devastated fish farms in northern Europe. Parasites have been another problem. As a result, the farmed fish are routinely fed antibiotics and washed with pesticides. Besides these chemicals, salmon feed is laced with red dye to give the flesh that characteristic pink colour.

Inevitably, some of these substances are released into the open sea, excreted through fish feces and washed out of the pens. There is a growing fear among independent researchers that they're creating antibiotic-resistant diseases in wild fish and the birds and sea mammals that eat them. There is also evidence that these chemicals may produce superbugs in humans. In 1997 nine people in Toronto were infected with a new strain of bacteria after handling farmed fish from the United States. The particular strain had never before been passed from fish to humans.

There are other concerns as well. Researchers at British Columbia's David Suzuki Foundation are worried about escaped Atlantic salmon killing Pacific wild fish, and about heavy concentrations of fish feces destroying the seabed beneath the pens and polluting nearby shores.[47] In a bizarre paradox, fish farming is actually increasing pressure on the ocean fisheries, not decreasing it, because many of the most lucrative species—shrimp, salmon, trout, bass and yellowtail—are carnivores and require fish protein to grow rapidly. It takes about five pounds of ocean fish, processed into fishmeal, to raise one pound of farmed fish. That's a huge net protein loss. In addition, the farmed fish are glutting the market and making it impossible for ocean fishers to compete.[48]

Ransom Myers, Chair of Ocean Studies at Halifax's Dalhousie University, believes that boycotting certain fish products is one way to offset government support for overfishing. The first species that should be the subject of boycotts, according to U.S. environmentalist Elliot Norse, include shark, Atlantic swordfish and marlin, bluefin tuna, orange roughy and Chilean sea bass—all for being severely overfished. He says that shrimp and salmon should be avoided too, because of the unsustainable way in which they are farmed.[49]

Ray Rogers believes it's going to take more than boycotts to save the fishery. He says we have to reanimate the ocean, to see it as a living thing, not just as a resource to be exploited. "The deepest thing you're struck by when you're slopping around at three in the morning in thick fog is that you're part of a force that is much more powerful than you are," says Rogers, "one you can't manage or control." Reanimating the ocean also means acknowledging how little we know about the creatures beneath the sea. It means recognizing the complexity of their lives and social structures. Rogers says cod are a case in point. "Cod are not individual decision makers," he says. "It takes a collective mass for there to be 'cod.' When they get below a critical mass, they cease to be cod. It may be that there are so few of them now that they don't know how to be cod any more. There is a social collective memory that used to be passed from the older fish to the younger fish. That's gone now. They're like teenagers bombing around the streets on a Saturday night. They're showing up in places they don't usually show up, as if they're lost."

It may be that understanding "codness" is a first step to understanding our own relationship with nature, and the role food plays in that relationship. How to translate that understanding into choices at the checkout counter comes next.

HOW TO SHOP ORGANIC

So you've made the decision to buy organic. Now, how do you find it? Here are some basic guidelines on what to look for and some suggestions for reducing your exposure to toxic chemicals when organic is not readily available.

If you buy organic from a store, a label offers important guarantees. The gold standard in organic labels is certification by an independent certification agency. Canada has forty-seven of them, and the label most commonly seen belongs to the Organic Crop Improvement Association. Others, seen often on organic food imported from the United States, include Farm-Verified Organic, California Certified Organic Farmers and Quality Assurance International. Their independence from government is a plus. When governments get into the organic act, they bring their own baggage. In 1998, for instance, the U.S. Food and Drug Administration tried to redefine organic to include sewage sludge fertilizer, genetic engineering and irradiation. Only the efforts of more than 200,000 people who took part in a write-in campaign blocked this effort to destroy organic's good name. No one has more of a vested interest in preserving the highest standards for organic than working farmers, who rely on the reputation of the label to stay in business. This is a case where self-regulation serves the public interest better than government.

A farmer who wants to be certified applies to a certification agency, which arranges for a professionally qualified inspector to visit the farm. All farm management practices are reviewed, and the inspector makes sure that chemical fertilizers and sprays haven't been used for at least three years. Once certified, the farmer must maintain a paper trail on purchases and practices to enable continual monitoring by the agency. Farmers can also take advantage of educational and other programs offered by agencies to facilitate continual improvement.

Exacting standards create a problem for farmers during the transition to organic. For their first three years, they face all the challenges of a new way of farming but don't qualify for the label that gets them a premium price for a premium product. As a result, some farmers who are moving towards organic follow pesticide reduction growing protocols, or Integrated Pest Management, known as IPM. The idea behind IPM is to reduce pesticide use as much as possible: attract birds and bats that prey on insects, keep a close eye on emerging problems so they can be isolated, and use pesticides sparingly. Produce grown in this way will often have the designation "ecological."

Companies that want to sell certified organic processed goods— like bread, frozen entrées and salsas—must, like farmers, have their operations inspected, and must keep the same rigorous paper trail. If most of the ingredients in a product are organic, then it can be called certified organic. If only some of the ingredients are organic, the manufacturer is allowed to list the organic ingredients but cannot claim that the entire product is certified organic.

If you're used to supermarket labels, the certified organic label is in a class by itself; most others are pure self-promotion. "Grade A," for instance, refers to size, shape or fat content; it bears little relationship to quality, healthfulness or safe farm practices. "All-natural" refers to whatever fantasy Madison Avenue hopes to conjure up in your mind. "Pure" sugar has none of the original nutrients and is 99.9 percent sweet nothing. "Brown," as in sugar or bread, refers to a colour, usually provided by molasses or caramel, not to an organic process. To keep the word *organic* from being kidnapped in the same way that *natural* was stolen from the counter-culture of the 1970s, it's important to keep your eye peeled for a certified organic label.

If you can buy food directly from an organic farmer you know and trust, a formal label is not the be-all and end-all. Labels play a role akin to brand names: in an anonymous market, they're a trust-mark you accept in place of knowing much about the personal integrity of the producer. When dealing directly with a trusted farmer, like when eating from your own organic garden, you don't need a third-party endorsement. An organic farmer may have a credible reason for not getting a formal label. Some feel the expense and rigmarole of using a label aren't worth it until sales reach a certain level, much like home-based entrepreneurs who postpone incorporating their business. Others just assume organic as a base-line while seeking a reputation and identity tied to their region or personal flair, much like Stilton cheese or French champagne. If the farmer is trustworthy, why get hung up on a piece of paper?

If you're not able to make a total switch to organic and have to resort to half measures, there are several ways to practise safe food and reduce your risks.

Buying local is usually a good bet. Food grown in the Third World has likely been sprayed with chemicals not permitted in Europe, the United States or Canada. The most infamous, DDT, is in widespread use. DDT sprayed on Central and South American plantations is carried away by air currents as far north as Canada, which accounts for the fact that the Great Lakes have DDT concentrations as high as they were when DDT was banned in Canada more than twenty years ago.[50] This will give you a feel for the exposure you're getting from last week's direct spray on your food. Food from the United States is much more likely than Canadian food to be grown from genetically engineered seeds or to contain growth hormones.[51]

Food shipped locally for quick sale is also less likely to have been sprayed with methyl bromide (to keep away moulds and fungus) than imported produce, especially from California and Florida. Methyl bromide is a suspected cancer causer. It's also a major culprit in the destruction of the ozone layer, which is linked to the rise of skin cancer. At the very least, local food is more likely to be fresh. The biggest losses of nutrients come from picking food before it's ripe, so that it can withstand the long haul, and from the losses while in transit.

Several scientific and public interest groups have developed "dirty dozen" lists of fruits and vegetables that receive the most lethal doses of chemical toxins. The lists are all quite similar. Strike these off your non-organic shopping list: apricots, bananas, bell peppers, cherries, Chilean grapes, cucumbers, green beans, lettuce, Mexican cantaloupe, potatoes, spinach and tomatoes. Tomatoes, in fact, top the list of foods treated with chemicals that are linked to cancer. The National Academy of Science in the United States estimates there's a risk of nine cancers per ten thousand consumer exposures.[52] Given levels of tomato consumption in Canada, that theoretically means that every family faces a chance of contracting cancer from tomatoes at some point.

Many people scrub their produce with dishwashing liquid and remove the outer layer of peels and leaves to try to reduce their exposure to toxic chemicals. There are limits to the effectiveness of this because some pesticides are embedded in the plant tissues. Also, be careful what soap you use for scrubbing food or plates. Several leading brands contain Nonylphenol Ethoxylates, or NPE, which the World Wildlife Fund considers a hormone disrupter. You don't want to be licking them off your food or plate.

Genetically engineered products are another category to avoid. The great majority of GE seeds have been altered for one of three reasons: they come with a built-in pesticide, as with New Leaf potatoes; they can withstand certain chemical sprays, as with GE canola, corn or soy; or they take longer to rot in trucks, warehouses and stores, as with genetically engineered tomatoes. None are bred for nutrition, health or taste. There is no consumer advantage. Since they're not usually labelled, you have few ways of knowing what you're eating until it is too late. In addition, literally thousands of processed foods may be made with genetically engineered ingredients. The list of thirty-six genetically engineered foods already approved by the Canadian government include several varieties of canola (oils and margarines), soy beans (oils, tofu products, fillers), corn (oil, syrup, cornstarch), squash, cotton seed and potatoes. Going organic on these items is your only safe bet.

As a general rule, the less animal fat you consume, the less exposure you'll have to poisonous farm chemicals and other toxic pollutants that gather in fatty tissue. If you can't afford organic meat and dairy, you might consider moving to a plant-centred diet. Grains, beans, nuts, fruits and vegetables contain a range of antioxidants, compounds that can heal damage from pollution and a goodly portion of fibre, which helps to flush toxins out of your body. Animal products are generally short of both antioxidants and fibre.

Fish poses another problem. Usually it is impossible to know if the fish you're buying is farmed or wild. It's more than likely to be farmed, making it a no more healthy choice than beef or chicken raised with hormones and antibiotics. If you have access to a local fisher or to one of the few inshore co-ops or certified organic fish farms, you're in luck. Otherwise, until there is a system for labelling sustainably caught wild fish, as there is for organically produced meat, milk and produce, consumers would be wise to eat fish sparingly. Healthier choices include sardines, flounder and sole. It's smart to limit swordfish, Atlantic salmon and lobster in your diet.

When you make the decision to go organic, you'll find that it's not as hard as you might think, nor as costly. Without wishing to sound like an ad for hair colouring, going organic might cost a few pennies more, but you're worth it.

CHAPTER 2

EAT SMARTER

EAT SMARTER

Most people have three problems with going organic: they don't have the money to buy it; they don't have the time to prepare it; and their kids, watching their friends gobble down pizzas and fries at lunch, won't eat it. The bread-and-butter problems of money, time and social support are holding back a large-scale shift to organic eating. Lack of motivation isn't the main problem; most people have already figured out on their own that junk food is junk and health food is healthy. Nor is there any shortage of anxiety; people are plenty worried about their guts, butts, energy levels and risks of disease. But no one's helping them out of the fix they're in. This chapter offers that help.

A new home economics will be at the centre of the move to organics. Home economics recalls the original meaning of the Greek word for economics: home management. Odd as it sounds at first, the next big improvement in the overall economy will come from boosting the effectiveness of how we spend our energy at home. Despite what government and business leaders tell us, advancement won't come from increasing output or productivity at work. We've doubled workplace productivity since 1969, which should mean that we could enjoy the comforts of 1969 while taking every other year off for holidays. Instead, the average person works ten hours a week more today, and most families have two income earners instead of the one common in 1969—all for a barely noticeable improvement in the standard of living. The doubled productivity has vanished down a black hole of microwaves, cell phones, energy bars, laxatives, antacids, heart pills, allergy treatments, Ritalin, Prozac, diet clinics and taxes to cover the spiralling costs of chronic disease, traffic jams and landfill sites.[1]

The next generation of health and economic advances will come from learning to consume more productively. The productive consumer, or "prosumer" (to use the hybrid phrase of futurist Alvin Toffler), will lead the way.[2] That's because the new home-based productivity will use the currency of time. It takes the old adage "time is money" and brings it into the twenty-first century, where "time saves money."

Time is a great equalizer. The rich can't use their money to buy a twenty-six-hour day. Their crock pots don't cook more quickly and their potatoes don't grow faster. Quality time is the precondition of healthy relationships. Shared, it can transform the lone drudgery of finding and preparing food into a good time. The more we democratize time, the more we equalize access to health and food.

Going organic will be affordable when we rethink the way we use our time. That's because it's time more than any other factor that's preventing a mass movement to organics. According to a poll released by the Canadian Dietetic Association, 40 percent of adults blame their poor eating habits on lack of time.[3] Organic food can be grown, distributed and prepared at low cost as long as people have the time they need.

This chapter offers a baker's dozen of practical suggestions that can help make organic food part of your life. We start with a few old-time penny-pinching tips, then sample some ways to get by with a little help from your friends, today's equivalents of neighbourhood barn-raising and quilting bees. If these ideas whet your appetite, you'll appreciate the logic of the last few suggestions, which show how employers and governments can save a bundle if they think outside the box and lend a hand to organics. Later in the chapter we'll present some profiles of people who have tried some of these approaches and who are happy to share their secrets for eating smarter.

THIRTEEN WAYS TO EAT SMARTER

1. Shop at a local store where you know the owner as well as the owner knows you.

You may not know the supermarket owners, but they know your unconscious mind better than you do. They count on you spending seventy dollars more than you intended to on each trip to their store. They know that when you buy strawberries on sale, you buy shortcake mix that's marked up, and when you buy hot dogs on sale, you buy mustard, relish and buns that are marked up. They know you let your guard down when you see fruit and vegetables displayed as you enter the door. They know you start by turning to the right aisle. They know a full shelf gives you a feeling of abundance and helps you relax about money; that's why they always have staff filling shelves, even when they're short-staffed at the checkout counter. They know that you slow down in wide aisles, so they put the high-profit items there. They know you'll likely buy meat and milk, so they line them along the back, making you walk across several aisles, each with an end shelf brimming over with items people buy on impulse. They know that eye level is buy level, and when the kids see the candy and gum right at their eye level by the checkout counter, you're going to give in rather than cause a fuss in public.[4] Fully 89 percent of the candies and gums sold at supermarkets are bought on impulse.[5]

When you buy organic food at a neighbourhood health food store, you can expect to pay more for individual items. But you won't be like a kid in a candy store, with eyes bigger than your stomach. When you ask where the laxatives are, the owner will point you to a fifty-cent bag of bran. And you'll save in driving time and line-ups at the checkout. Although your organic purchases will cost you more, you'll save on what you don't buy. Just look at the junk piled up in a lot of shopping carts and you'll know that the easiest savings for health and the pocketbook come from what you don't buy.

2. Eat low-fad foods.

Buy top value for bottom dollar with the proven techniques of bil-
lionaire investor Warren Buffett. He puts his money in underpriced
stocks that have lasting worth and steers clear of overpriced stocks
that have glamour but no underlying value. People who invested
$10,000 with Buffett in 1956 are worth $200 million today. Buying
food or buying stocks, it pays to find discrepancies between value
and what Buffett calls "nonsensical market prices."[6]

The best foods have bargain-basement prices. Barley, beans, beets,
cabbage, carrots, garlic, kale, oatmeal, onions, potatoes, sweet potatoes and turnips are not status items. That's because they're thick-
skinned, and can be transported and stored without much packaging. Processors know that, without packaging, there's no basis for
brand loyalty. And they know that advertising builds brand loyalty.
That's where money is made—in brands, not food. So the big-name
processors focus on adding value to the brand, as Madison Avenue
puts it, or nonsensical value, as Buffett defines it. Since no one is
adding hype to barley, beets and cabbage, they're good value.

People who blow their food budget on meat don't know beans
about value investing. Most people could afford organic if they used
meat as a garnish rather than a main course. Most beans are rich in
protein and a good meat substitute. They're superior to meat on
most other counts. Beans are good for the heart. The more you eat,
the more you get fibre, calcium, magnesium and B vitamins, all key
to healthy arteries. Beans are considered gourmet food in many
parts of the world. With a little experimentation and a good cookbook, they can be gourmet food for you too.

Beans, grains, root vegetables and organ meats are the staple
foods in most cultures, so they've been stigmatized along with the
poor people who eat them. Only in France have they escaped this
fate. Escargot and frogs' legs first got on the menu when nothing
else was available; now they're the symbol of classy eating. The
foods eaten by African-American sharecroppers in the American
Deep South—collard greens and black-eyed peas are two examples—are also undergoing something of a revival. A study of U.S.
dietary trends over thirty years shows that poor African-Americans
in the 1960s were eating healthier than rich whites today, and notes
that a new generation of affluent, health-conscious whites are

learning to appreciate sharecropper foods.[7]

Top chefs have recognized the value of poor people's food for generations. Alexis Soyer, England's most celebrated nineteenth-century chef, gave up cooking for elite gentlemen's clubs to organize soup kitchens in famine-stricken Ireland, and later worked with Florence Nightingale, cooking for wounded soldiers during the Crimean War. For low-cost but delicious meals, he wrote, the secret is to "use and not abuse nature's productions." In his book of famine recipes, he stressed that "it requires more science to produce a good dish at trifling expense than a superior one with unlimited means."[8] Food brings the knowledge economy into the kitchen. Knowledge is more democratic than money and can be distributed evenly among all income groups, making quality organic food accessible to all. This is the incredible lightness of beans.

3. Buy in season.

To every food there is a season. You pay a lot less when you buy in season because you're paying for food, not for the costs of transport and storage. Farmers sell fresh food at bargain prices, because the market is flush with competition. They'd rather sell cheap than lose their crops to rot. And they make more money selling to the fresh market than they do selling to processors and canners, who pay them a tiny fraction of the retail price. Apples sold to juicers, for instance, get as little as three cents a pound. You also get peak nutritional value when you buy local and fresh. Food that's been picked early to withstand long-haul transit can lose half its nutrients before it reaches your table. Fresh organic costs less than the combination of stale conventional and a bottle of vitamin pills.

Buying fresh and seasonal requires a change of shopping and cooking habits. Many people shop with a list to make sure they don't forget anything and to protect themselves from impulse buying. They work backwards, from the meal plan to the food. Going with the flow of the seasons works forward from what's available. Buy strawberries, apples and pumpkins when they're fresh, scrumptious and cheap, then find recipes to cook them in different ways. As we shift to fresh and local, a new style of monthly cookbook will come into its own. The chapter for May will feature early bloomers such as mustard greens and radishes; the chapter for November will feature late arrivals like kale, cabbage and squash. February recipes can focus on locally grown and stored fruits and vegetables and sprouts. We'll revive old celebrations that marked seasonal changes with feasts: maple syrup parties in March, strawberry socials in June, corn roasts in August. Thanksgiving isn't the only feast tied to harvests, it's just the only one we still celebrate. Buying in season can actually increase, not decrease, food variety, healthfulness and celebration.

4. Waste not, want not.

Organic foods deliver full value when you make full use of them. There's no need to peel the skins off organic produce because there are no chemical residues. Dieters can eat the apple in its skin and so get the full value of pectin, which sends a message to the brain that the body is filling up. Peels from oranges, lemons and grapefruit can be made into marmalades and used as cold remedies. Tea from grapefruit rinds, sometimes called "fruit quinine," clears congested lungs. Watermelon rinds make a mean pickle. When juicing joints go organic, they'll develop another revenue stream by selling products made from nature's packaging, namely peels. They can pass the savings on to two sets of customers instead of one.

Making foods do double duty was common before the chemical era. Check out the recipes in the old Girls' Annuals from World War I days: bread puddings made from stale bread, roasted squash seeds added to cereals, steamed tops of radish, turnip and beet for nutrient-rich greens. Mastery of such recipes was the stock in trade of what were called thrifty and progressive homemakers. Other cultures have never lost this attitude. Panzanella, for example, a Tuscan salad that's gaining popularity in North America, features stale bread soaked with sweet plum tomatoes, minced red onions, diced celery hearts and cucumbers that have been tossed with olive oil, red wine vinegar and red chili pepper.[9]

Organic foods become affordable when you use the whole food. What our grandmothers took for granted is what innovative economists are now calling "elegance" or "economies of scope." It's based on the concept of the old camping scarf that can be used as a pot holder, a wash cloth and a sunhat, depending on the time of day. Organic is all about elegance. It costs less because it creates more benefits. It needs cooks who appreciate elegance, for whom once is not enough.

5. Pay the extra cost of organic on the instalment plan.

Eat now, save later. Regard the extra money you spend on organics as an investment, not as an expenditure. The return on investment is perhaps best illustrated by what it could mean in the life of a school-age child, although organics will pay off for a person of any age.

An organic diet goes hand in hand with a wholefoods diet, a diet high in fresh, local foods and low in refined starch and sugar. This is in direct contrast to the diets of many Canadian children, according to a report issued by the Canadian Heart and Stroke Foundation in 1998. The Foundation issued a formal "red-flag warning" on the diet of kids from six to twelve years old. Only 20 percent eat enough fruits and vegetables. Only 28 percent eat grains high in fibre and complex carbohydrates. As many as 35 percent are obese, doubling since the early 1980s. Foundation officials said these children are prime targets for diabetes and heart disease in later life.[10] The medical bill for diet-related Type 2 diabetes is about $6 billion a year, for heart disease about $50 billion.[11] As well, overweight North Americans now spend $40 billion a year on diet treatments, which have a low record of success in reversing problems that set in during childhood.[12] Obese people are widely stigmatized; their career opportunities and lifetime earnings are significantly lower than the average. An investment in eating organic helps ensure that your child doesn't become a medical or social statistic.

A trip to the dentist highlights another financial benefit of going organic. The coarse grind and low sugar content of organically processed cereals and breads mean less tooth decay.[13] The pioneering dental anthropologist William Price found almost no cavities or need for braces among traditional people, who ate only natural foods.[14] While some of the financial advantages of going organic are only realized in the long term, others, like avoiding dental bills, mean savings in the short term too. After all, when there's a cavity to be filled, a trip to the dentist can't be put off.

Wholefoods may also help your child do better at school. Refined starches and sugars make up about a quarter of the calorie intake of most children, yet they wreak havoc with blood-sugar and energy levels, and create a deprived brain environment that no amount of right attitude can correct. When the body gets a dose of refined sugar, the pancreas produces too much insulin and blood-sugar levels drop. The brain receives less glucose, its essential fuel, leading to an inability to concentrate, loss of energy and mood swings. Barbara Stitt, a Ph.D. in nutrition with more than a decade of experience as the head of youth probation services in Ohio, concludes that "the American way of eating is precisely the sort of diet which will cause brain malfunction."[15] The complex carbohydrates in organically processed grains, by contrast, burn slowly and steadily, keeping the brain on an even keel. They can help provide self-control and a source of early self-esteem that will pay off over a lifetime of personal effectiveness and earning power.

Organic food also reduces expenditures for vitamin pills and over-the-counter drugs. Zinc lozenges, for example, are often bought as an immune booster during cold season. This trace mineral is one of the first to go in commercially processed beans and flours, but it's retained by organic processors.[16] And if the immune boost of natural foods prevents just one day home in bed, it's a big money saver for the parent who has to stay home from work to attend to a sick child, especially if that parent is self-employed.

There are other, smaller savings that are rarely considered: no need to scrub produce with detergent in an effort to get rid of chemical residues; no need to discard the outer leaves of greens, which are most exposed to sprays; if composted, the food scraps make toxin-free soil conditioner, avoiding a trip to the garden supply store. And none of these savings take into account that organic lets you avoid the risk of potential illness from years of ingesting pesticide residues and genetically engineered foods.

When you really start to think about it, there are all sorts of ways to finance organics with the savings on the hidden operating costs of conventional foods. You'll probably come up with many we've left out. Those savings constitute one of the best returns on investment you'll find.

6. Turn your kitchen into a profit centre.

To do this you need to make two budget calculations. First, figure out how much extra you pay for food just because you're pooped out from your day job and jammed for time. Don't be surprised if you spend over seventy-five dollars a week on take-outs and prepared meals from the supermarket, which you could have made from scratch for fifty dollars less. Second, figure out what your real take-home pay is for a day. Most people count their take-home pay as the money left after taxes and benefits are taken off the top, but they forget to add up the costs of commuting, work clothes, dry cleaning and eating at work. The cost of working also includes money spent on things you could have done without or done yourself if you spent less time at work. That list includes child care, cell phones used to juggle appointments, things you bought new because you didn't have time for repairs, money you spent to treat yourself because you were feeling down from exhaustion, and money you spent on the kids to appease your guilt over not spending more time with them. Our estimate is that the average parent of pre-schoolers actually takes home three dollars an hour. Most other people take home about five dollars an hour, a total of forty dollars a day. That makes minimum wage look pretty good.[17]

One way to increase your take-home pay is by taking a day off work. If you arranged to work a four-day week and take Fridays off, you'd lose a day's actual take-home pay of forty dollars and give yourself a raise by not spending the extra fifty dollars for take-outs and prepared food. Time off becomes a personal profit centre. If your first reaction to this suggestion is that your boss will never go for it, try to put that concern aside for a few minutes while we show you the potential savings. A little later in the chapter we'll face head-on the problem of getting time off work.

Supermarkets and take-out joints are now competing for "share of gullet," as it's known in the industry, in the same convenience food market. Convenience is doublespeak for time famine. It's the disappearance of free time that gives rise to the trend supermarkets call "home-meal replacements" or "grab-and-go capability." Basically, this is just-in-time delivery applied to food. Supermarkets first jumped on the prefab food wagon in the 1970s, during the shift to two-income families. That's also the decade when the number of fast-food outlets across North America shot up from 30,000 to 140,000.

It's time to review the math on this trade-off of money for time. People "might think ready-made meals mean an end to slaving at the stove," writes food anthropologist Jeremy MacClancy, "but all they are really doing is handing over the chains to a different master."[18] How much time is really saved is open to debate. The French actually spend less time cooking than the English, even though the French spend a fifth as much on prepared foods and enjoy a worldwide reputation for their cuisine.[19] Cutting back on salt, sugar and fat, the main ingredients in take-out and prefab foods, also buys a lot of time—like about ten extra years of good health and some nice meal experiences to go with them.

As soon as you realize that supermarkets and fast-food joints are not only competing against each other but also against you, you will see the competitive edge you can enjoy in your own kitchen. You're already paying for your kitchen in your rent or mortgage. Unlike supermarkets and fast-food outlets, you don't have to pay top rents and city taxes for commercial space. You don't have to pay a cent on every dollar to shareholders, or two cents on every dollar for head-office expenses and ads. You don't have to pay for styrofoam or other packaging. You don't have to pay union or even minimum wages. You break even at five dollars an hour.

Much of the cost of organic can be rolled into the savings of cooking from scratch. This is the corner the fast-food outlets and supermarkets have painted themselves into. The cash register in our heads needs to add up the cost of meals, which includes labour time, and not just the cost of organic ingredients, which pale beside labour costs. As we start to think in terms of meal costs, it's only a matter of time before organic home cooking becomes a profit centre.

7. Turn your lawn into a profit centre.

Canadians spend an average of three hours a week spraying $1.5 billion worth of chemicals on their lawns annually, and pay for 100,000 gallons of water each year to keep Kentucky grass green in Canada's climate. But there's no reason to let the grass grow under your feet.

The yard, which comes from the ancient Anglo-Saxon word for herb garden, was intended for prosumers. Ornamental grass became a status symbol around the homes of the wealthy during the 1800s. The more useless and wasteful something was, Thorstein Veblen explains in his *Theory of the Leisure Class*, the more it showed off the owner's wealth and fine breeding. The lawn was a piece of "conspicuous consumption," which screamed that the owner had enough money to buy food and waste space. Working people couldn't afford this pretension. Until the 1950s, backyard gardens kept many families in food. The Veterans Land Act, which offered low-cost land to soldiers returning from World War II, assumed that they would use the land to grow their own food in the event of another depression. Then came the prosperous 1950s and "keeping up with the Joneses." Working stiffs got a chance to show off yards that were as useless as those of the idle rich. The lawn became a monument to industrial society's division of space, where money was made at work and spent at home.[20]

Converting lawns to gardens does two favours to the environment. Firstly, the lawn is one of the most polluting technologies on the continent: the motors on lawnmowers are so dirty that the average suburbanite creates more smog cutting the grass than driving the car; and lawns are sprayed more intensively with chemicals than farms are.[21] Secondly, by replacing a lawn with a garden, the same space eliminates the pollution that comes from importing produce grown with chemicals.

Backyard gardens can pay for time off work with free food of the highest quality. New intensive gardening methods so compress the time and space needed to grow food that a family of four can eat veggies year-round for as little as four hours' work a week during the growing season. John Jeavons popularized "biointensive" gardens with his 1970s classic *How to Grow More Vegetables Than You Ever Thought Possible on Less Land Than You Ever Imagined*. He featured high-yielding crops such as Swiss chard and rutabagas.[22] Mel Bartholomew took these methods one step further in his book *Square Foot Gardening*, with plant-by-numbers instructions for sixteen carrots or onions, four lettuce or one tomato plant per square foot.[23] In *Small Space, Big Harvest*, Duane Newcomb provides detailed maps for planting to harvest two hundred pounds of produce from a five-foot-by-five-foot plot.[24]

Eliminating rows, which take up space and leave room for weeds, triples the output of a plot. Intercropping—snuggling cool-loving, fast-growing lettuce right beside heat-loving, slow-growing tomatoes—lets two grow in the space of one. Aiming high, with beans and cukes that grow off string, uses air space, not ground. Home gardeners can eat fresh most of the year by practising what Eliot Coleman calls "the four-season harvest." Broccoli, cabbage, kale, onions, radish, turnips and spinach survive cold snaps in early spring and late fall. With a blanket of mulch over them, carrots, brussels sprouts, parsnips, rutabagas and beets can be dug fresh all winter in many parts of Canada. They even taste better when the cold converts their starches to sugar.[25]

Edible landscaping doubles the gardening pay-off. Go for vertical integration. Use trellises to grow flowering food plants up sun-exposed walls, or hang containers with bushy plants off A-frames or eaves troughs or on tables close to the wall; they shade the house from direct sunlight and save cranking up the air conditioner.[26] Fruit and nut trees do the work of several air conditioners. They provide shade and give off water that sucks up heat during evaporation, the same trick our bodies use when they cool us by sweating. In the winter, trees act as windbreaks and can shave 15 percent off heating bills. Money may not grow on trees, but savings do. Experts say landscape design can cut home energy bills by a third.[27]

Rooftop gardens, perhaps over a flat garage or atop an apartment, are the latest in edible landscaping. The earth blocks out the heat in summer and keeps it indoors in winter. It also protects the roof from damaging UV rays. If the roof won't bear the weight of soil, try containers on tables, which eliminate the need to stoop and crawl while weeding. Basil, parsley, strawberries, grapes, beans, peppers, tomatoes and eggplants take to containers. So do figs, which can be brought indoors when it's cold and used for interior decorating and food. And plants in places where there were no plants before means less carbon and more oxygen in the atmosphere—an environmentalist's dream. A garden over every garage, a plant in every pot: it's a slogan worth shouting from the rooftops.

8. Turn your window sill into a profit centre.

Why buy vitamins in a bottle when you can grow them in a bottle? Ounce for low-cal ounce, sprouts pack more nutrients than either seeds or mature plants. Sprouted wheat has three times more vitamin E than wheat. Radish sprouts have thirty-nine times more vitamin A, nine times more niacin and seven times more folic acid than the bulb. Broccoli sprouts contain fifty times more cancer-fighting sulphorophanes than broccoli itself.[28] Sprout power built North American railways. The Chinese immigrants who did most of the work lived on them. They called their North American concoction chop suey.

A cup of sprouts can be grown for less than twenty-five cents' worth of seeds. In less than two weeks the sprouted seeds increase their weight six times and bulk up twenty-nine times. Your money goes for food, not chemicals, trucks, warehouses or packaging. No agribusiness can match the freshness, quality or cost.

The variety of seeds and tastes is enormous. For starters, try alfalfa, barley, broccoli, buckwheat, Chinese cabbage, corn, garlic, lentil, mung bean, onion, radish, rye, sesame, soy bean, sunflower and wheat.

Sprouts can be served in many ways. Beginners use them in salads and soups and as sandwich toppings. Enthusiasts are breaking the recipe barrier with sprout shakes, juices, cakes and breads. Substitute fresh sprouts for wilted imported vegetables in winter, and increase your nutrient intake while saving money and eliminating the pollution from incoming trucks. Tuck the savings away in a bottle and put them towards organic greens when they're fresh, local and better priced.

9. Turn a walk in a meadow into a profit centre.
Weeds are wild flowers with bad pr. Fiddleheads, blueberries, wild rice and a few others are acceptable, but as a class, wild plants can't get no respect. They're invasive, which means they grow like crazy, without any chemicals or tending. They are also a nutritionist's field of dreams, with more nutrients and taste than many domesticated plants. Weeds are most delectable in early spring, when leaves are most tender and sweet, and in late fall, when seeds are parched dry and easily picked. It's as if they were meant to be eaten during the shoulder seasons when fresh produce isn't around. Rediscovering weeds takes us back to the time when all foods were organic, when humans foraged for a varied diet of eighty-five different wild plants, before civilized beings took half of their calories from three plants: wheat, rice and corn.

Only chemical propaganda and cultural ignorance lead us to detest and spray weeds. Dandelions, often referenced in herbal medicine texts, have more calcium, iron, phosphorus and vitamins A, B and C than iceberg lettuce. Dressed up in olive oil, garlic, onion and basil, Dandelions à l'Italienne have European flair. Tossed in a salad with sorrel, they rate in *Gourmet* magazine. With radish and fennel, they can be found at Alice Waters's famed restaurant, Chez Panisse, in San Francisco.

Purslane is richer in iron than all vegetables save parsley, richer in vitamin C than all vegetables save green pepper, and also packs heart-healthy omega 3 fatty acids. It's prized in India and the Middle East. Burdock is strong in vitamins B and C as well as magnesium, sulphur, phosphorus, calcium and iron. Chickweed, which scores well on iron and phosphorus, is listed on the menu of one respected Quebec restaurant as Chinese watercress. Plantain is rich in vitamins A and C, calcium and sulphur. The seeds, which gave plantain the nickname Indian wheat, can be used in muffin and cereal mixes. Foragers' handbooks, most notably Eull Gibbons's classic *Stalking the Wild Asparagus*, can direct you to the likes of lambs' quarters muffins with may apple marmalade, and cattail flour biscuits with choke cherry jam. Recipes for chicory canapé and chickweed paprikash with milkweed are issued by the National Museum of Natural Sciences in Ottawa.

Wild fruits, nuts and berries suffer less stigma than wild greens. Saskatoons, blueberries, cranberries, rose-hips and raspberries are justly famous for taste. Saskatoons, which flourish throughout the Prairies, have three times the iron of imported raisins. Dried rose-hips, ripe for the picking throughout Alberta and eastern Canada, have thirty times more vitamin C than oranges, and good stores of vitamin A, calcium, phosphorus and iron. There are guidebooks, particularly those issued by the National Museum of Natural Sciences, that can take you well beyond these old favourites and introduce you to rose-hip sherbet, hazelnut cookies, elderberry jam and wine, and mountain ash jelly and brandy.[29]

Weeds stay true to their roots. They prefer abandoned fields and tracks. Montreal pop culture enthusiast Barry Lazar discovered "cornucopia de côte" along a west-end train track and biking trail, where foragers harvest milkweed shoots, dandelion leaves, wild grapes and wild flower bouquets, as well as boughs and grasses for celebrations of Sucot, the Jewish Thanksgiving. It's a "long thin line of urban anarchy," he reported, "a splendid example of how many people, with different interests, put a small bit of the city to good use."[30] Further east on Ste-Catherine Street, in one of the poorest neighbourhoods in Canada, Joe Maltest and his sons, Micmacs from the Gaspésie, hosted free Saturday-night banquets for the community in the summer of 1997. The sons cooked up a buffet of wild salad greens, steamed milkweed, pigweed and dandelion with butter and lemon, and organic potatoes they swapped for weeds. After dinner the sons and their friends made music, and Maltest held court, recalling how his mother used the milk in milkweed to waterproof moccasins. "You have crops available everywhere," he says. "Nature gives us all the food we need."

10. Think outside the box store.
Cut out the middlemen who take seventy-five cents on the food dollar. Buying wholesale puts you on the inside track, especially if you're an outsider. This is the secret to the success of many immigrant groups in North America, forging community connections that let them buy direct at wholesale prices. This "we're-in-this-together" instinct among disadvantaged groups is formalized in co-ops, mainstays of the Canadian economy and society outside of Ontario. The idea, says Wally Seccombe, treasurer of the Ontario Natural Food Co-op, is to create a social network that "can get more bang out of the domestic buck, and increase the efficiency of domestic work, so you can have more without increasing your income."

Community Supported Agriculture is part of this tradition. It's less formal and more direct than most co-ops, and features all the advantages of what Irish economist Richard Douthwaite calls "short-circuiting."[31] There are many variations to CSAs, but most work something like this: a hundred people agree to each buy 1 percent of a farm family's harvest, and to pay two hundred dollars in advance and two hundred dollars at the end of the season; over the course of the season, the farmer delivers fresh-picked organics to their door that would cost five hundred dollars at a health food store.

CSAs create a four-way win. First, farmers do well; they don't have to go to the bank for an advance, they know how much to grow and they don't lose any money to brokers. Second, eaters do well; they get fresh-picked organic produce for a price the stores can't beat. Eaters who are strapped for cash, or who love working their hands through soil, can do a day's work in exchange for food. The same prosumer math that can finance a day off work with a day's cooking from scratch applies to a day on the farm; an added benefit is that it's fun. Thirdly, food is no longer an anonymous commodity; it's personalized. It's also celebrated, on community farm days and at harvest parties. And lastly, the environment does well; it's spared the toxic chemical sprays, and the fumes from long-haul trucking of basic produce. If unions and social agencies got into boosting CSA through their networks, CSAs would number in the tens of thousands, as they do in Japan, instead of the five hundred or so that exist in Canada today.

The trick here is to use social connections to add to individual leverage. This allows individuals to access the economies of scale previously monopolized by centralized corporations. I'll borrow your pressure cooker on Monday, you borrow my crêpe maker on Tuesday. I'll throw extra chili in the crock pot for you on Wednesday, you make an extra batch of soup for me on Thursday. I'll give you my excess Swiss chard, you give me your excess zucchini.

Using information and connections to bypass middlemen is second nature in the emerging knowledge economy. When you order a book, car, bank transaction or insurance policy electronically, you're engaged in what Internet guru Don Tapscott calls "disinter-mediation"—bypassing the intermediaries who add cost but not value to goods.[32] By allowing producers and users to communicate directly, wholesale prices become the benchmark.

11. Start a community garden.
There are so many health, social, environmental and financial benefits to community gardens that it's surprising city planners haven't put them at the top of their priority list. Free organic food for the people who work them is just the icing on the cake.

Community gardens are what Toronto landscape designer Michael Hough calls "working landscape."[33] They offer what economists now call "free ecosystem services." They are the cheapest urban infrastructure to be had, and they pack more uses into a compact space than a Swiss army knife. When it rains on a community garden, water is soaked up by plants instead of rushing down sewage grates and creating underground flash floods that require expensive expansions of sewage mains and sewage plants. Compost, lawn clippings and fall leaves can be dropped off locally instead of being carted across the city. Compost is sometimes called the "twin sister" of community gardening, and it can cut garbage collection costs by 20 percent. The plants in community gardens get some evaporation and oxygen happening downtown, countering what's known as the "heat island effect" created by pavement. Dark pavement attracts and holds the sun's heat, intensifying summer heatwaves and leading people in office towers to crank their air-conditioners up to full throttle. Gardens also store carbon that otherwise goes into the atmosphere and exacerbates global warming. When people eat food from their own gardens instead of imports, they reduce the flow of long-haul trucks, which do major damage to city streets.

The social benefits are equally impressive. Community gardens are tools of what's called "proximity planning," whereby cities are arranged as urban villages so the world is at people's feet, basic services are within walking distance and main street businesses can be developed. Gardeners provide free neighbourhood crime-watch services, saving on policing costs. In U.S. downtowns they've become standard tools for city beautification and "gentrification from below," according to Sean Cosgrove, former Canadian board member of the American Community Gardening Association. Some refer to them as "empowerment zones," because they turn former eyesores into places of beauty, junk-strewn empty lots into symbols of hope. People used to being typecast as without—without jobs, skills, money, advantages—transform themselves into people who are with—with the skills to plan, grow and manage a community facility. U.S. community gardens serve as incubators for food- and landscape-based businesses. In Chicago and New York they're used as youth training centres. In San Francisco a garden run by homeless people sells twenty-six varieties of salad greens to local restaurants. This is social policy driven by the carrot, not the stick.[34]

Shortage of space is not a problem. There is no such thing as vacant lots, just vacant minds, the saying goes. Montreal, the North American leader in community gardens—with a mayor, Pierre Bourque, who rose to prominence as a result of championing the gardens—provides allotment gardens across the city. In Toronto, gardening is beginning to qualify as "passive recreation," deserving of a place in city parks. One park even features a bread-making oven where people from different cultures are encouraged to share their baking skills. One Toronto cemetery provides gardening space, as yet unclaimed by long-term occupants, in return for a tax deduction. In Fort Saskatchewan, Alberta, sheep are used to cut grass in city parks and offer an opportunity to raise meat. Victoria, British Columbia, is home to an experiment in "shared gardening" promoted by a youth service agency called LifeCycles. The organization links people who have yards but don't use them with people who could use one, perhaps matching a disabled senior with an unemployed youth looking for a gardening mentor and willing to do the spadework. The proceeds of the garden are usually split two ways between the land lender and the borrower. It's homesteading 1990s style, exchanging willingness to work for access to land.

This doesn't begin to exhaust the possibilities. Offices and warehouses surrounded by lawns could be given a tax deduction if they made space available on a temporary basis for neighbourhood gardens. Lots sitting idle for years, waiting for development approvals and financing, could be loaned by the season in return for a tax deduction. "Rooftops are a city's greatest untapped resource," says Toronto architect Monica Kuhn. Schools, hospitals and shopping plazas have roofs that could be leased to neighbourhood gardeners. In Switzerland all buildings over four storeys must provide a rooftop garden. In Portland, Oregon, every building application must present a rooftop plan. A wide variety of public and commercial buildings across Canada already sport green rooftops, including Vancouver's public library, Yellowknife's legislative buildings, the Mountain Equipment Co-op store in Toronto and several CP hotels.

The city of Pointe Claire on the island of Montreal rents out a dead-end street to neighbours who've turned it into a garden with 980 varieties of ornamental plants for year-round colour.[35] This fits with the trend towards "living streets" or "traffic calming," whereby a traffic lane is taken out of commission to slow down speeding commuters who jeopardize the safety of neighbourhood kids. Gardens help neighbours begin to reclaim control over their street and its community-building functions. How green is my alley.

Besides time, space is the essential ingredient for fresh, organic, healthful food at affordable prices. Community gardens create that space. Local governments can get them off the ground while promoting community spirit, encouraging individual self-reliance and saving ratepayers money. In Berlin, one of the most industrialized cities in the world, there are eighty thousand community gardening plots. A third of the world's people depend on such plots for their daily survival. Abundance is at our doorsteps. It is not the wolf we need to keep from the door, but cramped and stifling thinking that stops us from seeing the world of plenty that only awaits our respect and use.

12. Turn your workplace benefit plan into an organic profit centre. Earlier in this chapter we asked you to consider the idea of moving to a four-day work week and promised to give you some strategies for making it a reality. This is where those strategies begin. Smart employers who can do the math will drive the next innovation in fringe benefit packages: an "undertime bonus" that gives employees half-pay to take a day off work to grow, gather or prepare organic food. It will benefit employers as much as employees by reducing the costs of drug and absenteeism benefits. The fact is that employers already pay out as much in damage control as they would for an undertime bonus; they just don't get any benefits.

It's already widely recognized that the care and feeding of healthy employees can tip the scales for successful companies. Strong physical and emotional health can make the difference for high-performance industries on the cutting edge of the knowledge economy—software firms, for example. "In the next century," says McMaster University's John Lavis, a member of the Canadian Institute for Advanced Research, employee health will be key to "the human capital of the firm, contributing to improved work group productivity and firm competitiveness."[36]

The idea that your boss could be open to a four-day week is not pie in the sky. Many senior managers see at least part of the picture and are groping towards this new benefit package. Human resources

professionals see the writing on the wall, even though they're limited by an outdated concept of human relations that excludes nutrition. Employees "struggle to juggle" competing demands on their
time from work and family. This has become the top concern of
senior human relations managers. Some of the numbers on the hidden costs of fumbled juggles have already been crunched. Stress-
related disorders cost Canadian employers $12 billion a year, on top
of the $11.3 billion paid out for long-term disability, often stress-
induced.[37] Absenteeism, commonly costed as a corporate loss of one
and a half days for each day off, is incredibly high. In any given
week, one worker in twenty calls in sick. Absenteeism is highest
among obese people, people over fifty-five and women with children. When mothers have a struggle-to-juggle problem, they're
absent nine days a year; if they haven't, they're absent only two and
a half days.[38] Merely introducing flexible work schedules can cut
absenteeism by three days per person per year.

These realities have created a sea change among human relations experts searching for constructive solutions. "Traditional
work-family programs have been approached from a cost-contain-
ment and benefits perspective rather than as an investment in individuals to maximize loyalty and productivity," Doug Ross argues in
the profession's newsletter. Flexible work arrangements, he said,
are a "strategic investment" and "key management tool," not just
a perk.[39]

That thinking is behind employer participation in a
Saskatchewan government initiative to get some constructive
debate happening between workers and employers on the time
crunch. Wilf Hiebert of KPMG Management Consulting, who repre-
sents the business community, reports that the banks got interest-
ed when they added up the training and related costs of employee
turnover. It costs a bank forty thousand dollars every time an
employee quits. That's an expensive way to mishandle stress. As a
result the Royal Bank now promotes flex hours and maintains a
computer network for people looking for job-sharing partners. It
doesn't take much in the way of creative math to figure out that a
bonus to take a day off each week can avoid many costs.

Some employers are also looking for ways to control drug plans,
the cost of which has shot up over the decade at twice the rate of

inflation. An average thirty-nine-year-old costs $198 to cover; an average fifty-nine-year-old costs $450. Getting employees off drugs is a lot cheaper. Nova Chemicals in Corunna, Ontario, took a look at its drug costs for shift workers. Shift workers are in constant jet lag, and their employers have the drug bills to show for it. Problems with ulcers, constipation, bowel disorders and depression are endemic in this group, which now constitutes a quarter of the workforce. Nova coached workers on the importance of eating carbohydrates rather than fatty meals, so their bodies didn't have to work overtime on digestion when they were supposed to be sleeping. To help workers get off coffee, the company put a juicing machine and fresh fruit in the lunch room. Company costs for drugs dropped drastically, officials say.

Fully half the costs of drug plans go to treat five groups of illnesses and disorders that are more effectively treated with low-cost foods: heart disease, diabetes, stomach ailments, bacterial infections and stress. Vitamin C and zinc are proven cold and infection fighters.[40] Both likely are depleted in most non-organic foods. High blood pressure, a forerunner of heart disease, can be reversed within two weeks with a diet high in fruits and vegetables and low-fat dairy products, according to a study by the American National Institutes of Health. The study also found that the dietary approach outperformed hypertension drugs.[41] B vitamins are finally winning recognition for their role in limiting damage from cholesterol. Organically grown and processed foods retain the full range of B vitamins needed.[42] Diabetes can be prevented and controlled by a diet high in complex carbohydrates. It's cheaper to help people change their diet than to pick up the costs of bad diets in a drug plan.

Dietary improvement is especially critical to high-performance companies that depend on workers being razor-sharp, alert and hard-driving innovators while remaining calm and sensitive—a difficult combination. These are the employees who make knowledge companies work, in the fields of software and engineering design, for example. Helping workers live balanced lives so they can remain cool, calm and collected for that all-important meeting is a life-or-death matter for knowledge-based companies, Rosabeth Moss Kanter argues in her classic *When Giants Learn to Dance*.[43] It's as simple as this: when employee satisfaction and stress management at Sears Roebuck stores in the United States went up 5 percent, sales went up 1.3 percent and revenues up 0.5 percent.[44] That kind of revenue increase would normally require building two more outlets in an already overcrowded retail scene. Health is related to stress and satisfaction, and so is diet. This is why workers in high-stress jobs "carb up," just like marathon runners. The complex carbohydrates head off agitation and frustration by stimulating serotonin, says Massachusetts Institute of Technology's Judith Wurtman.[45] B vitamins have a similar effect on frayed nerves.

The best-known company to get the food–performance connection is Husky Injection Moulding Systems of Bolton, Ontario, the world's leading firm in plastic design. President Robert Shad is a strong supporter of environmental causes and naturopathic or nutrition-based medicine. The company employs 1,600 people. Salaries are high and the pace is intense. "People are pushing themselves to the limit," says Dr. Kim McKenzie, a chiropractor and naturopath contracted to work at the Bolton office once a week. "The meals support this atmosphere." The cafeteria buys mainly organic produce. Each day a different "peak performance meal" is prepared under directions from a staff naturopath. A typical lunch is quinoa and adzuki beans with zucchini, beets and mushrooms on the side, and herb tea. The meal is subsidized to sell at $3.50. The tea is free. Those who wish less healthy fare pay full prices. "You can see the difference in people in a week, even if it's their only healthy meal of the day," says McKenzie. Their bowels function better, their back tension eases, their concentration is higher and they wake up in the morning with a clearer head, he says. Husky's costs for prescription drugs are three hundred dollars less per employee than the industry average, and absenteeism is less than half the average.[46] Those savings are worth a hill of adzuki beans.

When a company is laying off employees, or "downsizing," it's an opportune moment to consider some of these suggestions, in particular the four-day work week. Usually, employers take the chainsaw approach, which is to get a hundred people in an organization with five hundred employees to take a severance and early retirement package. For a hundred employees, the cost is in the range of $5 million to $6 million. In exchange, the company loses senior and experienced people who think they have better options elsewhere, and retains employees who are demoralized. But there are better ways to spend $5 million than in severance packages. Why not offer all employees a fifty-dollar bonus to take an unpaid day off work each week? The company could avoid a demoralizing downsizing and meet its reduced payroll, and the five million in the severance kitty would stretch out for four years. The improved health and morale would do more to save the company than the staff cut.

Are these not the situations that benefit packages were designed for? Put the elements together: major reductions in absenteeism, drug bills, disability pay-outs and turnover costs, and major improvements in staff morale and performance. An undertime bonus that promotes organics is the quintessential benefits package for the knowledge economy.

13. Turn government taxes into an organic profit centre.
It's not necessary for governments to legislate shorter work hours and longer meal hours; all they have to do is click a few computer keys so they don't block the trend from happening. Governments have a number of policies that confirm the law of unintended consequences: they cause harm that wasn't necessarily intended. These policies are a barrier to individuals and companies working together to follow the strategies outlined above.

Let's start with payroll taxes, the deductions from employers and in some cases from workers that cover workers' compensation, employment insurance, pensions, medicare and the like. At $45.2 billion a year, they account for one tax dollar in six paid by private-sector employers and workers; yet they receive little public attention. Unlike income and corporate taxes, most payroll taxes are levied according to the number of employees. They are not progressive taxes, adjusted to ability to pay—quite the opposite. Huge oil companies pay few payroll taxes because their money is in equipment, not workers. Payroll taxes actually encourage employers to lay off workers, who cost them a payroll tax, in favour of machines, which gain them a capital tax deduction. Payroll taxes create another major problem as well: they make it cheaper for an employer to have current staff work longer hours than to hire new staff, for whom another set of payroll taxes must be paid. Statistics

Canada estimates that enough overtime is worked to justify hiring 169,000 workers, each of whom would stop collecting employment insurance and welfare and start paying into them. To solve this problem, all the government has to do is program a computer so that payroll taxes and benefits are prorated by the hour, not levied by the number of employees. Then employers would choose to cancel overtime and hire new staff. If a third of employees also decided to move to a four-day week, they would create so many job openings that unemployment could be eliminated. And if that extra time off were used to move to healthier lifestyles, government taxes needed to pay for medical care would go down.

Governments should also stop discriminating against one-income families and parents who workshare so that one can always be with the kids. Right now, two-income families with pre-schoolers receive subsidies that are not enjoyed by one-income families and couples that workshare. Fees for child care are tax deductible; but there is no equivalent deduction, worth about fifty dollars a week, for one-income families that took a cut in pay to avoid child care. Canada faced legal action at the United Nations for this piece of discrimination. Likewise, child care is heavily subsidized, but there is no equivalent given to parents who take an income cut to stay home with the kids rather than use child care. If there were equality in subsidies, one-income families would receive over two hundred dollars a week in assistance, which would make the move out of the workforce possible for many, especially combined with the prosumer strategies we've already outlined.

Behind these counter-productive tax policies is an industrial assumption that machines, not people, boost productivity. Therefore, governments give tax incentives to those who buy machines and penalize those who hire workers. In fact, a bicycle courier had to take Revenue Canada to court to have his meals qualify as fuel that could be tax deducted, the same as if he used a car and bought gas. He won, and exposed the bias of tax policies towards polluting machine energy.[47]

By prorating payroll taxes and benefits, and by giving equal tax and subsidy treatment to people who work full-time and to those who workshare or live on one income, the government could provide a level playing field on which people could make their own choices. But this requires a challenge to the cruel religion of industrialism. Primitive religions believed that human sacrifices, particularly of children, appeased the angry gods. They hoped that blood sacrifices would bring back plentiful supplies of food and other necessities. Industrial religion appears to believe that sacrifices of health will appease the angry gods of the market. There is no evidence that blood sacrifices ever worked. There are no angry gods, other than of our own making. Nature offers us abundance. Time is the resource we need to access that abundance. Take the time.

COLLECTIVE FOOD STRATEGIES THAT DELIVER HIGH VALUE

One of the most effective ways to save money and time is to get together with others and share the work. These tried-and-true collective buying and cooking strategies are sure to save you a bundle and build a sense of community at the same time.

Collective buying strategies

In an airy, modern warehouse in an industrial park in the west end of Toronto, half a dozen men and women scoot around with fork-lifts and trolleys. They're unloading shipments of soy milk and carbonated fruit beverages, and picking orders from sheets of paper stacked neatly on a tray in a corner. This is the Ontario Natural Food Co-op warehouse, thirty-three thousand square feet of veggie burgers, organic pastas, coffee, milk, even home-cleaning products—more than two thousand products in all. "We sell only natural and organic foods," says general manager Randy Whitteker. "In the mid-eighties we decided that we had to develop a niche." They started servicing big health food stores, and enlisted small groups to buy in bulk together.

While supplying health food stores is a major part of the business, the co-op also coordinates more than three hundred buying clubs in more than one hundred communities scattered across Ontario, including student buying clubs at several universities. Members pay about 4 to 8 percent over the wholesale price. They can buy in bulk if they wish, but they can also make small orders. Yet they save up to 30 percent off their food bill.

Kim De Lallo is the buying club representative at the co-op. Clubs must have at least five adult members, she says. Some have as many as eighty. The co-op puts out a catalogue that lists all the items they stock. Clubs send in their orders by phone or fax, and the complete order is delivered to one person's home. It's up to the members to unpack the boxes and separate the order. The money is then collected and sent to the co-op. De Lallo says that some clubs give each member a specific job; in others, one person takes most of the responsibility.

There are as many kinds of clubs as there are people who form them. De Lallo says many are run by women who are at home, looking after young children. "One person I know likes it because she thinks of it as shopping any time of the day or night," says De Lallo. "She gets her catalogue out after the kids have gone to bed and looks through it at her leisure. So for her, it gives her time, frees her up from shopping and gives her flexibility." Some members have disabilities that make it difficult to shop in more convention-al ways.

De Lallo says it's important to decide if a buying club fits with your life. "Some people love the retail experience," she says. "They love chatting with the store owner and looking at the labels." She says buying club members tend to be planners. They usually place their orders every six weeks and buy all their dry goods in advance. That means spending anywhere from two to five hundred dollars at once. But the savings are great, De Lallo says, and "if the kids ask for a snack, you've always got something in the cupboard."

Whitteker believes the co-op can encourage the growth of the organic market. "Our goal is to help local producers and processors understand what it's going to take to be successful," he says. "In our purchasing criteria, local and organic are high on the priority list for sourcing." Whitteker says consumer co-ops are very influ-ential elsewhere in the world. "Swedish co-ops are very large and powerful. They can dictate to the manufacturers what they want the products to be." In 1995, Co-op Switzerland, the largest food retailer in the country, had sales of $9 billion. It also helps farmers switch to organic agriculture.[48]

One way to cut costs of fresh organic produce—not usually available through wholesale operations—is to sign up for a food box. Food box programs are essentially large buying clubs where members pool their resources to buy fresh produce. The programs are available in a number of cities across Canada, including Toronto, Vancouver and Calgary. Some deliver directly to the door while others have a drop-off at a neighbourhood coordinator. The grandmother of them all is Toronto's Good Food Box, started in 1994 to provide low-income people with local, healthy, fresh food, outside the for-profit retail system. From a modest beginning of forty boxes a month, the Good Food Box now sells more than four thousand boxes, delivered every week through a volunteer network of two hundred coordinators. People of all income levels participate, lowering food bills while upping their intake of fresh produce.

Here's how it works. The Good Food Box puts you in touch with a volunteer coordinator in your neighbourhood. You decide what kind of box you want to order: the basic box, or the small or large organic box. A box designed especially for seniors has a range of fruits and vegetables already cut up. You pay in advance, anywhere from fifteen to thirty dollars a week. The box varies from week to week. Carrots, potatoes, onions, some fruit and greens are usually there every time, but there's a focus on what's fresh and local. In early spring there might be asparagus; in summer, a small watermelon, fresh basil, snow peas and vine tomatoes; in fall, fresh-pressed apple cider. For holidays, some organic Blue Mountain coffee beans may be tucked into the box.

Part of the savings in food boxes comes from sacrificing some choice for affordability and convenience. Customers get the best produce available at the best price. The savings average about six dollars a box. "A lot of people say they're trying things they've never had before," says Rob Horricks, a twenty-five-year-old entrepreneur who runs a one-person organic food box operation in Calgary. "People tell me they love the surprise of new products each week. They also appreciate the recipes." Horricks includes a recipe with his weekly newsletter so that people know how to use the ingredients included in the box. He looks for the best buys in organic produce, packs the boxes himself and then delivers to the door. "My customers tell me the time they save is one of the big advantages," he says. "They also tell me that because they're receiving the organic produce regularly, they're finding that they eat a lot more of it than they would if they had to buy it themselves."

The innovative Vancouver company Small Potatoes has expanded the concept of the food box to include fresh flowers, prepared meals—even a selection of B.C. microbrewed beer. Customers can order by phone, fax or Internet; they'll even take credit cards.

Companies like these offer high value for the food dollar and an opportunity to expand your food horizons. With a little imagination and a few willing friends, you can experiment with other strategies for stretching your food dollar.

Dinner clubs

If you're like Tamara Elliott, you want good home-cooked meals for your family, you want to save money, but you don't want to spend every afternoon chopping and stirring, just to be left with a pile of dirty dishes at the end. Elliott, a mother of two young children who also works part-time, started a dinner club with two other families on her block in east-end Toronto. "The idea was to free up time and energy by not having to cook two nights a week, yet still having a healthy and delicious meal," says Elliott. "We didn't think it would be a big money saver, but it did cut down on our purchase of convenience foods by saving the occasional pizza dinner when I was too tired to cook."

The three families came up with some guidelines, and lists of individual likes and dislikes. "We wanted to provide a balanced meal that would only require a salad to top it up," says Elliott. "Although only one of the families is strictly vegetarian, we agreed to cook well-balanced vegetarian meals, with some good source of protein." One issue was timing. Because all three families had busy and varied schedules, they decided that delivering a piping hot meal at 6 p.m. was not realistic. Instead they concentrated on more flexible meals that could be assembled according to the family's individual needs—perhaps a pasta sauce delivered with the accompanying pasta uncooked, or a casserole that needed baking or reheating.

Elliott says they made a list of dishes they wanted to try, and figured out how to prepare a triple serving with the utensils at hand. Some dishes were ruled out because they were just too complicated for an ordinary kitchen, requiring too many pots and burners. They made a rule that soup could be a main course only once a week, and they decided to rotate who would do the soup on a weekly basis. Each dinner-club family was responsible for the same night each week. If club members were away on their night, they could either switch with another family or prepare their meals ahead of time. Elliott says everyone took their responsibility very seriously, but no one was rigid. When one woman involved became pregnant and was suffering from severe morning sickness, the other two families picked up the slack.

Elliott says there were the occasional goofs, mistimed meals or dishes that one family loved and another wouldn't eat again. But all in all Elliott says the dinner club worked really well. "Not having to think about preparing a meal two nights a week was a real stress reliever," she says. "It also fostered a sense of community and introduced us to recipes we would never have thought of making ourselves." An added bonus, she says, was the way it increased the amount of vegetables everyone ate. "When I'm stressed out and in a rush, I'm likely to do something like garlic spaghetti and a salad. But we had meals brimming with vegetables on a regular basis."

Here are Elliott's tips for families considering dinner clubs. "Three is the ideal number, to give each cook enough of a break without requiring an industrial-sized kitchen," Elliott says. It's best if the participating families are about the same size; the chefs have a better sense of how much they need to make. Families need to enjoy the same types of food; if there are too many compromises, no one enjoys the meals. Everyone has to be willing to put in a similar effort and expense. Planning ahead and letting the others know what you're going to cook is a good idea; it cuts down on the chance of having pasta twice in one day. Collect casserole dishes from the other participants in advance; that way they can take back their own dishes and do the washing-up themselves. Most of all, there has to be goodwill and flexibility. There will be times when meals don't work out and people are inconvenienced, but people need to take that in stride.

Community kitchens

If you want to try a collective cooking strategy that puts a premium on cooking together a community kitchen may be the answer. And there are as many kinds of community kitchens as there are communities. Anne-Marie Abdul chops carrots and peppers in the common room of a suburban Toronto high-rise while someone watches her kids in the next room. She jokes with another young mother chopping beside her. They belong to the Trethewey Community Kitchen, and today they're making Caribbean fried rice with chicken and vegetables. Every week a dozen women and children meet in the common space of their housing complex to cook up a storm, socialize and share a healthy meal. "I love it," says Abdul, "because I can get a break from the kids. Plus I don't have to do all the cooking all by myself."

Thousands of people across Canada are joining community kitchens. From humble beginnings in Montreal in 1986, there are now more than three hundred in Quebec, four hundred in Ontario and at least a hundred in B.C. Although many kitchens cater to low-income people, the groups are diverse in membership and style. They include poor women, single men, seniors, the disabled, people with HIV looking to improve their health and people who just want to share a multicultural cooking experience.

In most community kitchens people cook and share one meal, and then have leftovers to take home. Everyone contributes to buying the food. For under two dollars per participant, they can have a nutritious meal; that's a lot less than eating fast food at McDonald's. A community agency often provides start-up support, ensures there's a good space with the right equipment, helps with shopping and menu planning, and works through any challenges that emerge when a new group of people get together to share cooking and eating. Community kitchens do stir it up, and not just in the pot. Talk turns to other issues, such as family violence, job training, recreation for the kids, improving the neighbourhood. And talk often leads to action: swimming classes for the kids, reclaiming the building lobby from drug dealers, referrals to community support services.

Debbie Field, executive director of FoodShare, Toronto, one of the agencies supporting community kitchens, says that when people break bread, they also break down social isolation. "I don't think it's an accident that this movement, which is about making people feel better about themselves, is connected to food," she says. "Food is a very healing thing in all cultures. Eating together makes us feel good. That's why we have festive meals at holidays, birthdays and weddings. The community kitchen movement is using an age-old cultural symbol—food—to help people feel less socially isolated."

In Peru, where the idea first developed, small groups of poor women got together to obtain cheaper vegetables and milk. It grew into a national network to lobby for social improvements. In many Peruvian communities the "popular kitchens," as they're called, are the only form of social assistance available.[49] They have become a focal point for community organizing in Canada as well. Quebec has an extensive network of community kitchens, supported by the provincial government. City and provincial public health units across the country provide facilitators and funding for manuals.

At the Trethewey Community Kitchen the room is filled with happy chatter as the women and children finish their meal. Before the washing-up begins, one woman rises to recount a Caribbean folk tale. The faces around the room are peaceful and attentive. "We need to know each other," says participant Lavina Cummings, "even for a day—to cook and laugh and have a good time."

LOW-COST FOODS THAT DELIVER HIGH VALUE

Just about every book about food has its favourite wonder foods, ones that pack a nutritional punch. We have ours too. They're foods that deliver on three counts: they're nutritious, they're delicious and they're cheap. Some have medicinal value that has only recently been rediscovered. Our list is short and incomplete because it's meant to be an introduction to foods that have been undervalued and often overlooked. But it illustrates the fact that food you can buy or make at bargain-basement prices offers top-of-the-line value.

Garlic

Now that it's gone uptown, no one turns up their nose at garlic any more. In a busy location along Richmond Row, theatre-goers and business executives in London, Ontario, hobnob at Garlic's Restaurant, which serves about forty specialties featuring the stinking rose—from cream of garlic soup to pasta with roasted garlic sauce and garlic pizza. The ice cream, topped with a chocolate-covered garlic bud and laced with caramelized garlic, is a sensation.

Garlic has become the ketchup of intellectuals. The challenge is to recover its history as the health food and flavour enhancer of choice among the hoi polloi. It's thought that the first labour strikes in history were waged by Egyptian slaves who wanted a daily garlic break while building the pyramids. The ancient Egyptians, as sophisticated in medicine as in engineering, respected garlic for its ability to build strength, improve blood circulation and fight colds. Later, the Roman proletariat developed garlic sauces to counter the effects of food spoilage. The classic English text on herbal medicine by seventeenth-century physician Nicholas Culpeper promoted garlic as the poor man's cure-all. Before antibiotics were discovered, garlic and moss were used to dress wounds and prevent infection. Early in this century Albert Schweitzer used garlic to fight dysentery at his African mission. But only in the past twenty years has garlic known the sweet smell of success among conventional medical experts. Since 1980 over 130 scientific papers have documented its powers to lower cholesterol levels, reduce hypertension, kill bacteria and boost the immune system.[50]

It now appears that garlic can even help prevent cancer. At Queen's University in Kingston, Ontario, Pok-Gek Forkert does her garlic research with a $500,000 grant from the U.S. National Cancer Institute. She's found that garlic protects tissues from the effects of toxic chemicals. Her findings have been confirmed in England, where studies at the University of Exeter show garlic can both detoxify carcinogenic substances and sabotage cancer cells in their quest to multiply. Garlic is considered especially effective as a protection against cancer of the colon and digestive tract.

Garlic has also gained a reputation for its power to treat colds and heart disease. Rich in vitamins B and C, as well as phosphorus, potassium and calcium, it boosts the immune system, and fights colds and phlegm better than more expensive drugs. The allein in garlic, difficult to make effective in pill form, has antioxidant properties that resist heart disease. Researchers have found that garlic dilates blood vessels and lowers blood pressure. Many scientists consider it a better blood thinner than aspirin, with none of aspirin's side effects on the stomach lining.[51]

A clove a day is widely recommended for general health purposes. Chewing on a sprig of parsley is an effective way to combat garlic's strong odour. Taste and economy are two more advantages of garlic. Garlic is regarded as one of the great flavour enhancers ever discovered. When cooked, some of the complex molecules in garlic become sixty times sweeter than sugar. Despite its growing reputation as a gourmet food, garlic is cheap and easily available. Add a few minced cloves, chopped parsley and some olive oil to spaghetti, and you can eat like the theatre crowd for vaudeville prices.

Soy

With soy, the proof is in the pudding. At age five Anika Roberts got most of her daily requirements for protein and calcium by tossing silken tofu, a cup of soy milk, two tablespoons of tahini, two tablespoons of apple butter and a banana in the blender. Eat dessert first is her motto.

Though soy and tofu are still identified with serious vegetarians, their low price, rich supplies of essential nutrients and proven medicinal value are winning over a wide variety of new eaters. Long a mainstay of Asian diets—soy beans were cultivated in China five thousand years ago, while tofu, discovered by mixing soy milk in sea water, goes back almost two thousand years—soy and tofu attracted the attention of Western medical experts when they noticed the low rates of cancer, heart disease and menopausal problems in Japan and China.[52]

Over 250 studies into soy have been conducted during the 1990s, and most point in the same direction. The chemical structure of soy contains phytoestrogens or isoflavones, which are similar in structure to the female hormone estrogen. These mild plant estrogens appear to have many positive effects on the body. They lower LDL or "bad" cholesterol. They are considered as effective as many prescription drugs in preventing strokes.[53] They play a role in limiting cancer sites in the body. Some experts claim that a diet more weighted to soy products could reduce breast cancer rates by a third. Increasing intake of soy products also seems to reduce hot flashes during menopause and to hold back the onset of osteoporosis after menopause. In men, soy estrogens may play a role in preventing the development of prostate and colon cancer.[54] The lower death rate from these diseases among Chinese and Japanese males has been attributed to soy.

As with oats, soy in North America is mainly fed to livestock. Since World War II, North American seeds have been bred with livestock in mind. More recently, soy bean growing has fallen under the domination of genetic engineers, who've created varieties that can withstand the herbicide sprays used to protect soy beans from weeds. Beans from these seeds have found their way into a wide variety of foods, including baby formulas, baby foods, whipped topping, coffee whitener and luncheon meats. It's unfortunate that a food with so many health benefits has been contaminated by genetic engineering. As we've argued before, the only way to protect yourself is to buy certified organic soy bean products.

In conventional farming, soy is grown in rows, like corn, a system that invites erosion and weeds. It makes more sense to stripcrop soy beans, with narrow strips of soy beans surrounded by strips of rye, oats, barley and alfalfa. This takes maximum advantage of the soy bean's ability to draw down nitrogen, a key component of fertilizers, from the air. Growing soy beans tightly packed between other crops in this way would also make herbicides unnecessary because there would be little opportunity for weeds to move in. The natural advantages of such a system are gaining the attention of farmers as governments phase out their subsidies to soy monoculture.

Low cost and healthfulness assure soy a central place in the daily diet of the future. Bringing home the tofu is a logical alternative to expensive and high-fat meat and dairy products, which aren't superior in protein or calcium. Soy products are coming on stream in a wide range of forms and tastes that North Americans can develop a hankering for. The versatility of the soy bean, and the sprouts, tofu, tempeh and "milk" drinks cultured from it, create an opportunity for neighbourhood soy stores that can cater to an expanding market for soy shakes, smoothies, puddings, burgers, miso soups, casseroles, stir-fries and ice cream. The market is so new that there are few established players to discourage new and small upstarts. And neighbourhood soy preparation offers a major taste advantage: fresh soy drink and tofu are to store-bought brands what fresh-baked bread is to a store-bought loaf.

Oats

Samuel Johnson, who compiled a famous dictionary of the English language published in 1755, described oats as "a grain, which in England is generally given to horses, but in Scotland supports the people." The thrifty Scots had it right, but the horsey set still dictates popular taste. Until it was found that the energy in the humble grain helped horses "feel their oats," it was considered too coarse for any but the coarse stomachs of the poor, who used it for gruel during the Middle Ages. On this continent, 95 percent of the oat crop goes to horses to this day. Until the 1980s, oat bran was added to dog food.

Jane Brody's *Good Food Book*, which refers to oats as a "nutritional Cadillac" and "the best buy for your food dollar," helped launch the oat revival. Available for less than a dollar a pound at bulk food stores, oats are rich in protein and complex carbohydrates and low in fat. They are a good source of B vitamins, vitamin E and several minerals, including calcium and iron. Oats also store well, thanks to natural antioxidants that protect them from going bad.

Although they are no longer considered an aphrodisiac (whence comes the expression "sowing your wild oats"), evidence on the health benefits of oats is so strong that food companies in the United States are allowed to advertise their therapeutic value. Oats were the first food to be so recognized. (In Canada, only prescription drugs can be sold with claims of medicinal value.) The main reason for this distinction is beta glucans in the fibre of whole oats, which help regulate cholesterol levels. There's wide medical agreement that oats can have positive effects on five major chronic disorders: heart attacks, cancer, diabetes, high blood pressure and obesity. And no one doubts that the soluble fibre in oats works as a natural laxative. Organic steel-cut Scotch oats are the least processed and most nutritious. It's generally better to eat whole, organically processed oats with the bran inside than the bran alone. Like commercial laxatives, the bran by itself tends to move the bowels by irritating them rather than filling them with soluble fibre.

Oat flour is remarkably versatile in cooking. It can be used for quick breads and cakes, and for thickening soups, stews and gravies. Oat flakes can be used in blended drinks like smoothies, casseroles and desserts. And when health, taste and affordability create demand for oats, the environment also wins. Oats are an excellent rotation crop on farms. They help control weeds and enrich the soil. That's why oats, like garlic and soy, deserve to be on our list of undervalued foods that deliver.

Whole-grain bread

When the ancient Israelites were under siege, the prophet Ezekiel told them to take "wheat, and barley, and beans, and lentils, and millet, and fitches, and put them into one vessel, and make thee bread thereof." Healthy bread is as old as the hills. Because it's a simple, tasty and low-cost way to get many essential daily nutrients, it well deserves to be on our list of foods that are good for your body, for your pocketbook and for the environment.

Ezekiel understood that good bread was essential to health; the ingredients in his recipe attest to that. Whole wheat is loaded with most essential nutrients, including micronutrients such as zinc, chromium and manganese, which are hard to get from other sources. Barley was a standard grain of biblical times, first domesticated as far back as 6000 BC. It had a reputation in folk medicine as a heart remedy, probably due to the fact that the hull, removed in the processing of modern pearl barley, contains beta glucans, the same substance that gives oats their cholesterol-lowering properties. Barley is also a good source of protein, niacin, thiamin, potassium and silicon. Both wheat and barley are good sources of vitamin B15, which helps improve circulation. It is missing in most foods, and is removed in grain milling. Beans and lentils are high in protein, plus phosphorus, potassium, some calcium and vitamin A. Millet, which in this country is fed mostly to birds, is rich in protein, B vitamins and several essential minerals, including iron and copper.[55] As for fitches—who knows what they are?

Although not all whole-grain breads are as nutritionally complete as Ezekiel's, they can still go a long way towards preventing a new generation of deficiency diseases. These diseases may be less obvious than the scurvy and rickets of the past, but they are every bit as serious. White bread milling strips out—"refines" is the word the industry uses—bran, wheat germ, B vitamins, vitamin E, chromium, magnesium, manganese and zinc from wheat flour. In total, about twenty minerals and vitamins are lost to a significant degree. These nutrients are the first to go in commercial bread making because they're either the wrong colour, like bran, or they're volatile and go off when stored for a long time. In this process, health gets short-changed. When bran goes, you can't, which is why laxatives sell well. When wheat germ and vitamin E are dumped, it's hard on the heart. The discoverers of vitamin E, the Shute brothers of London, Ontario, blamed the rise of heart disease in this century on commercial bakers who took this crucial vitamin out of flour.[56]

Former Harvard medical researcher Kilmer McCully also links the rise in heart attack rates in the 1950s to the first decade of hyper-processed breads and foods. In his book *The Homocysteine Revolution: Medicine for the New Millennium*, he agrees with the Shute brothers that many cholesterol and heart problems are caused by diets deficient in vitamin E. But his research emphasizes the role of the B vitamins as well—in particular vitamins B6, B12 and folic acid—all sensitive to processing. McCully's research indicates that if vitamin B6 is not present in the diet, a substance called homocysteine can build up and damage artery walls, leading to heart disease.

Other studies have also established a connection between homocysteine and heart disease, and even the dominant medical community accepts that elevated blood homocysteine is a factor in 10 percent of heart disease cases. McCully believes there is a reason why there has not been more research on the role of vitamin deficiency in heart disease. "The concept of under-consumption of vital nutrients that are lost or destroyed in food processing, preservation or preparation is diametrically opposed to the assumption that over-consumption of a major dietary constituent could be the underlying cause of arteriosclerosis," he says. In other words, the conventional understanding of the causes of heart disease blames the victim for overindulgence in rich foods, rather than looking to the processing industry as the source of foods that make us sick. Switching to whole foods that have not had their vitamins processed out "promises to be extremely effective without yielding excessive profits to the pharmaceutical companies." Companies that make significant profits from anticholesterol drugs are not likely to wholeheartedly endorse a remedy as simple and cheap as eating unprocessed foods.

Whole-grain bread doesn't need to be "enriched," a word that better describes what happens to the processors than the food. When you buy enriched bread, you're settling for half a loaf. Enrichment is doublespeak for the substitution of stable and inert chemicals for the real thing, sensitive vitamins and minerals. Enriched breads don't provide substitutes for everything taken out of the original. The trace mineral chromium, for example, is commonly forgotten. Apart from these slip-ups, recent findings in nutritional science discredit the entire strategy of chemical substitution. Without the invisible galaxy of minuscule "phyto-nutrients" that surround vitamins and minerals in their natural form, our bodies can't make full use of the vitamins and minerals.

The discovery of the central role of phyto-nutrients has been likened to Einstein's discovery of relativity. As this new scientific world-view sinks in, the old science behind chemical processing is doomed. Chemical processing, like chemical fertilizing, comes from a tradition known as "reductionism," a relic of pre-Einsteinian science. Break things down into parts that can be duplicated by chemical formulas that contain their essence, the reductionists say. But the role of phyto-nutrients confirms that the essence is in the whole, not the parts.

MORE LOW-COST HEALTHY TIPS

Home-made baby food
Parents who want to give their baby the best possible start and still save money would do well to steer clear of most prepared baby food, which is generally poor value for money. Besides, it's an area where

even the most inexperienced cooks can put do-it-yourself methods to work with great success.

What's in most prepared baby foods will come as a shock to many parents. In some cases there's more cornstarch or tapioca in the jar than there is fruit or vegetables. Other kinds are high in sugar and salt, despite warnings from the Nutrition Handbook of the American Academy of Pediatrics that sugar and salt are unsuitable for infants. Most lines of baby food come from food conglomerates that service people from the cradle to the grave, making baby foods the training ground for a lifetime of taste addictions.

The $70-million-a-year Canadian baby food market is controlled by Heinz, which has at least 75 percent of sales. Despite free trade, Heinz enjoys tariff protection that prices U.S. exporters (the best known of which is Gerber) out of the Canadian market. The Washington-based Center for Science in the Public Interest (CSPI) charged Heinz in 1996 with abusing its monopoly by loading Canadian baby foods with cheap fillers, and gouging consumers on price and quality. The nutrition advocacy group found baby servings of puréed banana in Canada contained only 30 percent banana, compared to 55 percent in the more competitive U.S. market. The group's survey found that of 95 Canadian baby foods, 79 were notable for overuse of starch fillers. Sixty percent of baby desserts were mainly sugar and water. "Although there is no proof that the fillers are harmful," Dr. Michael Jacobson said when releasing the survey, "it is certain that parents are paying real-food prices for them and not receiving the nutrients they expect."[57] Heinz claimed its research showed Canadian babies like starch more than U.S. babies do. (Perhaps this explains why Canadians are a bit stiffer than those extroverted Americans.) Since the starch abuse was exposed in 1996, Heinz has increased the fruit and vegetable content of its main line of products. Ironically, Heinz has been responsible for making organic prepared baby food more widely available. Recognizing a growing trend, Heinz bought out Vermont-based Earth's Best, a leader in the development and distribution of organic baby food, and, following the CSPI controversy, made it available in Canada.

Although organic prepared baby food is handy for travel and other times when convenience is required, home-made baby food is simple, fast and much less expensive. Buying a banana and mashing it with a fork costs a quarter of what a jar of puréed banana costs, according to Toronto nutritionist Sylvia Kerr, formerly on staff with FoodShare Toronto, which promotes at-home methods. Carrots can be puréed at home for a third of the cost of commercial baby food. Chicken can be prepared for one-tenth the cost.

If dinner clubs were ever adapted to produce baby food, we'd have the makings of an infant industry. There's about a $50-million-a-year price spread between the value of commercial baby food and its price. The difference is due to a variety of non-food costs, including bottles and labelling, advertising, distribution and mark-ups. That's a lot of money for little in the way of added value. Try this scenario on for size: A parent stays home one day a week and cooks a week's supply of food for five babies in a dinner club. Each parent pays the going retail rate for baby food, but the money goes towards organic produce and preparation time instead of ads, bottles and trucks. Every time four parents took a day off work to cook for such a club, a new four-day job would be created to replace them. At this rate, dinner clubs could create 20,000 jobs across the country, which is 18,800 more than at the Heinz factory in south-western Ontario. That's a baby step towards a new trend of cooking from scratch for improved value for the dollar in terms of health, self-reliance, free time and job creation.

Off-grade vegetables
Vegetables blended in a juicer or puréed for soups get top grades for taste, economy and nutrition. They're also a way to make good use of what's known as "off-grade" produce—cosmetically imperfect or odd-sized vegetables and fruit. The grading system used by the food industry and legislated by government has little to do with nutrition or healthy growing methods; it's all about looks. This emphasis on appearance means that blemished but otherwise perfectly good produce is left to rot in farmers' fields because it doesn't make the grade. This isn't small potatoes: cosmetically unacceptable produce can account for up to one-fifth of a farmer's crop.

Our obsession with looks dates back to the 1960s, when food stylists started to play a key role in the marketing of food. Food that looked great on the shelves and that photographed well in glossy ads gave supermarkets a competitive edge. Until then, shoppers had accepted food with minor blemishes or unusual shapes. Processors were also keen to promote the new Olympic standards of perfection in appearance and size: it gave them a ready source of cheap produce. Apples with small imperfections, for example, were no longer acceptable at fruit stands but had to be sold to juice manufacturers at a deep discount. Governments recognized that grading could be used to prevent collapsing prices in times of overproduction. So if it's been a good year for potatoes, the government will set new size standards at harvest time to prevent a glut on the market. Potatoes that don't meet the standard are left in the ground to rot.

The grading system is also a leading reason for the use of pesticides.[58] Thirteen of the sixteen sprays used on conventionally-grown Nova Scotia apples, for instance, are aimed at a fungus that leaves a slight scab on the outside of the peel, easily sliced off before serving. The scab doesn't affect taste or nutrition. The need for pesticides is compounded when rejected fruit and vegetables are left in the field to rot. Doing this effectively lays on a feast for pests, which fill up before hibernating for the winter and are then ready to reproduce with gusto in the spring.

Before grading was institutionalized, budget-minded consumers had scores of tricks for using perfectly edible off-grade foods. Fallen apples were used for cider. Misshapen vegetables were used in stews. Juices and puréed soups are modern adaptations, made possible by low-cost food processors and juicers.

Juicing is a tasty, convenient and economic way of getting the nutrients you need from vegetables. A powerhouse blend developed by Jay "The Juicer" Kordich is made with three carrots, one stalk of celery, one apple, half a beet, and half a handful each of wheatgrass and parsley. One eight-ounce serving meets your daily requirement for beta carotene, a well-recognized cancer fighter. This drink is also loaded with a heart-smart mix of B vitamins, which are gaining recognition for their role in clearing the body of cholesterol, and essential minerals.[59] Juices are an easy way to increase your intake of raw foods, known to be higher in nutrients than their cooked counterparts. They're also a natural for budget-conscious eaters because the nutritious tops of carrots, celery and beets, often tossed in the garbage, can be thrown in. Many juicing enthusiasts favour going easy on fruits, which are best eaten whole. Their high natural sugar and fibre content makes them delicious just the way they are. Because of their high sugar content, juicers say fruit should only be used to add flavour to vegetable juices. On its own, the concentrated sugar in fruit juice is difficult for the body to process.

We look forward to the day when consumers, processors and governments see past the look of cosmetically imperfect produce. A move to more juices and blended soups would mean farmers could sell food now left in the field to rot. Perhaps we could start with special discount bins aimed at the juice and soup market. And we would like to see reforms to the grading system to inform consumers about the healthfulness of their food, not about its looks.

Many foods we undervalue today have been the staples of traditional cooking for generations. As packaged and prepared foods take over a bigger share of the market, the knowledge and skills needed to cook with the basics is being lost. But there are still some persistent people who, through necessity and happenstance, are preserving and passing on these skills.

CIA GADD'S STRATEGIES FOR EATING CHEAP AND WELL

Ben and Cia Gadd know how to live high on a low food budget. Professional mountain guides in Jasper, they take rockhounds and wild-flower enthusiasts on Rocky Mountain climbs. High Country trekkers need food that's light but indestructible, that can be passed around and eaten on a boulder, and that carries enough nourishment to help them go the distance. Cia Gadd's Mount Logan Bread, named by a friend who used it on the trail to the mountain range bordering Alaska and the Yukon, fills the bill. It's a nutritious mix of whole wheat flour, sesame and sunflower seeds, wheat germ and molasses. Baked without milk, it can survive ten days in a backpack without crumbling or going bad. Served with peanut butter and jelly on a rest stop, "it's like I just served caviar," says Cia. "You just don't want to drop it on your foot."

An accomplished cook who's won contests with her recipes, Cia

Gadd raised two ravenous boys who grew up to be world-class athletes on the uncertain income of a mountain guide and nature writer. Ben Gadd is author of the standard *Handbook of the Canadian Rockies* and a leading critic of rampant commercialization in Canada's national parks. Fortunately, Cia Gadd's personal history made her heir to three indigenous North American traditions of low-cost cooking: Pioneer Deep South Make-Do, Depression Midwest Leftover, and Sixties Earth Mother.

She was born into one of Maryland's oldest families and was taught to cook by grandmothers whose family recipes were heirlooms from the earliest days of pioneer settlement. Of necessity, pioneer cooks learned to rely on ingredients that were locally grown and required no refrigeration and a minimum of store purchases. Elbow grease and ingenuity made up for expensive exotics like yeast and sugar.

When she left home to go to university in Colorado in 1967, Cia got a chance to study cooking in the school of hard knocks. Raised by an affluent family to become a delicate southern belle, she gave it all up for love of the Rockies and a fellow student, Ben Gadd, who invited her on a backpacking weekend a few weeks after classes started. Her parents wouldn't hear of their nineteen-year-old taking part in premarital camping, so the couple eloped. Knowing they would be broke, the Gadd family gave the newlywed students some books that had got them through the tough times of the 1930s Depression: *Food Economy Recipes* and *Plain Desserts*, by Mrs. Knox of Knox Sparkling Gelatin Company, taught cooks to "eat plenty, wisely and waste nothing"; *Old Pennsylvania Recipes* preached the same message. Cia Gadd picked up two other golden oldies to help her cook for two on $9 a month: Janet Hill's *Cooking for Two, A Handbook for Young Housekeepers*, written in 1917, was loaded with sweet homilies; how-to tips came from the 1933 edition of the Hood milk company's *Hood Basic Cook Book*, which featured dairy products, whole grains and edible weeds. Almost all cookbooks of those days featured penny-pinching methods and recipes. Meals that were light on the pocketbook were essential when most working-class families had to get by on the male's income, and when food accounted for a full third of family expenditures, about three times more than the portion of income spent on food today.

Climbing mountains was easier than climbing out of poverty,
so the cookbooks were carted along when Ben Gadd decided to
resist the draft for military service in Vietnam. In 1969, the Gadds,
now a threesome with an infant son, arrived penniless in Calgary.
Though Ben Gadd got a job right away—"If you could say 'geology'
and 'computer' in the same sentence, you were hired in those
days," he says—$400 a month had to cover starting a household
from scratch, feeding a family of three and soon four, and meals for
other draft resisters who needed a place to stay until they got on
their own feet.

The youth counter-culture was in full swing at the time, and
food was as central to it as sex, drugs and rock 'n' roll. Cookbook
classics of the 1970s, such as Frances Moore Lappé's *Diet for a
Small Planet* and Laurel Robertson's *Laurel's Kitchen*, promoted
authentic, unprocessed grain- and vegetable-based meals as the way
to save the planet; saving money wasn't the driving force of the new
food ethic. But most participants in the counter-culture had more
time than money, so meals based on unprocessed grains and veggies
made economic, as well as ethical, sense. For many, there was little distinction between thrift and political correctness, between
scrimping and scruples.

Cia Gadd's alternative cooking borrowed freely from both
Depression-era and sixties traditions. Her granola was always
cooked from scratch, her dried-fruit leathers were home-made,
with dented fruit bought at bargain-basement prices, and her
window sills offered a harvest of sprouts.

In food, as in computers and telecommunications, the 1970s are
almost as long ago as the 1930s Depression or the colonial eigh-
teenth century. The way most North Americans eat today, as much
as the way they work in offices, is almost entirely an invention of
the past twenty years. Think about the microwave, the time crunch
of two-income families, the dominance of prepared meals and fast
foods; or think about the proliferation of health obsessions, food
allergies and diet fads. The widespread nostalgia for grandma's
cooking and old-time comfort foods suggests we can still hear the
echo from older traditions that offered richness as well as thrift.
Retracing our path on that old trail, as Cia Gadd knows, can take
us to some high places.

HOW A MOM ON SOCIAL ASSISTANCE
BUYS ORGANIC

Jane Upham brings mugs of spiced tea out to the picnic table in the patch of green behind her home. It's the first really warm day of the year, and Upham's five-year-old daughter and a friend are happily digging in the mud and watching a beetle. Upham is a single mom living on social assistance. She rents a ground-floor apartment so that she can have access to the yard and grow some of her own food. Like many moms, she juggles child care and a full-time skills upgrading course with the daily routines of food shopping and meal preparation. The big difference is that her budget is tighter. Yet she manages to buy and eat mainly organic food.

Upham's reasons for buying organic are straightforward. "I simply can't afford to be sick. I'm getting older and I have a young child," she says. "Buying organic just feels better to me. I don't like the idea that as human beings we believe we can come up with a better way to grow things than nature can."

Upham's commitment to organic food has evolved over a couple of decades. When she was young, she lived in a co-op with eighteen people. Although completely inexperienced, she took on managing the kitchen, which meant shopping for and preparing three meals a day for the entire group. The household was vegetarian, and broke. Upham learned how to cook healthy and cheap. Those skills have allowed her to buy organic today, even on a tight budget. "The funny thing is, it's not that difficult or time-consuming, but does it ever save the bucks," she says.

While running the communal kitchen, Upham learned about buying bulk. She stocked big jars of honey, flour, beans and lentils. She also bought off-grade fruits and vegetables. "I would go to small wholesalers and they would allow me to buy whole crates of misshapen carrots, lettuce with a few wilted leaves, apples with scabs, that kind of thing. To some extent, this would dictate what I cooked." So Upham learned to ad lib. "I had to make things taste good. These were people in their early twenties with big appetites who were used to a pretty traditional menu. I might make a meal one night of lentils with cheese melted over it, with some carrots, and a big salad. I'd make more than enough because we always had people dropping in. The next night I might mix a little mustard and ketchup together, layer the ingredients in a casserole dish with some tomatoes, and bake it. I'd get rave reviews. If we still had some extras, I would throw it all into the blender with some milk, tamari and spices, and make a nice cream soup for lunch the next day."

Upham has updated these methods to life with a child and figured out a lot of ways to stretch her food dollar while buying organic. She and her daughter enjoy nachos with avocado and salsa, so she makes her own salsa and grows all the ingredients herself: hot and sweet peppers, tomatoes, an assortment of herbs. "I've also grown zucchini, potatoes, celery and lettuce. I grow mint and make my own mint tea. I steam dandelion greens for dinner. There are always plenty of dandelions around."

As a treat for her daughter, Upham buys organic sunflower seeds and mixes them in a bowl with tamari, paprika and a little garlic. "Then I put them on a cookie sheet in a moderate oven for about an hour and a half. I stir them every so often, and put them in jars when they cool. It's a great snack for kids, and very high in zinc, a nutrient kids are often lacking."

She also does a mean popcorn. Instead of butter and salt, Upham mixes a little butter and canola oil, and adds tamari and nutritional or engevita yeast. "A lot of people think kids won't eat the yeast," she says. "But my daughter and her friends love the stuff. Sprinkle it generously and add a little cayenne for the adults."

Her adult friends prefer another one of Upham's creations. "I go to the local falafel restaurant and ask if I can have the ends of their pita bread," she says. "When they make falafels, they chop off a half-moon-shaped piece of pita and discard it. Rather than throwing it away, I can pick up a big three-pound bag of pita pieces for about a dollar, sometimes for nothing." Upham brushes the pita pieces inside and out with a little olive oil and then sprinkles on herbs such as oregano and rosemary, and a little Parmesan cheese. One minute under the broiler and they become a gourmet treat.

"I also make my own granola," says Upham, "all with organic ingredients. I use rolled oats, sunflower seeds, sesame seeds, wheat germ, some coconut, a few flax seeds and some lecithin. I mix it all with a little canola oil, and pop it in the oven at 350 degrees until it starts to brown, about an hour. Then I add some honey and put it back in the oven for a few minutes." Upham says the trick is that by adding the honey at the end, you don't have to stir the mixture or worry that it's going to burn.

Upham has also become something of an expert at cooking with beans. She says it's a lot easier than most people realize. The trick is not to overload yourself with too much kitchen work in one day. "I divide up the work. I bought a slow cooker for five bucks at the Sally Ann a few years ago. I can put the beans on and go out for a while, knowing the pot is safe. When the beans are done, I just put them in the freezer. That way, they're ready to use when I need them."

Another time saver is a premade nutrient-packed pancake mix of organic ingredients. Upham grinds up sunflower, sesame and flax seeds, and mixes them with flour, baking powder and salt. Sometimes she adds a little buckwheat flour, wheat germ or milk powder. She stores the mixture in the fridge, and then just adds an egg, some oil and milk when she's ready to cook the pancakes. "My daughter and I have started doing variations with the pancakes. Sometimes we add a little tomato sauce and some cheese, and fold the pancake over like a panzerotti. We call them pizza pancakes."

Upham spends about 20 percent of her income on food for herself and her daughter. That amounts to about $1,300 a year for each of them, well below the $1,600 that the average Canadian spends on food each year. Although welfare cutbacks have forced her to make painful and pointless sacrifices, Upham has been able to use her cooking skills to stretch her pennies to cover many organic purchases. Upham is convinced that spending the extra money on organic will help ensure a healthy future for her daughter.

One of the cost-saving measures Upham took for granted was breastfeeding her daughter until the age of four. Breast milk might be the most undervalued low-cost food of all.

MOTHER'S MILK

It takes a village to raise a child, the saying goes, but it takes a workplace to support a breast-feeding mom. Yet few employers think new moms deserve any special breaks, least of all the one-hour daily break for nursing recommended by the International Labour Organization in 1919. In this unsupportive climate, breast-feeding rates drop like a stone over the first year of a child's life. Less than 5 percent of babies are still being breast-fed on their first birthday.

If we respected the needs of children, breast-feeding would be the norm for at least two years. Four years was the norm for most of human history, and is still common in many pre-industrial societies. In fact, breastmilk offers additional physical and emotional advantages to infants older than six months. That's when substances in breastmilk that protect against childhood cancers start to click in, says Gabrielle Palmer, an international authority on breast-feeding.[60]

Most kids start on a partial diet of solid foods by six months, and they need the special enzymes in breastmilk to help with digestion. The extra immune boost in breastmilk becomes more important when babies start making their way into the wide world, crawling everywhere, putting their fingers into everything and then sucking them, playing with children who have colds, eating prepared foods that may contain harmful bacteria. Dr. Jack Newman, director of the breast-feeding clinic at Toronto's Hospital for Sick Children, speculates that nature took this need for enhanced immune protection into account by tripling the levels of antibiotic-like lipozyme in human milk after year one. And as kids take their first hard knocks, falling on their faces as they try to walk, learning that the world does not revolve around them, the loving touch of mom's breast becomes a "rock of security," Newman says. "They need to know that mom is still there." For all the amazing physical properties of breastmilk, Newman says that security, which is as crucial at eighteen months as it was at six, is the single most important thing breast-feeding offers.[61]

Breastmilk offers other protections as well. Breast-fed babies have lower rates of juvenile diabetes than formula-fed babies. They also receive important fatty acids through breastmilk that play a role in neurological development. Research conducted by Roger Masters at Dartmouth suggests that lack of breast-feeding may be associated with juvenile delinquency. Compared with breast-fed babies, children raised on substitutes absorb five times more manganese, which is linked with learning disabilities and aggressive behaviour. "It's the breakdown of the inhibition mechanism that's the key to violent behaviour," Masters argues.

Contrary to the popular stereotype, on today's world scene breast-feeding is more common among working women than among stay-at-home moms, says Gabrielle Palmer. Women in the Third World commonly carry their babies with them while working in agricultural fields, and feed them on demand, she says. In North America, progressive companies have found that breast-feeding-friendly policies are a surprising profit centre. Breastmilk is "the gold standard" of infant nutrition, says Boston workplace lactation consultant Marsha Walker, whose clients include insurance giant John Hancock. Breast-fed babies catch fewer colds and suffer half as many ear and lung infections, so the absenteeism rates of moms who breast-feed are lower than for moms who don't. If the employer pays for employee health and drug plans, the savings are staggering. The tab for drugs to combat child ear infections alone comes to $100 million a year in Canada. Christine Hoey of Kaiser Permanente, a health maintenance organization that provides health care to many U.S. companies, says that a breast-feeding mom provides her employer with $1,400 in savings during the first year of her child's life. Companies that cater directly to the public, such as Sears department stores, have also found that breast-feeding facilities help to attract shoppers who are breast-feeding.

It's pretty simple stuff to develop company policies that accommodate breast-feeding. Companies that let nicotine addicts duck out for smoke breaks can figure out how to let new moms duck out for a while too. All it takes in the way of facilities is a private room with a comfy chair and a footstool, a place where moms can bring their babies or express their milk into a bottle. It also helps to provide running water and a refrigerator where expressed milk can be stored. Top-of-the-line facilities provide breast pumps.

Some say breast-feeding is viewed as a problem because it involves female employees only. If a male executive took a midday break to express his milk, the argument goes, it would be called a power lunch. Aside from gender bias, the deck has to be cleared of some deep-seated cultural and psychological issues before we can get workplace breast-feeding on track. Getting a sense of these issues also helps us understand some of the complexities behind sound food policies and practices. There's an interesting link between the dehumanization of our food system and the dehumanization of work.

We get a hint of the unconscious hang-ups that surround breast-feeding by observing the intense pressure to wean babies onto solid foods. "We wean very early," says Dr. Shirley Gross, director of the Edmonton Breastfeeding Clinic. "It's all part of our conviction that to raise a child successfully is to foster independence," she says. "We pressure our kids to walk early, to talk early, to eat early. We tend to deny our kids their babyhood."[62] It's as if we fear that unless we establish distance in the food system, and rupture the child's direct access to mother and nature, the child won't become a socialized individual. Society has to establish a hold early on, otherwise the child will be sucking up to mom all its life and not sucking up to the proper authorities.

Julia Kristeva has put these subconscious and irrational fears on her psychoanalyst's couch in a number of arrestingly insightful books, ably summarized by Kelly Oliver in the anthology *Cooking, Eating, Thinking: Transformative Philosophies of Food*. For Kristeva, the female breast has been commonly seen as dirty, sinful and disruptive—the male obsession with hooters is just the flip side of this—because breasts don't respect the Berlin Wall that separates Nature and Society. Culturally, this is what distance in the food system is all about—suppressing the closeness of body, food and nature. "Western culture sustains itself by establishing borders between abject corporeal nature, which oozes and flows and defies categorization," Oliver writes, "and civilized society composed of clean and proper individuals."[63]

From this perspective, the obsession with early weaning and breastmilk substitutes is part of a war over symbols. Removing the baby from the breast separates the baby from the sole authority of the mother and from a direct route to nature. The child is "free" to be influenced by society. Unfortunately, this strategy for promoting individual development is inherently dehumanizing—what other word can we use to describe a preference for food that comes from the breasts of another species, the cow, rather than our own?—and contrary to the child's physical and emotional needs. Oliver says it's time for a rethink of a strategy that "turns the nourishing breast and mother's milk into a threat." Oliver's strategy for personality development is to treat breast-feeding as an opportunity to nurture individuals with loving and secure relationships from their earliest days. "We can create a new discourse in which mother's milk is a symbol for a social bond based on love of an other as oneself," she writes.

What does all this have to do with workplace programs to promote breast-feeding? The sharp break demanded between child and mother, child and nature, anticipates the sharp division between work and life itself, one of the cornerstones of industrial society. The industrial strategy for increasing efficiency is both the division of labour in the workplace (on assembly lines, for instance) and, more profoundly, the division of work from the rest of life.

Sociologist Alice Rossi once asked what would happen if social, workplace and medical policies were recentred on the biological realities of healthy reproduction. She argued that it would lead to a radical change, "a society more attuned to the natural environment, in touch with, and respectful of, our own body processes, that asks how we can have a balanced life with commitment both to achievement in work and intimate involvement with other human beings." Many powerful groups think technology can overcome biology and the need to adapt to it, she concedes. But in her judgement, "by far the wiser course to such a future is to plan and build from the most fundamental root of society in human parenting, and not from the shaky superstructure created by men in that fraction of time in which industrial societies have existed."[64] This is what a humanized food system and humanized workplace are about.[65]

CHAPTER 3

POWER SHOP

POWER SHOP

Consumers have the power to change the food system. Every time you make a purchase you have a chance to exercise that power. Your decisions can influence change in both the kinds of products that are sold and the kinds of businesses that sell them. In this chapter we'll show you how a new trend in consumer power can help create a new food system.

The food market place is being transformed by superpower shoppers. A new breed of tough customers is the shoppers' version of what 1997 Nobel Peace Prize winner Jody Williams dubbed "the new superpower." Williams was cheering the citizens movement that lined up reluctant governments behind a treaty banning military landmines. The movement was considered naive by pragmatic politicians, until the worldwide outpouring of grief for the late Princess Diana demanded some form of tribute to her crusade on behalf of children butchered in fields strewn with landmines. The elements of a successful campaign fell into place as if out of nowhere. By the end of the year, 121 countries had signed on to tiny Canada's big initiative. No one could have imagined this kind of turnaround five years ago, foreign affairs minister Lloyd Axworthy told the crowd celebrating the treaty. Political sovereignty "has become more diffuse, and no longer the sole domain of governments," he said. Independent citizen groups representing the general public have "demanded and won a place at the table" traditionally monopolized by the biggest players, Axworthy said.

In case anyone thought the landmines treaty was a fluke, the new superpower did a repeat performance the next year. A plan to ban public control over global corporations through a Multilateral Agreement on Investment, or MAI, was scuttled. With only the Internet to link them and leaked documents to work with, volunteers in public interest groups around the world built such public opposition to the cosy deal that the sponsors threw in the towel.

This new superpower of independent citizens has become the counterpoint to the dwindling ability of governments to protect the public interest in an era of global corporations. We predict that food will increasingly be at the centre of the action. More responsive, decentralized, community-based businesses will soon have their day in the sun.

Few would pick Canada as a country likely to succeed in such a momentous transformation. Canada has the most economically concentrated food sector in the western world, and such concentration can often resist new trends.[1] Consumers and citizens have little input or representation on government agencies that deal with food and consumer protection. Food consumers have no rights under the federal Charter of Rights or provincial human rights codes. Of the biological needs for life—air, water and food—only food is run exclusively by the for-profit sector and has no consumer champion in government. Governments get away with this because Canadian consumers aren't organized on this issue, in stark contrast to producers. No political party profiles consumer issues. And environmentalists are so dead set against consumerism that they've never bothered to define environmentalism as fundamentally a consumer rights issue.

But that's changing. Angus McAllister, of the polling firm Environics, has been following ecotrends in Canada and twenty-nine other countries for a decade. The environment, he warns business and government clients, "is not top of mind" with the public but is still "close to the heart." Strong majorities believe corporations are destroying the planet, worry that their health is at risk, think chemicals do more harm than good and want governments to pass stronger environmental laws, he says. People are holding to these views despite a systematic decade-long campaign by business, media and politicians to discredit environmental science and priorities. The great majority don't look to big solutions, but to small, immediate actions they can take personally. Two-thirds feel empowered to do something direct and positive, such as buying green products. They are "taking matters into their own hands," the pollster says. At the same time, however, they feel "stuck" by the limitations of what they can do on their own, and want to be "enabled" to do more by companies or governments. If there's no response, a backlash is in the works, McAllister warns. Today's lull, he says, is just the quiet before the storm.[2]

THE POWER TRIO:
BOYCOTTS, BUYCOTTS AND NICHES

Boycotts

Without much in the way of organized appeals or fanfare, one Canadian in four boycotts at least one product at least once a year for ethical reasons.[3] They see it as an act of citizenship. They're casting their dollars like votes. The corporate supporters of government deregulation didn't count on this. They didn't anticipate that consumers would reregulate them much more strictly, especially around such issues as child labour, which happens to be endemic in food production as well as in the manufacture of running shoes and clothing.

The Alar Scare, or more properly the Alar Rebellion, revealed the lay of the land in 1989. Apple growers in the United States sprayed Alar because it made apples fall from trees over three, instead of six, weeks. This made mass-production harvesting more efficient and gave apples a nice ripe look. Though it had been known since 1980 that Alar was linked with cancer, governments couldn't bring themselves to do more than study the issue. Then CBS television ran an exposé researched by an environmental organization and promoted by actress Meryl Streep. Apple sales collapsed instantly, growers begged the government to save their reputation by banning Alar and the manufacturer voluntarily withdrew Alar from the U.S. market, diverting sales to the Third World.

Boycotts happen. In the media village they don't have to be painstakingly organized; they can be sparked by a small group with limited resources. Without warning, they come on like a tornado, indifferent to the size of what's before them. They are above the government's law, responding to a higher law of the public good. And they engage what supermarket executive Paddy Carson calls "the power of one to make a difference." He likes to remind fellow executives that the Boston Tea Party, featuring seventeen protesters who dumped overtaxed British tea into the Boston harbour, sparked the American Revolution and caused a shift to coffee that Americans maintain two hundred years later.

The bigger the corporations are, the harder their stock falls if there's a boycott. The clue to their weakness in the face of boycotts comes from an analysis of the merger movement that has put such concentrated economic power in so few hands. The 1990s merger wave is different from the ripples that preceded it in the previous hundred years. Competition is more intense than ever. Gluts, and collapsed prices, are worse than ever, as any hog, wheat or oil producer will tell you. Just like the giant who collapsed while chasing Jack down the beanstalk, these megacorporations can't carry their own weight. An average employee at a non-financial corporation works seven hours and forty-six minutes a day recovering the cost of running a business and only fourteen minutes generating profit.[4] Far from creating a more controlled world, megacorporations have created a hair-trigger world where a tiny blip in demand can precipitate a crisis. Whereas size matters for firms, it doesn't for boycotters. That's why the market can be goosed with a gentle squeeze.

The soft, if bulging, underbelly of corporate giantism is evident in supermarkets, where Loblaws alone snags one Canadian food dollar in five. Eight chains divvy up $48.3 billion in sales a year. But there are two sides to every story, and it doesn't take much to rattle supermarket carts. In the late 1990s supermarket share of food purchases dropped for the first time since the 1950s. Competition for food dollars, and the steady consumer traffic that food sales bring in the door, is fierce. Department stores and drugstores have food stalls. Discounters like Costco get business when people stock up on staples. Restaurants and fast-food chains compete for everyday meals. If just 2 percent of shoppers switch to any number of health food alternatives, at least one of the Big Eight will do a bellyflop.[5]

Goosing an oversupplied market with a boycott is much more effective than lobbying politicians. That's how a dozen Friends of the Lubicon in Toronto turned around seemingly impossible David-and-Goliath odds to win justice for a small Native band in northern Alberta. The federal government refused for fifty years to negotiate Lubicon treaty rights. Alberta leased their traditional lands to the Japanese multinational Daishowa in 1988, which got set to log ten thousand square miles of forest. In 1991 the Friends approached take-out chains that used Daishowa cardboard for packaging, and suggested it was easier to switch suppliers than fight a boycott over complicity in the genocide of Native peoples. Daishowa lost $14 million in sales to forty companies. In 1996 it sued the Friends for libel and got a court injunction to stop the boycott. The company lost face in the media, which denounced the strong-arm tactics as suppression of free speech and association. In 1998, Daishowa faced a humiliating court judgement that threw out the injunction and awarded the company a few dollars for the damage done to its reputation by over-the-top rhetoric about genocide. The boycott was called off when Daishowa postponed logging until it could settle with the Lubicon.[6]

There's a lesson here about working with competitive market forces when politicians won't listen up. The market offers more opportunities for influence than governments, which hold all the cards in dealings with citizens and none of the cards in dealings with global corporations. Governments are forbidden, for instance, under the rules of the World Trade Organization, from banning imports of products on the basis of unethical or environmentally dangerous production methods practised elsewhere. But consumers can still exercise free choice and, through boycotts, ask retailers to do the same.

Buycotts

Buycotters go out of their way to buy from those who try to do the right thing, not just punish those doing the wrong thing. Usually, this takes one of two forms. The more traditional comes from groups that see "trade, not aid" as the way to help impoverished Third World suppliers of tea, coffee, chocolate and the like. Alternative Trade Organizations promote "fair trade" by offering a just price to producer co-ops in the Third World. The newer form of buycotting is local. Typically, an organization of consumers works with producers who want to change for the better but need some help while they're learning.

That's what Julia Langer of the World Wildlife Fund is doing. She figured that if environmental organizations could help create a consumer base for earth-friendly foods, farmers might reduce their use of chemicals without change being forced through legal means. To this end, she brought together a unique coalition of environmentalists, apple growers and apple-juice processors to work on marketing an ecological apple juice. Apple growers in Ontario's Beaver Valley agreed to participate. Chemical agriculture is the norm here. Some refer to the area as Death Valley, a reference to the high rate of cancer among orchardists. But the farmers agreed to try what's called Integrated Pest Management, or IPM, which reduces pesticide use significantly by incorporating some methods used by organic growers. Environmentalists have gone along with IPM, reasoning that a 50 percent reduction in chemical sprays is a good start, and better than insisting on zero and getting nowhere. An ecological apple juice went on the market in early 1998. Langer is negotiating with processors and fresh-apple retailers to expand the project. She's also developing similar projects with potato and canola farmers. The success of these ventures depends entirely on the concept of consumer buycott.[7]

Treats are often among the first items to be buycotted. People see treats as reflections of their personal preferences, not just their physical needs; so they're willing to do something a bit out of the ordinary that they wouldn't do for carrots and potatoes. Coffee is a good example of how this works. Coffee is second only to oil among world exports. Coffee bushes grow naturally in shaded forests, but major growers prefer sunny plantations. Where once South American coffee bushes nestled among over 40 species of trees, home to some 150 species of birds, they now line fields. Yields are higher, but so is use of pesticides and chemical fertilizers. Half a kilo of chemicals are applied for every kilo of coffee produced, and residues from nineteen pesticides have been found on beans tested by the Natural Resources Defence Council. Unable to afford the chemicals, peasants with small holdings, who were once sustained by the trade, are going under. As well, the Smithsonian Migratory Bird Center has documented declines in the 97 percent range for some bird species.

Canadians have 15 billion opportunities each year to reverse this trend—one for each cup of coffee they drink. A small co-op called Just Us, based near Wolfville, Nova Scotia, roasts and sells organic beans from a farm co-op that's guaranteed a fair base price. In 1998, two years after start-up, Just Us (their phone number is 1-800-NOT THEM) did $500,000 worth of business in Canada. "We want people to buy our coffee because it's great coffee," says Just Us staffer Ria March, "then appreciate it because it's fairly traded."[8] Applying the principles of buycott to other foods as well can not only ensure that you're getting quality products, it can also send a powerful message to retailers.

Niches

Aside from considerations of conscience, food tastes have gone upscale of late. The yuppies of the 1980s were the first to expand taste horizons. They created the first significant market niches based on the tastiness of food prepared without gravy or ketchup, served in an ambience that offered more than clean washrooms and Formica table tops.

Niche marketing has governed the entire North American economy since the 1980s. It has an impact far beyond the number of people in any or all niches, because designer products respond to deep-seated trends. In an era when prices for raw commodities are nosediving, niches provide a place where value—service, or some other differentiating factor—can be added and prices maintained. Advances in marketing allow companies to zero in on precise customers. New technologies allow small batches to be made for about the same cost as items cranked off an assembly line.

Food has been affected dramatically by this trend. Less than twenty years ago there were two kinds of bread, white and brown, and two kinds of coffee, regular and double-double. Now, umpteen varieties of bread compete with bagels, croissants, pitas and foccacia, while coffee drinkers weigh the merits of café lattes, espressos and mocchacinos. Companies stuck in the mass-production, mass-marketing straitjacket—Kellogg's, Campbell's, McDonald's, for instance—are in crisis mode, experiencing the death of a thousand niches.[9] Expect these crises to broaden and deepen. Niche markets will unravel the industrial food system and replace it with a craft system in tune with micromarkets.

Beer was the first success story of niche products geared to educated taste. Craft brews, often based on old family recipes and marketed with a local, underdog image, account for about 8 percent of sales in the $10-billion-a-year suds industry. Craft beers cost a bit more per bottle, but since many of their drinkers are getting long in the tooth and no longer wish to chug-a-lug themselves into oblivion, a few high-taste beers can be nursed through the evening. Small-batch methods have been perfected to the point where even restaurants and pubs can brew quality beers. There are over seventy brew pubs across Canada, with one Toronto club, C'est What, offering hemp beer.[10]

Winemaking is moving in the same direction. Small B.C. and Ontario wineries regularly win international awards. Some farmers can boost their incomes by making specialty wines from their produce. Bill Redelmeier of Southbrook Farms, near Richmond Hill, Ontario, is Canada's second-largest wine exporter. When the cool summer of 1992 left him with a glut of berries, he made Framboise. He's since expanded into a range of blackcurrant, blueberry and specialty raspberry dessert wines that have won international awards. Redelmeier features Richmond Hill on his labels, donates a dollar from each sale to local community events and offers discounts to customers who bring their bottles back for refilling.[11] Donald Ziraldo, the Niagara winemaker who produces Inniskillin, also combines growing and processing, and gives back to his community by sponsoring the Shaw Festival and Brock University's new department researching winemaking in a cold climate.[12] Both winemakers typify a trend identified by Gene Logsden, U.S. champion of rural renewal through a small-farm renaissance. Logsden calls it the "new yeomanry" of entrepreneurial farmers, who've given up on lousy prices for anonymous commodities and are selling personalized products directly.[13]

Niches have also brought new life to restaurants. Canada has sixty thousand restaurants, 41 percent of them less than ten years old. "Chef" is one of the fastest-growing occupations in the country.[14] Many chefs are artist-entrepreneurs who work closely with local food growers to get the highest-quality ingredients. The trend is most pronounced in B.C., where "the Gourmet Trail" in Vancouver, Vancouver Island and the Gulf Islands has become a tourist destination. At Sooke Harbour House, Sinclair Philip serves only salads picked from his own kitchen doorstep, where four hundred varieties of fruits and veggies bloom. He also does a brisk sale of his own bottled balsamic vinegar aged in local woods.

The restaurant revival is also associated with redevelopment of once-threatened city cores in Montreal, Kingston, Edmonton, London and a number of other cities.[15] Downtown businesses can't compete with suburban malls and box stores by selling the same old dry goods, but by converting downtowns into gathering places and watering holes, they're reinventing urbanism. Niche operations work on the principle of "the more the merrier": the more choices, the more people drop by to sample them all. The niche economy also has a win-win relationship with the local community. Main Streets can't survive without vital neighbourhoods around them, so Main Street revival and the rejuvenation of inner cities are linked.

Away from the din of main streets, chefs are also setting up in residential neighbourhoods. This trend challenges the economic wisdom that holds that only high-traffic areas can support businesses and the town-planning dogma that residential neighbourhoods must be free of all commerce. In Toronto's troubled Parkdale area, Leslie Gaynor, a laid-off social worker "looking for a way to get out of the rat race and into the human race," opened up Mitzi's in the first floor of her home on a residential street. With seats for eighteen and a menu featuring premium coffees, ice creams and light meals, Mitzi's quickly became a hang-out. People who previously just lived near one another became neighbours in the fullest sense of the word. A play space for kids encouraged at-home parents to drop in for adult company and a hit of java during the day. "People are looking for places where they can have contact, say hello to their neighbours and get connected, instead of living within the four walls of their house all the time," says Gaynor.

Restaurants that double as hang-outs are as old as the British coffee shops of the 1700s, dubbed "nickel universities" because of the drawn-out discussions that took place over one of the central ingredients of a great nation, a good five-cent cup of coffee. This reflects one of the central cultural functions of meals, as a setting for companionship. Instead of high traffic and fast turnover, corner bistros such as Mitzi's thrive on repeat business and low rents on residential streets.

Small operators have it all over the big chains when it comes to what the business pundits call "customerization." It's true that they don't have the mass-production economies of scale that drive down costs when billions of burgers are sold. More important, they don't have the dis-economies of scale, the uniform rules and standards needed to centralize control over an inherently personal service in an inherently unpredictable business. This is the "Cheers" factor—the preference people have for a friendly place where everybody knows their name. Big companies have a hard time moving customer service in that direction. The division of labour means workers have one job that requires all their attention, and that turns customer chit-chat into a disruption. Some companies think friendly behaviour can be ordered up. One Vancouver supermarket ordered checkout clerks to establish eye contact and smile at customers as they were ringing up the bill. A spotter from headquarters nabbed a worker for failing to smile, and the worker was disciplined. The union protested. As it turned out, the checkout clerk had just returned from a funeral.

Toronto inventor Robert Curran coined the term "nano-businesses" to describe self-employment possibilities that need minimal capital to start and that can be grown with a small band of loyal customers. Nano-businesses are about niches where entrepreneurs find a place to express their values in their day jobs because they offer something meaningful and unique. However modest the return by Bay Street standards, they generate a healthy profit in human terms.

Dream equity has made food the business of choice for disadvantaged groups. Food businesses have what economists call "low barriers to entry"; they don't take millions of dollars to start. They can fly on a wing and a prayer, some sweat and some blood. With fifty customers, an aspiring farmer can lease five acres and launch a Community Supported Agriculture operation. A caterer to families with food sensitivities can run the service from a small kitchen.

Women are three times more likely to open a new business than men; almost half a million have gone into business for themselves since 1991.[16] Immigrants can also turn their heritage to advantage in the food business. For all their exotic offerings, supermarket chains don't stock basic staples used by many immigrants. As a result, most cities have a thriving Chinatown and Little India, centred around food stores and restaurants where the entrepreneurial skills of immigrants are transplanted. Immigrants enjoy few opportunities in the straight corporate world, where their language, culture and credentials aren't valued. In the food and restaurant industry the tables are turned, and a distinctive heritage translates into a unique advantage. Mid East Food Services in Windsor, started on adrenalin, now sells over $4 million worth of pitas a year. "This was the type of business where we could still relate to our people," says co-owner Paul Hanna, "and that we had a little knowledge of." In Toronto, Iranian refugee Manoucer Etminan went from waiting tables to starting his own Persian bakery. With $6,000 borrowed from friends, he's built a $10-million business. Some of his loaves sell for seven dollars, but he provides the recipes for free on his Web site. He has two rules for baking success: old-fashioned ways are best, and relationships are everything.[17]

Youth are another disadvantaged group checking out self-employment in nano-businesses. Hire yourself first. Politicians gung-ho for training schemes have got the wrong fix on youth unemployment, concludes a federal government study by University of Alberta sociologist Graham Lowe. The big problem isn't that skills are too low to fill available jobs; it's that jobs offer too few challenges to match the skills of youth. Most starter jobs are so mind-numbing, Lowe says, "we're actually reducing our human capital." Jobs need to be upskilled so they "use the knowledge that is available."[18] In the absence of such change, young entrepreneurs are going it on their own. The trend gives some astute executives the shivers. "The biggest threat to the long-term prosperity of a corporation these days is not other large firms," says Robert Spinrod, who was vice-president in charge of innovation for Xerox. "It's the guys in the garage shop down the street who come up with something out of the blue and take everyone by surprise."[19]

Niche markets invite Canadian businesses to break out of their colonial mentality. Mass production discouraged Canadian entrepreneurship because people thought Canadian markets were too small. Our problem lies in thinking too big. If we think smaller, in terms of businesses that can be supported by tens or hundreds of customers, we will see opportunities one niche at a time. If a restaurant with seating for eighteen can provide rewarding employment for two or three, if a farm family with fifty CSA customers can do well, what is the limit to job growth?

Unlike boycotting and buycotting, which rely on deliberate ethical decisions by shoppers, niches rely on diverse and educated tastes, and innovations in small-batch production. But these niches extend the possibilities of shopping around an impersonal economy that divorces social and spiritual values from economic activity. "It seems to me," says Tom Webb, a co-op activist who directs the extension department at St. Francis Xavier University in Antigonish, Nova Scotia, "that it's an exciting, revealing, tough, worthwhile, lifelong adventure to reintegrate ethics and economics."[20]

BOYCOTT GENETICALLY ENGINEERED FOOD

A gentle but forceful boycott can put the genetic engineering industry out of its misery before it does irreversible harm. A boycott offers the unique and historic opportunity to keep more genes in the bottle before they're let out. With most of the health and environmental disasters of this century—dioxins, PCBs, CFCs and nuclear power, for example—damage was not recognized before entire industries had become dependent on the products, and before toxic releases did irreparable harm. Perhaps because of these experiences, an international movement to boycott genetically engineered (GE) foods has developed quickly. Canada and the United States are the only major Western nations not to have well-informed, widely supported and militant movements against genetically engineered foods. Involvement of the Canadian public could tip the balance, at the very least by inhibiting one of the most reckless promoters of genetic engineering in world councils today—the Canadian government.[21]

Genetically engineered foods can't find buyers in most of the world's markets. Japan only gives entry to GE corn. The European Union, over the protests of the Canadian government, insists that all foods be labelled as to whether they do or do not "contain genetically modified commodity." It's anticipated that any foods labelled with "do contain" won't be moving off the shelves quickly, except to be returned to the sender. A number of prominent processors and retailers, such as Iceland Foods in Britain, refuse point-blank to carry any GE stock. "Consumers are being used as guinea pigs without their knowledge," says Iceland Foods corporate chair Michael Walker. He predicts that GE foods will prove to be a greater calamity than mad cow disease, and may come to be recognized as the "most dangerous development in food production this century."[22]

European resistance to GE crops cost Canadian canola farmers $30 million in lost sales in 1998. Farmers who used unmodified canola lost out as well, since they went along with the Canadian government's recommendation to pool the entire canola crop, a reflection of the government's position that no labelling of GE foods is needed. "If we thought there was a health and safety concern with these foods, they would not be getting into the marketplace," says Margaret Kenny of the Canadian Food Inspection Agency. "Trust me, I'm from the government" does not translate well in Europe, however. Major GE companies have bowed to market realities and are segregating and labelling their crops, so at least other sales can be salvaged. In 1998, AgrEvo delayed introduction of its GE soy bean, known as "Liberty Link," until European opinion stabilized, to the great relief of U.S. soy bean producers who were worried about $9 billion in lost sales.[23] H.J. Heinz, the largest buyer of Ontario white beans, has made it known that it doesn't want GE product, since GE beans could jeopardize Heinz sales in Britain, where the company now enjoys over half the market. That has put a hold on commercial GE research on beans at Guelph University, one of the centres of GE research in Canada.[24]

The stock market judgement has been equally harsh on GE, or biotech, as it's grouped in stock markets. "Dead in the water," "zero growth" and "goose egg" typify comments from stock analysts watching the sector in 1998.[25] Its performance throughout the decade earned the biotech industry a reputation as a "money-destroying machine." In 1996, for instance, 1,300 U.S. biotech firms swallowed losses of $4.6 billion. Governments, however, are standing behind the industry, as they did with nuclear power. The U.S. government hands out about $4 billion and Canadian governments about $400 million each year, refusing to pull the plug on this life-support system.

There are several reasons why Canadians should join the international boycott movement. First, genetic engineering carries a high risk of catastrophic environmental damage. Many people feel the reputation that precedes Monsanto, a key industry player, demonstrates their lack of the environmental responsibility needed in such an experimental field. Monsanto, a giant in the chemical spray industry before it got into the GE business, is notable for having marketed PCBs and Agent Orange to the world. The company is named in connection with a score of toxic sites requiring clean-up identified by the U.S. government.

The various arranged marriages between chemical and seed companies to form GE companies also arouse fears about vested interests to develop seeds that promote chemical dependence. About 75 percent of all GE research, according to Dr. Vandana Shiva, one of the world's foremost biotech critics, goes into seeds that can tolerate heavy doses of a particular company's sprays; Monsanto's soy beans that tolerate Monsanto's Round Up herbicide is one example. Andrew Kimbrell, a leading critic of genetic technologies in the United States, worries that GE seeds will unleash "biological pollution" on a scale the world has never known. Chemical pollution is at least diluted over time and space, he says, but biological pollution—Dutch elm disease, purple loosestrife and zebra mussels are examples—gathers strength and does devastating harm. There are already reports of "gene-jumping"—of genes in genetically engineered crops mixing it up with weeds to create "superweeds," akin to the "superbugs" that have been created by excess use of antibiotics. It's unlikely that quality-control levels in the industry or government can protect against this. In 1997, for instance, Monsanto had to recall sixty thousand bags of bioengineered canola seeds from Canada because the wrong line of genetically modified seed had been inadvertently released. By the time of the recall, some of the seeds had already been planted. The incident was not reported to the public by any major media or government agency.[26]

Genetic engineering threatens grave economic damage to farmers and eaters, especially in the Third World. Patents are indispensable to GE success, the only way a company can recoup the millions it has invested in research. As a result, seed and chemical companies are taking out patents on anything that moves, even when it's patently absurd. Companies have taken out patents for soy beans, India's basmati rice and cherished neem tree, and scores of plant varieties nurtured over the millennia and long considered the common property of all peoples. Any who use a patented seed must pay a licence fee to the patent owner. Shiva refers to this corporate strategy as "bio-piracy."

In North America, Monsanto signs contracts with farmers who buy its seeds. These contracts prohibit the farmers from saving seed for next year's supply, as has been done by farmers since the beginning of agriculture. Collecting seeds at the end of the season saved farmers money, and also allowed them to adapt seeds to their particular climate and conditions. But this tradition doesn't fit with the needs of seed companies. Monsanto, for instance, has been referred to sometimes as the "Microsoft of agriculture," reaping unending profits every time a crop is grown by controlling seeds, just as Microsoft controls computer software. The costs of buying seeds, paying licensing fees for seeds and buying chemicals to go with the seeds are especially frightening in the Third World, where tiny farms with modest surpluses are the norm. Two-thirds of the world's food is raised on farms of less than three acres. Such farms will be driven into bankruptcy, and the people who depend on them will be driven into starvation, if GE seeds become standard.

Genetic technology raises ethical challenges that humans are not yet ready to consider. "This is the first branch of science born on Wall Street," says Shiva. Corporations, with minimal regulation from public agencies, have the reins on the future of what used to be called life. Their lawyers have won major court cases that define life as patentable. Many animals "created" by GE methods are formally referred to as "bioreactors," as if they were machines. Many genetic alterations are unspeakably cruel to the animals involved, forcing them to live lives—if they may be legally defined as having lives—of agony, one example being the painfully engorged udders of some cows on Bovine Growth Hormone. "This industry says it is about progress," says Kimbrell, "but that's an incomplete sentence. Progress toward what?" This is an industry that threatens cosmic pollution, which could undermine the basis of morality and human relations to other creatures.

Boycotting the industry on an item-by-item basis is impossible in Canada, thanks to government and industry policies that prevent labelling and segregation of GE products. According to Dr. Richard Wolfson of the Campaign to Ban Genetically Engineered Foods, GE canola, corn and soy beans can be found in thirty thousand food products, including baby food.[27] Until labelling and segregation of genetically engineered products are required in Canada, GE boycotters should buycott organic.

LOCAL LABELLING

Residents' Choice promises to be the fastest-growing name brand in the country, where the name stands for Jill up the street, who makes the best relish in town, and Tom down the road, who makes great butter from wild crab apples and choke cherries. Local labels are already on products in three Ontario communities. Peterborough's "Kawartha's Own, Locally Grown," Renfrew County's "From The Ottawa Valley," and Windsor's "Bounty of the County" show what happens when farmers, tour operators, unions, social agencies and Main Street business groups support local food businesses. In British Columbia, Cathleen Kneen and the non-profit dynamo FarmFolk/CityFolk are developing a campaign to establish Food Policy Organizations across the province to promote local food heroes.[28] Local labels are essentially a promotional tool to draw attention to what small, local processors are cooking up. They're spearheaded by a local organization—a public health unit, a union, a merchants' association—that recognizes a community and economic development opportunity.

Local labellers believe that food grounds a local economy. Since everyone has to eat every day, food-based businesses are relatively recession-proof, and don't suffer from the uncontrollable boom-bust cycles that plague other industries. Food is also rich in what are called "multiplier effects." If the $20 you spend at a local restaurant goes to buy $20 of food from a local grocer, then goes to buy $20 of food from a local farmer, then goes to a farmer's taxes that pay $20 to a local teacher, who then goes to the local restaurant and starts the cycle again, the effect of one purchase is multiplied many times. By contrast, $20 spent in an area dominated by importers and exporters has little multiplication going for it; it's likely to leave town in short order. Local labels strive to nurture the community ties, loyalties and linkages that keep multiplication happening. Money is like manure, they say. It needs to be spread around.

There are other reasons why local labellers start by boostering local economies with food. It increases local pride and identity. Tourists like it; they want craft, not Kraft. Local is also fresh and nutritious, carrying low transportation, packaging, storage and refrigeration costs. Local farmers and processors also know local taste preferences. Going the extra mile to service customers may just mean walking down the street. And local is where the jobs are. Agricultural researcher Brewster Kneen's study of Ontario buying habits shows that fifty thousand growing and processing jobs could be created overnight if Ontarians ate the same proportions of local food today as they ate in 1971.[29] John Warnock's study suggests similar job creation possibilities in B.C. if people bought 47 percent of their food in-province, as they did in the early 1980s. Both believe there's a good chance of going far beyond what was achieved in the past.

Some unlikely institutional practices keep local purchasing from happening. Tourists in Thunder Bay who try fresh wild fish at a Lake Superior resort might be surprised to find where they came from. One hotel owner apologized that his stock came from a fish farm in Manitoba, arriving after being flown through Toronto to Detroit to Thunder Bay. Local fishers aren't into supplying small orders to fussy resort owners, he said. Or take the case of Russel Pocock, one of Canada's first organic farmers. He lives in the Eastern Townships of Quebec and tried selling his produce at a local supermarket there, only to be told that all orders were filled from the Central Market in Montreal. Some time later he recognized his vegetables at the local store and decided to track what happened. It turns out that the Massachusetts broker he sold to had in turn sold the stock to a Chicago broker who then sold it in Montreal's Central Market, whence it returned home. There are a thousand stories like this in the naked city.

Suffice it to say for now that centralized institutions such as supermarkets don't source locally. Inventory is best controlled from the chain's head office, the industry dogma goes. Some chains' buyers prefer to handle all deals through one broker who can provide year-round supplies; that pretty well cuts out Canadian farmers, who can't grow through the winter. The virtual monopoly that allows supermarket chains to get away with such decisions means all roads lead to Florida and California. Toronto, according to Ontario Food Terminal manager Bill Carsley, regularly places as either the biggest or second-biggest purchaser of California and Florida produce on the entire continent. Branch-plant food for a branch-plant society.

Some government programs encourage local purchasing. Ontario sponsors a "Foodland Ontario" logo, backed with heavy advertising on the advantages of fresh produce. Some Ontario jails give preference to local farmers and processors, a marked shift from the early 1980s, when Ontario institutions were the major Canadian buyers of juices from the apartheid regime in South Africa. Most provincial liquor boards give premium shelf space to local wineries. B.C. Ferries, the largest single food buyer in the province, spends 80 percent of its $60-million yearly budget on local food. It's as simple as stipulating freshness and quality when tendering contracts. Quebec encourages school-meal programs to source food locally. Generally, however, taxpayer money leaks as badly as any, despite the payback to taxpayers when local jobs are created.

Though local labelling organizations lobby public bodies to do more local purchasing, the focus of their efforts is on building new partnerships that give community-based networks some zing. Farmers' markets, buyers' clubs and public meetings are common ways to connect directly with buyers. This approach leaves it to individuals to make the right choice, once presented with labelling information and given an opportunity to choose. Personal and informal channels are critical in the free trade era, since free trade agreements make it illegal for most governments to discriminate against foreign producers. But it's not illegal to advertise that something is grown or made locally. Nor is it illegal for individuals to give preference to a local favourite—yet.

Imagine if people bought half their food locally, says Lynn Jones. She's a public health staffer in the Renfrew health unit that helped sponsor "From the Ottawa Valley." The local economy would be strong, with family farms and small businesses able to steer clear of stormy international business cycles. And, as Jones says, food would be "fresh and wholesome, reflecting the short path travelled by food from the field to the table."[30] Perry Pearce, a farmer in Ontario's Essex County, agrees. Agriculture is second only to the auto industry for jobs in the area, he says. "It is good to see that people are coming together and focusing on what we can do here where we live," he says. "We are thinking globally, and acting locally."[31]

ANNEX ORGANICS

In a warehouse in a derelict industrial neighbourhood near downtown Toronto, Lauren Baker and Jonathan Woods pull handfuls of sprouts from a barrel and tuck them into small resealable bags. The sprouts are their own special mix—a spicy blend of french green and crimson red lentils, marrowfat and green peas, and mung beans—and they're a favourite of customers across the city. Baker and Woods, along with Tracey Loverock, make up Annex Organics. They're the only certified organic food producer in the city. That's right, *in* the city. Their "farm" is a rooftop, a small greenhouse made of scavenged material, and this storage area at the back of a warehouse. And it suits this trio of young entrepreneurs just fine. "I wanted to be an organic farmer," says Woods, "but I'm an urban person and I didn't want to live full time in the country." Annex Organics is the perfect compromise.

The three owners of Annex Organics, all in their mid-twenties, are committed to breaking down the traditional boundaries between country and city, food producer and food consumer. Most food comes from the country, transported to food stores in refrigerated trucks. It's not the most efficient or environmentally sound way to grow food for urban dwellers. The Annex Organics trio believes there's great potential for urban agriculture, and they are ready to lead the way. "The urban farm is part of a larger greening movement," says Baker. "This is commercial agriculture that's helping to green the city. And it makes sense. There's so much unused space right here in the city. Rooftops are effectively free land. They're all over the city, acres of them, and they're right where the customers are. Because we're right here too, we know what our customers want, we talk to them every day and see how they like the produce."

Woods says there are other advantages. The city is relatively warm, so the growing season is longer than in surrounding rural areas. The city is also a great source of organic waste material. The fertilizer that Annex Organics uses comes from food waste from the Good Food Box program, just below their feet, and the Chinatown food markets. Woods has been known to climb into church belfries to shovel out bird droppings. "Urban agriculture makes good use of the city's waste," he says. "Waste is transformed back into food. It's a closed loop."

Sprouts are Annex Organics' mainstay throughout the year. Besides the "mixed legume crunch," as they call it, they grow alfalfa sprouts and seedling sprouts of peas and radishes, which make locally grown greens available all through the winter. The business now services more than two thousand customers. But the low-tech growing system can handle a much larger capacity. It's all surprisingly simple. On a rack made of old wood palettes sit up to seventy-two twenty-litre buckets. The buckets were scavenged from Chinatown garbage cans, cleaned, and adapted to sprout production simply by drilling a few drainage holes. The seeds are rinsed twice a day. Scavenged barrels sawn in half collect the nutrient-rich water that flows through the sprouts. Within a week or two, the sprouts are ready to harvest.

"This must be our hundredth version of this," Baker laughs, "and now we're considering moving to larger barrels with a different watering system." Since Annex Organics' founding four years ago, most of the time and expense have been devoted to experimentation. Urban farming is still a new concept. There are no instruction manuals; it's all trial and error. Woods points to two bushel barrels topped up with sawdust. "That's fish emulsion, a rich natural fertilizer made from fish heads, bones and tails. I've finally figured out how to make it work and not stink to high heaven. It's something of a triumph for me this week. Just try to find instructions on how to make that."

Jonathan Woods started Annex Organics in 1995. As a zoology student, he took a course on the geography of agriculture that transformed his thinking. He became convinced that agriculture was an unrecognized environmental issue, falling under the shadow of more dramatic issues such as clear-cutting pristine forests. He also felt he could make a difference, and make a living at the same time. He came up with a list of possible enterprises—making wild teas, collecting mushrooms—but finally gave rooftop farming a try. With the support of Mary Lou Morgan, a visionary food activist in Toronto, he exchanged his computer skills for a chance to experiment on the rooftop of her food-box packing operation. With financial support from FoodShare, Annex Organics got off the ground. "The first year I put down a layer of cardboard, plastic and compost, and got these tiny stunted plants. It was pretty discouraging. But by last year we covered our expenses and sold about $1,000 worth of food."

All the experiments are now paying off. Besides the sprouts, the rooftop farm produces thirty-nine varieties of heritage tomatoes, as well as peppers and eggplants. Annex Organics also makes and sells its own potting mix, worm castings, a mineral fertilizer mix, seedlings and other gardening supplies. They're growing herbs and edible flowers. They teach gardening workshops and provide consulting services on urban agriculture issues such as composting and pest management. Developing all these skills keeps the business viable and gives them the ability to generate income throughout the year. Unlike most farmers, who are forced to take unrelated jobs in the off-season to make ends meet, the three owners of Annex Organics use their off-season work to buttress their skill and knowledge. As a result, Annex Organics makes enough money today to provide a modest living for the three owners, as well as several part-time jobs for workers who help with packing.

The centrepiece of the operation is upstairs. Baker and Woods nimbly climb two metal ladders that lead to the roof. There, spread over five thousand square feet, are tomato, pepper and eggplant seedlings. They're being grown in a system the trio refers to as "hybrid hydroponic." The plants set down roots in both soil and water. Most of their nutrients come from the water, which is infused with fish emulsion and other natural fertilizers. A conventional hydroponic system is a sterile environment. In this hybrid, the soil lends complexity and diversity, encouraging the micro-organisms that help plants to thrive. They settled on this growing system for a very practical reason. "Soil is too heavy to lug up to the roof," says Baker. "Also, the water flows through the system, so it's a less labour-intensive way to provide nutrients." The result is beautiful produce—so fine, in fact, that it has attracted the eye of several top chefs in Toronto.

"How much we three can physically do is our limitation right now," says Woods. "With a small crew and limited space, we don't want to take on more customers than we can service. But the demand is definitely there," he says. "So many of the chefs we talk to are really into the idea, especially the heritage tomatoes. They don't mind paying the premium. It doesn't make a big difference to their bottom line to spend $2 a pound for our tomatoes instead of $1 a pound for tomatoes that taste like crap. It makes sense to them, and it gives us a good price."

Baker adds that they're just starting to be confident that their technologies are reliable and consistent. "Once we have the systems down, and have a good year with them, then we can pass them on, or contract them out to other groups. An essential part of what we're trying to do is to create really simple technologies, with scavenged material and very little start-up money, so that people can make a decent wage. The start-up costs are high in terms of labour, but at the end of the summer you're harvesting quite a valuable product."

It's valuable because of its originality—tiny red and yellow currant tomatoes, purple, brown, and red beauties up to two pounds—and because it's certified organic by the Ontario Crop Improvement Association. Organic crops in the city may seem like a contradiction at first glance. Most people assume that urban areas are polluted, and there's no doubt the soil surrounding the warehouse is not safe to grow food in. "It's a question we're often asked," says Woods. "But we don't touch the surrounding soil. We make our own from compost material. As for air pollution, plants don't metabolize common air pollutants such as carbon monoxide or sulphur dioxide. The fruiting part of the plant is especially pure. The fruit is part of the reproductive process. The plant produces the purest thing it can so that it can reproduce successfully." Heavy metals are another known urban pollutant that people often ask about. But Woods says they fall to the ground adjacent to roads. Being heavy, they stay put. Rooftops gardens are far above the problem. By making their own soil, using closed systems and farming high above the road, Annex Organics meets the criteria applied to any organic farmer in the country.

Now that they make a living, their dream is to turn industrial rooftops all over Toronto vibrant green. "We would love to have satellite gardens all over Toronto," says Baker. "We're now starting to experiment with aquaculture, finding ways to use our nutrient-rich run-off to grow marketable fish. Tilapia and carp are two of the species best suited to this, because they thrive in close quarters. One day we'd like to have a showcase centre with a rooftop garden, tanks of fish, sprouts in barrels, where we could teach people more about urban agriculture and how viable it can truly be. We're proving that this is a viable way of producing food commercially." They're also blazing the trail in what's known as "neighbourhood technologies"—inexpensive and simple technologies that create business opportunities and break down the barriers to the world of entrepreneurship.

"We believe that urban agriculture can be a source of meaningful employment for us and for others," says Baker. "That, in fact, is a big part of our goal. We're trying to be strict about taking weekends off and working regular hours, even though there's tremendous pressure to work twenty-four hours a day, seven days a week, when you're starting a business. We're committed to this because we believe it can lead to what we think is a good, balanced life."

Annex Organics breaks every rule of conventional farming. The cultivated area is minuscule compared to any country farm. The inputs required are almost as minimal. They have no refrigerator and no delivery truck. Yet here on an industrial rooftop, previously not considered worthy of anything, there's a thriving business, run by youth without any major start-up costs or bank debts. And it can spread. On urban industrial rooftops all over North America there are jobs to be had—new, challenging, cutting-edge jobs that can pay a fair wage. "In August, at harvest time, this whole roof is a sea of green," says Woods. "The bees are buzzing about, the tomatoes are ripe and beautiful. You can look through all that greenery and see the CN Tower looming nearby. That, to me, says it all."

FOOD BUSINESSES
THAT SERVE THE COMMUNITY

Service is what counts in the food business. Here's a cook's tour of what can be done when companies run with a "double bottom line" that includes service to the community as well as profit. Because of the long and intimate connection between food and community, food is a natural home base for such companies. And because the growing, preparation and sale of food draw on a variety of skills and skill levels, there's room for everyone to contribute and a way for every community group to help out.

*   *   *

Providence Farm in Vancouver Island's Cowichan Valley is owned by the Sisters of St. Ann. It's anything but a cloister to about five hundred people with physical and developmental disabilities, who come each week to nurture their personal and gardening skills. The facility includes a two-acre market garden, a two-acre orchard, a plant nursery, a seniors' garden, a retail outlet and a coffee shop. Some come to pick up a skill or experience that can help them land a job. Some come to meet new friends, others to regain confidence in their own worth and abilities. Expenses are largely covered by sales from the market garden and nursery.

"I left the farm on a high," Des Kennedy, one of the country's leading gardening journalists, wrote after a tour. "The dedication of the staff and volunteers, the tremendous support from across the community, and the enthusiasm of the workers left me thinking that what's most astonishing is not how brilliantly this facility works, but that there aren't more like it across the country."[32]

*   *   *

In Moose Jaw, Saskatchewan, Don Mitchell coordinates the Churchill Park Greenhouse Co-op, a twenty-five-year-old job-creation project geared to former residents of the provincial facility for people born with developmental handicaps. The co-op operates out of two greenhouses beside the old residence, and grows bedding plants that are sold in local Canadian Tire outlets and at farmers' markets.

It's a finely crafted business, meeting a wide variety of needs and requiring cooperation from a diverse group of people. To bolster the self-confidence and pride of employees and to avoid the stigma of sheltered workshops, the staff are unionized. Automation is kept to a minimum, partly because the co-op's main aim is to provide jobs for people who might otherwise be unemployed and who might be excluded if high-level technical skills were required. Pesticides are not used, partly because the co-op wants to promote sound environmental practices and partly because chemical sprays pose an exceptional workplace hazard for vulnerable individuals.

Mitchell's long-standing commitment to community-based economics—he's the author of the 1970s classic, *The Politics of Food*, and a former Moose Jaw mayor—comes through in the strategy to build a business that replaces imports rather than competing with existing local companies. The co-op spends over $60,000 a year in the community for supplies, and pays $10,000 in local taxes. Annual sales in the $170,000 range support ten workers for much of the year. Their incomes are supplemented by federal employment insurance and a small but significant grant from the province. Whatever the political stripe of the party in power in Saskatchewan, the grant has been considered money well spent, since it supports a self-help effort by people who might otherwise be on long-term social assistance. Instead of welfare dependence, the co-op offers personal development and independence.

As the interview with Mitchell draws to an end, a worker interrupts him to ask where the flats for new plants are. Mitchell answers slowly and calmly, repeating the directions three times. "When he started twenty years ago, he was too shy to speak to anyone," Mitchell says later. "Now he's a group leader."

*   *   *

The Raging Spoon Café drives its workers sane. The popular restaurant on a trendy strip in downtown Toronto hires "survivors" of psychiatric hospitals, people often deemed crazy by conventional rat-race businesses. The restaurant is run on classic business principles. "If there's a job to be done, it has to be done," says chief cook Stuart Lubin, "because first and foremost we're a business." The decor is churchlike, with attitude. The booths are renovated pews. Walls are painted turquoise, lime green and purple. The menu features loony latkas, wackos natchos, crazy gravy and bin burgers.

The Raging Spoon is one of eleven businesses sponsored by the Ontario Council of Alternative Businesses, or OCAB, with support from the provincial ministry of health. The government pays the salaries of two managers; the staff of eleven are paid out of earnings. "This is my first job in seven years," says waitress Lenore Owen. Before, "I always felt cast out and alone, and I was afraid to apply for a job in a 'normal' environment."

The supportive atmosphere repays the government grant many times over. Former psychiatric patients employed in survivor-run businesses reduce their hospital stays by 40 percent, have lower bills for medication and don't need welfare, says OCAB organizer Donna Caponi. "Part of the challenge is to try to figure out how to make the economy work for different people in society," says David Reville, a survivor who went on to become a distinguished provincial politician. Providing opportunities for people to "talk less about their psychiatric problems and a lot more about business," he says, "that's pretty brilliant."[33]

*   *   *

Field To Table is a non-profit organization in Toronto that started out delivering Good Food Boxes supplied direct from wholesalers and farmers to low-income families. People strapped for cash or starved for company came to the warehouse to help pack individual boxes in return for a "free" box of food. Every week a small crew prepared a tasty lunch for the volunteers. That gave managers Mary Lou Morgan and Debbie Field, who each personify the term "social entrepreneur," an idea for a spin-off business. They set up a training program to teach professional cooking skills to people trapped

on welfare, and built a professional kitchen in the warehouse basement. In 1997, Field To Table Catering Company was born, employ-
ing three of the graduates. They rent the kitchen on an hourly basis,
which gets around the thankless task of a single mom going to a
bank for a start-up loan to cover kitchen equipment. The kitchen is
also leased to individuals starting up catering companies, in the
hopes they'll hire Field To Table staff when they get a big order. The
kitchen is known in the community economic development field
as an "incubator": it gives a warm starting place for entrepreneurs
who need a little help getting out of the cold.

The catering company features a wide range of authentic cuisine
from around the world. It's been a big hit with the conference
crowd. To rave reviews by attendees and the media, it's catered university gatherings, meetings sponsored by the federal justice minister, and a gigantic public banquet honouring Jane Jacobs, the
international superstar of the liveable cities movement.

* * *

Across town in Toronto's west end is Rivers, a stylish eatery
staffed mainly by at-risk youth and street kids looking for their first
break. The restaurant is one project orchestrated by All-A-Board
Youth Ventures, the dream of two individuals, former church youth
worker Tom Freeman and Jennifer Keesmaat. Behind the restaurant
they run a woodworking shop, where stools, cutting boards and storage chests are crafted from scrap wood that would otherwise go to
waste. The shop also provides job experiences and a supportive work
environment for at-risk youth. Both the restaurant and the shop rely
on quality and service, not charity, to bring customers in the door.

A woodworking shop and a restaurant might seem like an "odd
couple" except that sawdust and food scraps go together to make
compost. The compost is used on a rooftop garden above the restaurant. The garden is the third All-A-Board business venture. It will
provide quality, fresh food to the restaurant, and employ yet more
people. Clusterings of companies that can use each other's waste
solve two problems at once: they cut waste disposal costs and they
cut costs of purchasing new materials when recycled will do. They
also help solve an environmental and landfill problem for the city.[34]

* * *

Calgary is a major centre of citizen initiatives and volunteer-driven projects. The Winter Olympics staged there were known for the extent of volunteer community support as well as for the sporting activities. It's also home to many innovative food businesses. A number of them provide job opportunities for people normally excluded from the mainstream economy, thanks to a local currency established in 1995. A community development agency, the Arusha Centre, issues local money that promotes bartering. An "Hour" of the local currency is equivalent to $10 of Bank of Canada money. Members exchange hundreds of goods and services—listed alphabetically from accommodation and accounting to window washing and yard maintenance in the bimonthly tabloid—in exchange for this local scrip. The system allows people to buy luxuries they couldn't afford in cold hard cash—crafts, for example—as well as basic necessities such as food and moving services. They earn the Hours for these swaps by offering their services or products to someone who pays for them in Hours. No formal employer or intermediary is necessary. If one person has a skill and another person has a need, a deal is as good as done. Money shouldn't stand between people and a beautiful thing, local-currency buffs argue. Skills and need are infinite, they say. It's only money that's scarce, so do your business in Hours and make some money, literally.

A lot of deals get cooked up this way. A typical issue of the *Bow Chinook Barter Bulletin* includes listings for fresh-baked bread and pies, prepared meals for people with sensitivities to milk or wheat, cooking and gardening lessons, chocolate mousse, chocolate almond tofu cheesecake, organic beef, home-made beef jerky, organic jams and salsa, and veggie burgers made from scratch. Members can also use combinations of Hours and direct labour to pay for a share of food from a local Community Supported Agriculture project.

The local currency supports the Multicultural Collective Kitchen, a catering company that involves people from seven language and ethnic groups. The new Canadians started cooking together in order to practise English in a friendly environment. "We can laugh at each other's mistakes without fear of embarrassment," says coordinator Marichi Antonio, originally from the Philippines. "And foreign cooking is an area where immigrants are experts, so they feel more confident sharing with other Canadians than they would if their language difficulty defined the interaction," she says. Meals from the collective kitchen won so much praise that the group was soon catering conferences of community groups, which traded meals for Hours, and to major corporations such as Mobil Oil and Husky, which paid in Ottawa money. Collective kitchen members use the local currency to trade for accounting and moving services, and for food.

*   *   *

We've presented just a small selection of food-related businesses around the country that serve the community in more ways than one. There are certainly others near you. Using your food dollar to support them is buycott in the best sense of the word. It's clear from even this overview that this is not charity, but good value for your money. Supporting businesses like this also turns one of the basic commandments of industrial society on its ear: the artificial division between economy and society. This commandment, brought down from the mountain by Adam Smith, states that businesses make money and that's it. Governments look after social problems and that's it. But when life is ordered that simply, a lot falls between the cracks. A new generation of businesses, rooted in and loyal to communities and enduring human values, is coming soon to a table near you. While these businesses are all innovative, some, like the maple syrup industry, harken back to deep traditions of Canadian history.

MAPLE SYRUP

Maple syrup is a sweet reminder that there's another way to tap into nature's growth economy: the working forest. It's been a symbol of alternative and authentic living since Helen and Scott Nearing became prophets leading us back to the wilderness in the 1930s. From their Vermont homestead, they wrote *The Maple Sugar Book* in 1950, a classic on how to live simply and well. Cash from maple syrup sales sweetened the financial pot for any needs they couldn't fill with their own inventiveness. The Nearings also recognized that maple syrup was the mascot of what's now called

agro-forestry or perennial agriculture, the ultimate farming in harmony with nature. The maple tree is "self-seeding and self-perpet-
uating. It is a crop that needs neither sowing nor hoeing. Maple
trees are self-supporting, need not be fed, watered, curried down, or
housed," they wrote. "They need no cultivating, fertilizing or
spraying."

If the benchmark for stumpage fees on hardwood forests were
based on the amount of marketable syrup maples can produce
between their fortieth and two hundredth years—not counting the
forest's value in storing carbon, cleansing water and holding down
soil, or the value of edible hickory, beech and oak nuts there for the
picking, or the wild turkeys who gorge themselves on these nuts—
the logging royalty on each maple would be $1,600. Selling hard-
wood forests for anything less confirms the thin veneer of bogus
economics.

Maple syrup time is now cherished as a rustic industry, a trip
down memory lane. But it doesn't take much to reposition the
industry in the forefront of a value-added economy. Maple sugar
producers have a job that people pay to watch. A quick look at the
gate of the Bruce Mills Conservation Area near Toronto shows that
when sugar producers double as tour guides, storytellers and edu-
cators, they triple their income. In season, the staff at Bruce Mills
get several hundred families to fork over $20 to get into the park,
take a sleigh ride through their acreage, talk to the boilers and sample boiling maple toffee thrown on the snow. After the sampling,
most families pay $10 to take a litre home. By multiplying income
that way, a twelve-acre wood lot yields $10,000 a day.

On L'Isle d'Orléans, in the St. Lawrence River off Quebec City,
farmers make a go of it by keeping half the island in forest. The
farmers sell syrup in early spring, asparagus and strawberries in
early summer, corn in the fall and firewood just before the snow
falls. This multiseasonal strategy also sustains a dynamic tourist
and gourmet restaurant economy, which turns maple syrup into
elegant liqueur and desserts.

Since maples thrive in mixed forests, not monocultures, there's
an incentive to find food uses from other species that grow in the
forest. Birch beer, a favourite of Queen Victoria, is one possibility
for enterprising microbrewers. Some health enthusiasts use birch

syrup as a spring tonic. "Carolinian Crunch," a snack made from hardwood forest nuts, is another obvious seller.

The reforestation agenda isn't limited to the backwoods. In Toronto, Don Williams of Eastbourne Street, also known as the Eastbourne Sap, has tapped into the possibilities of edible landscaping by charging neighbours $10 a litre for boiling down the street's yield. The private-label syrup goes like hot cakes at a street brunch. "It's a nice way to meet the neighbours," he says.

Maple syrup is not a health food, but it does contain less sucrose and more minerals—notably potassium and calcium—than refined sugar cane. And it has a taste that industrial sweeteners can't beat. It's the mineralized impurities, not the sucrose, that gives the sap its flavour. "Luckily for sugar makers," James Lawrence and Rex Martin write in *Sweet Maple*, "the flavouring compounds in the syrup are so complex that they can't be duplicated chemically."

When we begin to think like a forest, we can learn from the maple that economics doesn't have to be limited to bitter truths about earth's limited resources. When you buy maple products, you're using your consumer power to endorse the view that economics can be a treat, as long as we know where to tap into the wealth.[35]

REAL NON-FOOD FOR A CHANGE

Nothing is so powerful as an idea that's been around for a long time. Farm-grown fuel, clothing, building materials and chemicals were all common before the era of petrochemicals. A pot-pourri of traditional organic products are making a comeback for two reasons: people want authenticity, and entrepreneurs see opportunities for new products. It's once again considered acceptable to use flowers to brighten and freshen the air in a room instead of a plug-in deodorizer that off-gases petrochemicals, and to clean grime with vinegar and baking soda instead of lemon-scented Mr. Chlorine. Some people even heat their homes with wood stoves instead of electricity from coal and nuclear power plants, and buy clothes made from cotton and wool instead of petroleum-based fibres. Truly, no grass was growing under the feet of the people who first sold us on synthetic alternatives to natural materials. They were better marketers than the proverbial hustlers who sold coal to Newcastle.

Beyond these better-known options, an entirely different range of farm-grown products can take us back to the future. Some farmers are already on the ground floor of businesses that will define the new century: construction planks and lumber for furniture made from straw, paper made from weeds, plastic made from hemp, fuel made from milk waste. Many of these farm-grown products can replace materials we now take from delicate natural systems, such as forests, and thereby reduce the stress on wild lands. Others can replace synthetic products such as petrochemicals, which give off smoke and toxins.

Here's a quick round-up of new uses for crops that are outstanding in their fields. They provide farmers and rural communities with job opportunities that take them well beyond the food system; they create more jobs in more places for a greater variety of workers than petrochemical industries; and they bolster trends that make it easier to grow high-quality food. The changeover will be as easy as **ABC**.

A is for agriboards, made from crop residues, not trees. Residues are stalks and straw left after the food has been picked. Farms produce about 10 million tonnes of residues a year. Though inedible, the cellulose in these residues can be turned into useful products that give farmers a second income from the same crop, create jobs in rural areas and displace products that consume natural resources. In Elie, Manitoba, Isobord buys straw from a co-op of 350 nearby farmers and converts it into strong, smooth boards suitable for cabinets and shelves. Unlike wood manufactured from sawdust, straw boards don't need toxic binders to hold the residues together, thanks to the natural gluelike lignins in the plants. The only off-gas is the scent of wheat. It's estimated that agriboards can replace 65 percent of the lumber used to make homes and furniture, and reserve wood from trees for uses where its unusual strength and beauty are warranted.[36]

A is also for agro-tourism, the latest in dude ranching. Farming is restful for the soul if it's only done on holidays, and it increases respect for what goes into food. Farmers who've studied up on Tom

Sawyer can put their paying guests to work on simple chores. Many organic growers have signed up with Willing Workers On Organic Farms, which refers "wwoofers" who'll work for room, board and some tutoring on organic tricks of the trade. Not a bad way to see the country.

Sharon Remple has another approach to agro-tourism. She works with managers of historic sites to preserve and expand her personal bank of traditional wheat seeds, which have been all but exterminated in the headlong rush to standardization. A consultant specializing in agricultural diversity, her first contract was with a historic mill in British Columbia, where she convinced the curator to grow and grind flour from authentic historical grains. Near her home in Edmonton, thousands of tourists spend a day at a historic Ukrainian village, where guides look and talk the part of early settlers. Beside a sod hut built into a hill, where a mother and her children spent their first winter while her husband made some cash working on the railway, lies a one-acre stretch of the once-famous red fife wheat, courtesy of Remple's seed bank. This was the first wheat bred to survive harsh Prairie conditions, and it made Canada the "breadbasket of the world." As a result of the drive for uniformity, the red fife seed is now banned for sale by the federal government and its Canada Wheat Board. A historic seed, which may contain genetic material needed by breeders of the future, hangs on to life because one woman used the opportunities of the tourist trade to grow seeds she's stored in her kitchen refrigerator.

A is also for aromatherapy, and the rosy future awaiting those who use farms to source delicate fragrances and medicines. Business is blooming in the natural oils and fragrance industry, to the tune of about $4 billion a year across North America. Flowers aren't just a pretty smell. The Egyptians of six thousand years ago recognized the curative power of perfumes. The founder of Western medicine, Hippocrates, favoured a daily bath with fragrant oils. In biblical times, wise men travelled far and wide on camelback in search of precious herbs and oils. Wise women who kept the tradition up during the Middle Ages found themselves burned at the stake for witchcraft, which put a damper on research for quite a while. However, today's medical researchers are rediscovering flower power. At the Smell and Taste Treatment and Research

Foundation in Chicago, Dr. Alan Hirsch uses a variety of scents to treat people with a range of disorders, from claustrophobia to chronic obesity. There's been a major expansion of shops selling bath and massage oils and basic first-aid kits—lavender, tea-tree, peppermint, chamomile, eucalyptus, geranium, rosemary, thyme, lemon and clove—for everyday cuts, bruises and sniffles. Craftspeople can arrange aromatic flowers and spices in artful baskets or pillows for the gift trade.[37]

B is for biomass—plants and plant residues used as fuel to heat homes. Keeping the home fires burning with wood is the oldest use of biomass, dating back at least 2.5 million years to the campfires of pre-human homo habilis.[38] Biomass has become politically correct of late, because it maintains a balance between carbon that's burned and released to the atmosphere as carbon dioxide, and carbon dioxide taken back by plants. Coal and oil can't do that. Farm residues can also fire up electric power stations. In Minnesota, an alfalfa growers' co-op feeds the alfalfa leaves to cattle and sells the dried stems to a seventy-five-megawatt electric power plant.

It's not widely known that wood heat used in 1.5 million homes already provides 4 percent of Canada's energy—twice the amount provided by nuclear power. The superior economics of wood heating are so obvious—natural gas, oil and electricity can cost up to double what it costs to heat with wood—that convincing people to split wood, not atoms, isn't a problem. As with most natural products, there are always follow-up uses. Fireplace ash provides free conditioner for the radish section of the garden, and a free and environmentally friendly alternative to salting sidewalks in the winter. In many cases, wood can be replaced with crop residues. Pellets made from compressed switchgrass and straw are already economic. Many people prefer pellet stoves because automatic thermostats can drop the precise number of pellets into a fire to maintain steady heat and let people sleep through the night without the need to stoke the fire.

Agriculture linked with forestry has been the norm throughout history. Forests were central to the livelihood of European farmers throughout the Middle Ages. Besides being the source of firewood, they provided habitat for edible plants and animals, the most valued of which were pigs that knew their way to truffles. Pioneers in southern Ontario planted Osage orange trees as fences. The trees doubled as windbreaks, tripled as food for livestock and quadrupled as dyes for clothing. Acorns and beechnuts were fed to sheep, goats and turkeys. Butternut and hickory produced high-protein candy when coated with maple sugar. Today, this reintegration of forests and agriculture, known as agro-forestry, is used to raise water tables, prevent water erosion on hilly slopes and approaches to creeks, and provide off-season income from firewood and lumber sales.

B is also for biorefining. Traditional distilling of food crops produces just one product, either beverage or fuel alcohol. Biorefining, as distinct from distilling, can produce a variety of products that make biorefining financially viable and competitive with oil refining. Mohawk Oils, for example, is advertised throughout the Prairies as Mother Nature's Gas Station. The 10 percent ethanol it uses in its fuels is supplied by a biorefinery in Minnedosa, Manitoba, which processes both ethanol and Fibrotein wheat flakes from spring wheat. The ethanol takes up the starch in the wheat; what's left is high in protein and fibre. Fibrotein is a big hit at Edmonton's Three Blondes and a Brownie, which markets wheat-flake brownies for their nutty flavour and moistness, as well as their low cholesterol. "The long-term strategy is to have the ethanol plant run as a back-door operation for the food manufacturing," says Fibrotein sales manager Brian Crowe. Commercial Alcohols Inc. follows the same biorefinery strategy at its $153-million facility in Chatham, Ontario. As well as supplying Sunoco with ethanol, the refinery produces pharmaceuticals, industrial alcohol, disinfectants, livestock feed and beverages.

Cheese waste called whey is another hot prospect for alcohol fuels. A biorefinery strategy applied to dairy production could milk products for everything they're worth, including whey, sometimes referred to as the crude oil of the twenty-first century. When fuel value can be extracted as well as food value, the potential for environmental savings and job creation with farm-based fuels doubles. Likewise, perennial crops such as prairie grasses and Jerusalem artichoke have great potential as energy crops, and require few of the energy inputs required by grain and corn.[39]

B is also for beeswax. After bees mind their own business of pollinating flowers and fruits, flying fifty-five thousand miles to make a pound of honey, there's beeswax left over—yet more reasons for farmers to lay off the chemical sprays that kill bees and instead organize crop rotations around buckwheat and clover. Unlike standard petroleum-based candles, beeswax candles give off a pleasant odour as well as light. The stubs can be used to wax sticky clothes drawers, for furniture polish and for kids' crafts.[40]

C is for the C4 species of plants, beloved of botanical efficiency experts looking for plants that can supply paper. The term C4 specifically refers to the plant's chemical makeup. C4 plants have special qualities that allow them to grow quickly in harsh climates and poor soils. Many weeds and native prairie grasses are C4s. Most commercial crops—apples, wheat and beans, for example—are C3s. Important business opportunities turn on this difference.

C4 plants such as switchgrass, a grass that grows on poor soils, make the greatest amount of paper from the poorest and least amount of soil. A Montreal-based sustainable farming organization called Resource Efficient Agricultural Production, or REAP, grew ten tonnes of switchgrass on one acre. That got the attention of pulp-and-paper executives, who face severe shortages of nearby timber for pulpwood. The pulp quality from switchgrass was high, according to an ecstatic report in the industry publication, *Pulp and Paper Canada*. Domtar in Montreal conducted two years of successful experiments with switchgrass.

Pulp fiction has it that paper comes from trees. But when the ancients got tired of carrying written messages on stone tablets and wanted some lighter reading, they invented plant-based paper. The Egyptians used papyrus. *Bible* is a translation of the Greek term for "pithy centre of the papyrus plant." The first mass-circulation newspapers mixed plants and cast-off clothing for paper, whence the standard put-down "radical rag" came. Then came the cheap and sensationalist dailies of the late 1800s, printed for the vulgar masses on paper made from trees. The impurities in wood pulp yellowed when exposed to sunlight, and thus was born "yellow journalism." Today, wood pulp accounts for all but 10 percent of the world's paper. But there aren't enough trees to carry a wood-based paper industry much beyond a decade. Today's low paper prices are a sign of plentiful government subsidies, not abundant forests. Those looking to the future are exploring pulp from plants. In

California, major dailies use waste rice straw. Grain straw works for low-grade scribblers. Hemp and kenaf already supply niche markets with high-end paper used for cigarettes and currency and for documents that will be archived. Switchgrass mixed with hardwood pulp meets needs for medium quality.

Aside from sparing trees, plant-based pulps avoid pollution problems in the paper industry. Toxic chlorine bleaches are used to take gummy lignin out of trees. Lignin holds trees upright in the wind and fights off bacteria hungry for tree sugar, says Dr. Carl Houtman of the U.S. Department of Agriculture forest products lab in Madison, Wisconsin. Plants, by contrast, don't need much lignin, because they're short and less sappy.

When paper companies stop barking up the wrong cellulose source, forests will no longer be squandered for toilet paper and scratch pads. The mills get guaranteed supply, since farmed crops grow twice as fast as trees. The pulp price is reasonable, and transportation costs are much lower. Mills can be built in cities where their customers are and source their pulp from nearby farms, or companies can maintain their present mills and grow pulp right up to their doorstep. Plants and plant residues come in predictable sizes, which makes engineering controls easy. Farmers get a good price for pulp, about twice what they get for ethanol. And crops such as switchgrass grow like weeds, needing little maintenance, fertilizer, pesticide, herbicide or ploughing.[41]

C is also for cosmetics. A cross-check on the petrochemicals and coal tars people massage into their skin with Dr. Robert Gosselin's *Classical Toxicology of Commercial Products* indicates that many cosmetics should come with a skull and crossbones on the package. Food-based cosmetics, with natural vitamin E and selenium for example, can be massaged into skin at competitive prices. Food-based cosmetics also reduce financial anxiety wrinkles on the faces of farmers. Oats to be used in cosmetics sell for $100 a pound. Goat milk fetches a pretty penny in moisturizing soaps. Whey left over from cheese production can also be transformed, say Agriculture and AgriFood Canada's Jean Tester and Pam Forward, promoters of opportunities that make full use of "farmers' gold."[42]

C is also for cordage, as in Manitoba Cordage Company, the former government corporation that made hemp rope for the British navy. Rope, not dope, is the mind-set of modern hempsters, who see hemp as a wonder crop that can be turned into as many as fifty thousand products. These products can replace petrochemicals and precious natural resources with an annual crop that's easy on the land. People have had high hopes for hemp since it was first cultivated in Asia some ten thousand years ago. It was the first crop Europeans farmed in Canada. Pharmacist-turned-farmer Louis Hébert planted hemp in Quebec City in 1609. The early governments of New France, Nova Scotia and Ontario ordered pioneers to grow the all-purpose crop and subsidized its marketing, because ships couldn't set sail without hemp for rope and canvas. *Canvas* is the rough English translation of the Arabic word for canvas, *cannabis*. Until recently, however, growing hemp was illegal in Canada because of its association with marijuana. A ground-breaking conference in 1996 co-sponsored by the Bank of Montreal convinced the federal government that hemp had tremendous economic potential. "Non-narcotic hemp can be used for so many purposes and has so many spin-off benefits," Senator Lorna Milne told the media after hearing from Ontario hemp pioneer Geoff Kime, "that it is impossible to estimate in any other way than to say 'Jobs, jobs, jobs.'" Canadian farmers are now issued permits to grow hemp from special seeds that contain no drug effect.

Hemp has many qualities that endear it to farmers. It commands a high price, somewhere in the range of $750 an acre. It can grow in many soils and climates, though it prospers best in fertile and well-drained soils. It grows so fast—two feet a week in the early summer—that herbicides are unnecessary. It's so effective at preventing weeds that it's used as a rotational crop in Europe to clean weeds off fields. Hemp is also resistant to most insects, so pesticides aren't an issue. The deep tap root requires minimal irrigation and breaks the hardpan of deeper soil, giving topsoil a break from shallow-feeding grains and vegetables. However, hemp is a heavy feeder on nitrogen, phosphorus and potassium. That makes it best suited as a rotational crop grown on relatively small patches by farmers who can use it as an income booster, rather than a one-crop mainstay. This is the vision of Canada's first legal hemp grower in several generations, Joe Stroebel, who sees the plant's high price as a way to help beleaguered family farmers increase their incomes and still prac-tise sustainable farming.

Hemp's astounding versatility intrigues several industries. Hemp is a case study of how multiple functions avoid waste and create niche business opportunities. The woody inner core, or hurd, is more than half cellulose, suitable for paper and plastic. When used for paper, the pulp needs little, if any, chlorine. Hemp paper holds ink so well that costs for ink in printing are reduced. The fibre is so strong that hemp paper lasts for centuries and can be recycled many times. The dregs of the hurd can be sold for fuel and animal bedding. The outer bark, or bast, goes to textile and carpet industries, where the same qualities that brought fame to historic Irish and Belgian linens and the original Levi Strauss jeans can be rediscovered. Hemp eliminates the need to import cotton. Cotton is the most pesticide- and transport-intensive crop in the world. Fibre quality suffers if hemp is grown to seed, but the oils crushed from seeds have a range of food and industrial uses. As a salad or cooking oil, hemp oil offers eight essential proteins and three essen-tial fatty acids. The oil is popular in high-end soaps, cosmetics and balms. Hemp oils made the paints used by the great European mas-ters. The Hemp Pedaller in Washington State sells hemp oil as a lubricant for bike chains. Hemp oil can also substitute for diesel fuel, which has union and management leaders in the mining industry excited because diesel fumes are linked to high cancer rates among miners.[43]

We are coming out of the Age of Stone, Bronze, Iron, Steel and Oil, and entering a strikingly different Age of Plants. It puts agriculture and biology at the centre of a new economy that grows economic fuel rather than fuels economic growth. It breaks the link between economic growth and exploitation of more resources. Instead, much of the growth comes from full use of materials already pro-duced for another purpose. Farm materials also break the link between products needed in a modern society and pollution. Farm-grown fuel and paper, to give but two examples, dramatically reduce pollution associated with modern lifestyles.

There is literally no limit as to what can be made from farm products. Earlier in the century, automobile magnate Henry Ford made a car entirely out of soy, flax and hemp, a research passion of his that got scuttled when hemp was made illegal. Modern engineers and tinkerers have almost sixty years of lost science to make up—but then, that's where the new jobs for fresh-thinking people are. Most important, farm-based materials provide jobs and incomes which support sound farming practices that provide healthful food.

CHAPTER 4

AVOID GASSY FOODS

AVOID GASSY FOODS

Global warming is arguably the most serious environmental problem we're facing on this planet today. It is the result of too much carbon dioxide, methane and nitrous oxide being released into the earth's atmosphere, creating a greenhouse effect. Heat from the sun is trapped and the earth's temperature rises. Burning fossil fuels such as oil, coal and gas produces most of the greenhouse gases in our atmosphere. 1998 was the hottest year since reliable record-keeping began 140 years ago and the number of tropical storms is way up. Recent findings by Britain's Hadley Centre for Climate Change show that water shortages, creeping deserts, flooding and violent weather can all be expected with increasing frequency.[1]

Why write about global warming in a book about food? Because conventional food production and distribution is responsible for about 25 percent of the gases that contribute to this greenhouse effect.[2] There is no other industry that comes close. But it doesn't have to be this way.

There's no excuse for the food system being a smokestack industry. Food rightfully belongs in the front ranks of renewable, solar-powered industries. Crops and animals can be raised on soil, air, water and sunlight—what nature provides—without chemicals made from fossil fuels. Soil can be tended so that it stores more carbon dioxide than trees, keeping that CO_2 out of the atmosphere. Crops can be planted, maintained and harvested with energy-efficient equipment. Food packaging can be manufactured from agricultural waste that's now burned off in fields or dumped in landfills. Basic food staples can be grown within a two-hundred-mile radius of most Canadian homes, rather than be trucked across the continent. Food scraps and even sewage can be recycled and used to renew the soil from whence they came.

In this chapter we'll show that doing right by food not only improves the planet; our personal health and economic well-being also improve. That's why food is a natural in the counter-offensive against pollution and global warming. As individuals, we can reduce the amount of greenhouse gases pumped into the atmosphere by 20 percent just by changing what we buy. As you read on, you'll find dozens of practical, everyday tips to do just that. Actually reversing global warming, rather than merely slowing it down, is possible if governments and corporations come on side. Later in the chapter we'll lay out how we think they can become part of the solution rather than part of the problem. But to begin, we'll take you on a food tour with a difference.

DIRTY BUSINESS

Farming is usually pictured as a postcard-perfect industry. When the media need a quick shot of pollution, they use file footage of smoke belching out of factory furnaces or haze shimmering over traffic jams on Toronto's Don Valley Parkway. Never a cornfield or cattle barn. This squeaky clean image of agriculture is what allows politicians to use farmers to launder money that will go right into the hands of equipment and chemical manufacturers. To explain what we mean, here's a stereotype-free tour of one of Canada's heaviest and dirtiest industries: the food sector.

A modern farmer is backed up by as much heavy equipment and heavy-duty chemicals as any steel or auto worker. Most chemical fertilizers come from natural gas, which is a fossil fuel. When gas fields are tapped, they off-gas profuse quantities of methane, which molecule for molecule is twenty times more potent in its effect on global warming than carbon dioxide. Natural gas fertilizers are delivered to farms by trucks, which burn up 20 million gallons of fossil fuel just to make the delivery. Once in the soil, natural gas fertilizers off-gas nitrous oxide, far and away the worst greenhouse gas, about two hundred times more potent than carbon dioxide. Many pesticides are made from mixtures of fossil fuels and chlorine. Chlorine is almost a pure energy product, made by splitting salt molecules using electricity. Most electricity comes from burning fossil fuels, especially coal, the dirtiest of them all. Tractors, combines and chisel ploughs are made of steel and rubber, both of which require heavy inputs of fossil fuel energy to make and transport to the farm. The machines all run on fossil fuels. The equipment disturbs the soil, releasing soil carbon to the air, where it combines with oxygen to form carbon dioxide.

Food processing and packaging are the next step. Here too, fossil fuels take centre stage. Processors cook and pasteurize many foods, a fast and cheap way to keep them sterile over long periods of storage. Packages are made light and compact so the food can be hauled great distances at minimal cost. But lightweight packages are heavyweight energy users. Aluminum, central to most light containers, is made using huge amounts of electricity. Plastic, another packaging favourite, is from fossil fuels and chlorine. Paper and cardboard come from the destruction of trees that stored carbon and held forest soils against erosion. The pulp-and-paper industry is itself a major user of fossil fuel energy and chemicals.

Moving right along, the next step is about 1,500 miles. That's the average distance travelled by the food that rests on your table. Most food travels by truck. Trucks, like tractors, are made of energy-intensive steel and rubber, run on the dirtiest and cheapest fossil fuels, and ride over pavement and cement that give off about a ton of global warming gases for every yard put down. Trucking promoters get a lot of mileage out of defending long-haul trucking of food as a necessity during Canada's harsh winters. But the trucking is heavy in all seasons, not just in the winter. And the massive government subsidies allotted for highways and trucks are not available to help develop local alternatives such as greenhouses and improved storage systems which could extend the growing season in Canada.

Next stop is the supermarket. Supermarkets make super profit margins on convenience foods, usually overpackaged and frozen. Supermarket freezer sections, most left open to the warm air twenty-four hours a day, are energy pigs. Since superstores have decimated neighbourhood-based full-service groceries, most customers drive there, perhaps unaware that short car trips are the single biggest source of urban air pollution. Because it's a chore to drive to the supermarket, most people stock up for a week at a time, which means they need a big refrigerator at home. The fridge is commonly the least energy-efficient appliance and biggest electrical user in a home. The frozen food is thawed and reheated in the microwave. The plastic container and the food scraps are usually tossed in a plastic garbage bag, then trucked to a distant landfill. Smothered and deprived of oxygen, the food rots, giving off the tell-tale stench of methane. Because methane is such a powerful greenhouse gas, local landfills are among the worst global warming culprits across the country.

Meanwhile, back home, the food moves through your digestive tract. If it's flushed down a standard toilet, it's carried away with three times more water than is needed to do the job. The water comes from municipal pumping stations, commonly the second-biggest electricity expense of local governments. At the sewage plant, the sewage gets a shot of electricity-rich chlorine before it's dumped in lakes and rivers to poison fish.

This is a food system that requires more calories of energy to grow, process, distribute, cook and eliminate food than there are energy calories in the food itself. In a nutshell, this is what it means to call a food system unsustainable. A simple can of corn requires one hundred calories of fuel energy for every calorie of food energy. The industry average is well over ten to one.[3] Which wouldn't be so bad if we lived on ten planets; the big problem is that our pollution has no place to go. We are nearer to running out of air to store the pollution from fossil fuels than we are to running out of fossil fuels. This is what global warming and rising epidemics of lung disease and breathing disorders tell us.

Governments and big corporations both insist that going pollution free will inflict terrible damage on our economy and lifestyle. But there's something they know and aren't telling: governments subsidize polluters every step of the way, giving them a huge and artificial advantage over competitors who try to do the right thing. When the politicians say they'd like to do something about pollution, read their tax tables, not their lips. We're hard pressed to name one traditional government subsidy or tax break that doesn't steer farmers in the wrong direction.

When farmers do the math on fuel- and chemical-intensive practices, they don't work with numbers from the real world. Farm fuels, fertilizers and chemicals are free of most taxes. At income-tax time, the cost of equipment is written off as capital depreciation, and the cost of fuel, fertilizers and chemicals are written off as expenses. Contrast this with organic farmers. They don't buy much of the above, so they don't qualify for those tax breaks. They may hire a helper to do the work other farmers handle with fuel and chemicals, so instead of a tax break they get hit with payroll taxes, the penalty governments impose on businesses that employ people instead of chemicals and machines. This is just one among several examples of how government discrimination artificially drives up the costs of organic production to make it uncompetitive relative to conventional practices.

This craziness is repeated in the food processing sector, where packaging accounts for a significant portion of the total cost of a product. Packages made of recycled materials are better for the environment than packages made of "virgin" or new material. This is because it takes less energy to make recycled packages; if less energy is used, less fossil fuel is burned, and less CO_2 goes into the atmosphere. But most food processors don't buy recycled packages to wrap their products in because they cost too much. They cost too much because of unfair tax advantages enjoyed by companies that make packages from new material. These advantages give them a head start of 15 cents on the dollar, according to Jack Mintz, a University of Toronto management professor who produced a study on the subject for the Canadian Council of Ministers of the Environment.[4]

Subsidies to truckers are next. Trucks bearing California fruit and vegetables to Canada barrel along U.S. highways with a subsidy equal to U.S. $6.81 per gallon of fuel burned. Within Canada, every mile a truck travels is subsidized to the tune of 2 cents for every ton hauled. The damage they do to the pavement, especially when they lift an axle to negotiate city streets, is billed to local governments, which receive nothing in taxes from truckers.[5]

Long-distance trucking means that the main competition facing local market gardeners comes from California and Florida. But it's not their sunny climes or even their exploitation of migrant labour that give these states their competitive lead; it's more subsidies. California is mainly desert. It couldn't feed itself, let alone export, but for water irrigation subsidies that average out at $150,000 per farm per year. A $1 bunch of beets from California contains $6 worth of water subsidies.[6] Although Americans have not hesitated to block Canadian imports that they deem as having an unfair advantage, the Canadian government has never protested the unfair competition faced by Canadian fruit and vegetable growers.

These subsidies help explain why B.C. residents can afford fresh-pulped orange juice taken from Florida to New Jersey by train, then hauled in refrigerated trucks across the continent, rather than make the switch to pricier local cranberries, richer in vitamin C and grown in more environmentally friendly wetlands. Subsidies also help explain why the Niagara fruit belt, some of the best fruit land in Canada, is being paved over—perhaps so local farmers can wave at truckers whizzing by with fruits and vegetables from a one-time desert in the United States.

Subsidies like these are the rotten apple at the bottom of the barrel, contaminating everything around them. Just avoiding this collateral damage would save enough public money to finance the greening of agriculture and issue a major tax reduction to all tax-payers. Here's a rough tally of the damage:

- According to Jack Mintz's tax fairness report, commissioned by federal finance minister Paul Martin in 1998, the federal tax department could save up to $4 billion a year in legal and accounting expenses by simplifying tax forms and treating a dollar as a dollar, with no exceptions for fossil fuels and the products made with them.
- Consumption of fast food would likely drop when hamburgers are priced at $6, the real cost for the hundred gallons of water, two pounds of feed, one cup of gas, and one and a quarter pounds of soil lost to erosion that go into each burger.[7] This drop in hamburger sales would make a nice dint in the $15 billion a year now spent on treating heart disease.
- The Ontario Medical Association says air pollution causes health problems across Canada that cost $12 billion a year to

treat.[8] The major cause of air pollution is burning fossil fuels.

- Fuel and transport subsidies have what economists call an "opportunity cost": they soak up money that could be spent on other things, like education, for instance. Over and above what drivers pay in licence fees and gas taxes, Canadian taxpayers subsidize roads at a rate of about $5 billion a year, an expenditure that's never questioned when health-care funding is cut. While it makes sense to ship compact and expensive computers by truck, only subsidies explain trucking bulky and cheap lettuce halfway across the continent.

- Eating food trucked from afar costs Canadian jobs. Agricultural researchers have calculated that at least 100,000 jobs could be created across the country in growing and processing local food if consumers ate as much local food as they did twenty-five years ago. If those jobs took people off unemployment, the savings to public money would be in the range of $10 billion a year.[9]

- The financial cost of neglecting global warming is not zero. Though the specifics are controversial, there's no doubt that some of the costs associated with unusually high rates of forest fires, floods and other "natural" disasters—estimated at $138 billion in 1998—are due to fossil fuel abuse. Any one of these events comes with a multimillion-dollar bill.[10]

All this adds up to a fair chunk of money. It doesn't have to be this way. We'd like to present three options that have the potential to turn things around:

1. A hands-off approach to corporate welfare—no subsidies and no tax breaks for anyone. In a truly free and self-regulating market, where all producers take responsibility for their real costs, disposable packages and long-haul trucking will be displaced by local processors who sell basic staples in reusable containers.

2. Reverse the subsidies; use them to encourage consumers to support environmentally friendly businesses. This might mean subsidizing the cost of food at the checkout counter but not its packaging or transportation. The difference in price between local food sold in reusable containers and imported food wrapped in disposable packaging would speak for itself.

3. Cancel all current food system subsidies, and provide a yearly $25,000-per-farm scholarship that rewards farmers who

follow basic practices of land stewardship. Such practices aren't rewarded in the market, and they need some incentive. Without some monetary reward such as this, the temptations are too great to treat nature like a gigantic take-out. This base income would encourage small, diversified farms, and invite newcomers to give farming a try. If the newcomers dropped off unemployment or social assistance rolls, the $25,000 farm scholarship effectively costs nothing. Several European countries are toying with this policy. And there's no need to get hung up on implementation details; they've already been worked out by John Girt in a paper commissioned in 1990 by federal agriculture and environment ministers.[11]

These options are all realistic and workable. But in the short term, it's going to be individual farmers, processors, distributors and eaters who will take the lead in avoiding gassy foods and reducing the effects of global warming. To paraphrase an oft-repeated saying: Don't ask what the government can do for you; ask what you can do without government. The home front is where the action is for the time being. Individuals can honour Canada's global warming commitments at the 1997 world conference in Kyoto by reducing the fossil fuel content of their foods—and they can get better food in the bargain. We're convinced that personal reductions in the range of 20 percent are eminently achievable. Read on for our "how-to" suggestions, sprinkled with profiles of individuals who have taken the 20-percent solution to heart.

EAT RAW FOOD

Eva Leach grates an apple over the mixture in her breakfast bowl. For years she's had this morning ritual. She grinds and soaks oat groats and millet, grates an apple and adds a teaspoon of lemon juice. Sometimes she throws in a handful of nuts. In the summer she adds ripe berries. She pours milk over the mixture. Her daughter prefers it with a dollop of whipped cream. It's traditional muesli, first developed in Switzerland, a breakfast cereal made entirely of raw ingredients. For Leach, eating a raw breakfast is the only way to start the day. "I just don't feel right without it," she says.

All over the continent, restaurants are sprouting up that specialize in raw and "living" foods. In place of the standard stoves and grills, there are sprouting racks, juicers and dehydrators. The menus feature the likes of raw carrot cake with lemon cashew frosting,[12] sprouted wild rice salad, and cold tomato soup with avocado, lime and fresh corn.[13] While these restaurants specialize in vegetarian fare, meat enthusiasts can enjoy raw Italian carpaccio, a thinly sliced raw beef dish, or the Spanish ceviche, seafood marinated in lime juice. Increasingly popular is Japanese sushi and sashimi, fresh raw fish transformed into miniature works of art.

Raw food enthusiasts say their approach to eating offers greater resistance to illness and aging and a key to greater "aliveness." They say malnutrition is not just the result of too little, or the wrong foods. The natural energy present in any food in its raw state is destroyed by cooking, they claim.[14]

It's well established that cooking destroys nutrients. Certain vitamins are sensitive to heat. Water-soluble vitamins such as vitamin C and the B family are especially vulnerable. Green peas lose at least 30 percent of their vitamin C and 20 percent of their thiamin (a B vitamin) in cooking. Boiled cabbage can lose as much as 75 percent of its vitamin C. Broccoli loses 20 percent of its vitamin C and 15 percent of its available calcium when cooked. Even fat-soluble vitamins such as A, D and E can be affected by heat. Up to 50 percent of the vitamin E in food can be lost in frying or baking.[15]

Eating in the raw also preserves crucial enzymes. Enzymes are protein-like substances that act as catalysts in the body's chemical reactions. They exist in our bodies by the tens of thousands. They break down and assimilate food, build and repair tissue, and manufacture more enzymes to continue this vital work. Raw food contains enzymes; cooking tends to destroy them. When we eat cooked food, according to biochemist and nutrition researcher Edward Howell, the body has to give up its own enzymes for digestion. This depletes the body's reserves, which causes us to age faster and be more vulnerable to disease.

Cooking is so ingrained in our civilization that it's hard to get your head around the idea of eating raw. Social anthropologist

Claude Lévi-Strauss, in his book *The Raw and the Cooked*, argues that fire was the first invention. It led humans to perceive themselves as separate from, and masters of, nature, he says. That's why it's invested with such power in our imaginations, from the fire and brimstone of hell to the forges of industry. "Raw," on the other hand, is associated with something that's unfinished, lowly—raw resources and raw sewage, for example.[16] In an age when global warming threatens our very existence, we need to re-examine our cultural hang-ups around things raw. There are health benefits to the entire planet when greenhouse gas emissions associated with cooking are reduced.

Raw food enthusiasts encourage moving to a diet that is 80 percent raw. But eating just 20 percent raw will have an impact on both your health and the environment. Eating less cooked food at times of peak energy use, such as breakfast and suppertime, reduces the need for dirty coal-fired generating plants to be fired up to meet the extra demand. Peak electricity use is just like rush-hour traffic: we make our roads extra wide, building additional lanes at huge cost, only to use them for two hours in the morning and two hours in the afternoon. Similarly, our energy supply is geared to the maximum load. That's why the cost of having that extra capacity accounts for as much as one-quarter of the electricity bill, even though it's not being used most of the time.

Many of the foods we eat have been heated even before they reach us. Tomato sauce, for example, has been cooked and cooled before we open the bottle or can and heat it again. Frozen vegetables have often been blanched, doused briefly in boiling water to inactivate the enzymes, before freezing, which requires energy too. Then comes the packaging, the metal and plastic, that don't have to be put around raw food.

Raw food has an illustrious past. The first known proponents of eating raw were the Essenes, a monastic Middle Eastern group said to have influenced Jesus Christ. Ancient texts reveal instruction in the use of raw foods to achieve mental, physical and spiritual health. Today their traditions are kept up in Essene bread, a raw flatbread made of sprouted wheat berries and flax seeds. Many of the most enthusiastic pioneers of raw food in this century started eating that way to cure personal health problems. The famous humanitarian Albert Schweitzer attributed his recovery from diabetes to a diet of raw foods. Health-food guru to the stars of Hollywood's golden age, Gaylord Hauser, turned to eating primarily raw foods after regaining his health as a youth, when all medical authorities had given up on him.

Besides boosting your own health, and the planet's, making the move to more raw foods will support local growers, who are best at ensuring peak freshness.

ENERGY-EFFICIENT KITCHEN APPLIANCES

Apart from experimenting with new ways of eating, there's a lot you can do about your kitchen habits to meet a 20-percent reduction in greenhouse gas emissions. It's not unusual for kitchen appliances to burn up $500 worth of fossil fuel energy a year, whether they be electrical or gas-powered. Fridges and freezers are the biggest guzzlers, accounting for almost a quarter of all energy used in a home. Fridges are sometimes referred to as "the silent thief" for just this reason. The stove comes next, accounting for about 10 percent. Luckily, of all the energy-efficiency changes that can be done to a home, kitchen improvements are among the easiest to install and the fastest to pay off in personal savings.

Almost every home has one fridge. About one house in five has a second, often reserved for a few cold ones, about the most expensive way yet invented to avoid warm beer. Most people couldn't live without at least one fridge; our current food system requires them. Food companies don't make money selling grains, pastas, beans and produce that can be stored without refrigeration for several days. They make their big mark-ups selling convenience foods and animal products that have to be kept cold and under wraps all the time, which makes big fridges more of a necessity than they should be.

Smart kitchens start with energy-efficient fridges. The best new fridges run on about half the energy of pre-1991 models. That means you can get your investment back several times over the life of your new fridge. The payback is so good that many progressive utilities in the U.S. (but unfortunately none in Canada) give away free fridges rather than go to the greater expense of building more power plants to supply inefficient models. Someday, home design specialist David Goldbeck speculates, someone will invent a way to keep fridges cool in fall and winter by piping in free cold air from outside.

Heating appliances can also be modernized. New stoves have reflectors under the elements to bounce back the heat that's otherwise wasted; this increases efficiency by as much as a third. Convection ovens cut heating bills by about a quarter, and many people say the food cooks more evenly. A stove with all the efficiency bells and whistles can reduce energy costs by up to 30 percent. That means it can pay for itself a few times during its lifetime.

Many dedicated appliances are more efficient than combination stove-ovens. Electric frying pans and kettles use all their energy to heat the food and water, because they don't have to heat the elements first. Elements lose at least half their direct heat to the air around them. A compact toaster oven is better for grilled cheese sandwiches or a few baked potatoes than a standard oven, because there's less air to heat for no purpose.[17] Thermos-style jugs keep coffee hot without the bitter taste that comes from leaving the heating coil on.

The microwave is often touted as an energy miser. Indeed, it does use less energy than stovetops on many individual items, although the taste doesn't usually justify it. But the reality of microwaves in most people's lives is that they're used mainly to reheat coffee that should be tossed and to thaw food quickly that should have been thawed slowly in the fridge. Microwaves are tied in to a fast-food system and a hectic lifestyle. At the very least you can buy one without a built-in clock. Clocks require that energy be flowing constantly. It's estimated that if we unplugged all home appliances when they weren't being used, eight nuclear power plants in the United States could be mothballed. In addition, the waste energy and electromagnetic fields these appliances give off when on standby, sometimes referred to as "electronic smog," are widely suspected of being dangerous to health, especially for children and pregnant women—yet another reason for keeping energy use as low as reasonably possible.[18]

Eco-cooks rely on steamers to produce crisp, succulent vegetables. These vegetables cook at lower heat without drowning in water, and delicate vitamins stay in the food rather than being leached out. In some cultures it's common practice to stack steamers several layers high, with foods that cook more quickly on top. This energy-efficient method developed on continents where fuel was scarce. Not only does this cook several dishes at once, but it has the health benefit of requiring little or no oil. Quite simply, when food is not directly in contact with the heat source, it doesn't stick to the pan.

A pressure cooker is another useful addition to the ecological kitchen. A standard wedding gift for economy-minded couples during the 1940s, pressure cookers fell out of fashion when careless handling blew off their tops and left many a meal on the ceiling. But the problems have been worked out, and modern brands are perfectly safe. The tight fit of the lid locks in steam, causing pressure to build and temperatures to shoot up well over the boiling point. The pressure cooker eliminates the need for canned precooked beans and boxed precooked grains, according to pressure-cooking authority Lorna Sass.[19] Dried beans and grains can be speed-soaked and cooked in a matter of minutes—one minute for pintos, three for chickpeas, five for risotto rice—instead of hours. Pressure cookers make bulk beans and grains both cost- and time-effective. They leapfrog the need to precook and can or box, saving on energy-intensive resources. And because beans are usually shipped in cans half filled with water, transportation efficiency can be doubled. All told, pressure cookers can cut the energy demands of beans and grains by as much as half, while cutting costs almost as much. As for taste, Sass says juices, nutrients and flavours are locked into stews and soups, not carried away in steam or leached out during a long boil, so less salt and fat are needed.

Apart from trying new technologies, a lot of savings can come from changing the way we use the technologies we choose. Fridges are commonly placed too close to the stove, which means their motors have to work harder to stay cool. Efficiency decreases when dust bunnies build up by the motor at the back, so yearly clean-ups are a good idea. Keeping fridges and freezers full, with jugs of water if necessary, also helps. Water retains cold better than air, and saves the motor having to do all the work. Some people save as much as $40 a year with this trick. Window shopping in your fridge, dawdling with the fridge door open to warm air, often adds as much as 4 percent to electrical costs. Over at the stove, baking with shallow casserole dishes exposes more surface area to direct heat, which is highly efficient. So is putting lids over boiling pots. The reason why a watched pot never boils is that heat escapes when there's no lid.

What foods we buy can also make a difference. Dry goods put less demand on both in-store and home freezers and fridges. Lack of preservatives isn't a storage problem when you eat fairly soon after you buy. Preservatives, like big fridges, are examples of measures we're pressed to take because they fit with a supermarket-dominated system. Trying to fit with a world climate system requires different habits. If you shop on Main Street more often, you don't have to load up for the week. You buy what you need when you need it, and avoid the frustration of keeping stuff in the cooler until it goes bad because you forgot it was there.

FOOD WASTE

Waste is a verb, not a noun, says Abby Rockefeller, co-developer of the Clivus Multrum composting toilet. Rockefeller has figured out a simple way to turn food's end-product into clean, safe, earthy-smelling humus, a crucial component of soil. Technologies like the composting toilet can take what our food system calls waste and convert it to new uses. Better still, these technologies can significantly reduce the greenhouse gases going into the atmosphere.

Food waste can be divided into three categories: packaging, kitchen scraps and sewage. Let's start with packaging, which comes in several forms. Some packaging we throw out after one use; paper and plastic wrappings and tetrapaks are good examples. Some is recycled—plastic containers, cans and glass bottles, for instance. Some is reused, like Tupperware-style plastic containers and mason jars. When it comes to the environment, disposable and even recyclable packages are big problems.

The major purpose of packages is not to store or transport food but to sell it under a brand name. The package is advertising for the brand. It's the brand name, and advertising promoting it, that adds to the food's price. Packages also support centralized processing factories. Processors want packages that are light, durable and compact, suitable for the long haul to markets across the continent. Tetrapaks and light plastic bottles are the industry ideal, although their weight and durability come at the expense of the environment, since manufacturing them is energy-intensive and polluting. These packages are affordable for processors because taxpayers pick up the expense of getting rid of them after one use, through garbage disposal or recycling programs. The $500 million spent each year in Canada to dispose of or recycle food packages amounts to a huge taxpayer subsidy to centralized processors. Apart from encouraging practices like long-haul trucking that harm the environment, it makes no economic sense. Why should any municipality give a subsidy to a processor who provides no local jobs and contributes nothing to the local economy? If processors were required to pay the full cost of their packaging decisions, including disposal, we would see some changes in packaging design pronto.

Angry shoppers in Germany decided to take matters into their own hands. They stood in checkout lines and ripped excess packaging off items they wanted to buy. In the face of this consumer revolt, processors agreed to take full responsibility for their packages and sponsored an industry-wide co-op to collect, recycle and sell back the materials. As a result, plastic containers are now reused an average of thirty times in Germany—which is thirty times more than in Canada. When you insist on minimal and reusable packaging, you create benefits that are not created by conventional recycling and waste disposal. You cut local taxes and you support local processors using locally grown food to serve local markets. These home-grown businesses could afford to compete with the big guys if they were given a truly level playing field.[20]

Kitchen scraps are the second category of food waste. Most kitchen scraps are the packaging that nature provides—the skin on an orange, the hull on a seed. In our current system, most of these scraps end up in garbage dumps. When food scraps are landfilled, they become part of a toxic brew known as leachate. Moisture dripping from the scraps collects traces of toxins from leaking batteries and other items in the garbage. The moisture makes its way down to the water table and eventually into our drinking water. The scraps themselves rot anaerobically (without oxygen), because they're smothered by other materials. In that state they give off methane, a potent contributor to global warming. Even without counting the fuel burned in trucking food scraps to the dump, the sheer rot in landfills is responsible for about 5 percent of greenhouse gas emissions in Canada.[21]

One of the easiest and most effective ways to reduce pollution and greenhouse gas emissions is to treat food scraps as a resource to be valued. There are many benefits when the goal is not just to reduce waste but to convert it to a value-added product. For example, if workplaces and apartment buildings segregated food scraps from other garbage, it could be collected for use as pig feed. Pigs are scavengers that do well with food scraps in their diet. Major facilities, including many Canadian Pacific hotels and Toronto's Commerce Court, now have their food scraps picked up by pig farmers, saving a tidy penny in disposal costs.[22] Food scraps can also be fed to tilapia, one of the few fish that can be raised healthfully in captivity. The Asian and African communities in Toronto import fifty thousand pounds of tilapia a week; these fish could be raised locally. When food scraps are recycled as animal feed, they don't go into dumps and they don't produce methane. The result is less global warming emissions.

Some workplaces are experimenting with red wrigglies, worms that turn food waste into enriched soil conditioner. The worms live in bins filled with food scraps and unbleached paper towels. The red wrigglies are ideal indoor composters because they are odour-free and can "finish" a hundred pounds of scraps within three weeks. The worms have also become a hit at schools, where they devour scraps from school lunches and serve as object lessons in nature studies. Metro Hall in Toronto uses this system for turning veggie and paper scraps into potting soil for indoor plants. So does a major Calgary office tower, which retains a home-based business, The Compost Queen, to supervise worms in two bins in a small room in the basement parking lot. The landlord saves on waste haulage and on fertilizer for potted plants and outside gardens.

Compost can be a lot more than fertilizer for potted plants and gardens; it can restore contaminated lands. It's been successfully used to treat land at a U.S. air force base in the Carolinas. When compost was ploughed into the land, the organisms existing in it broke down the tough toxic compounds from airplane fuel leaks into harmless materials. German microbiologists tried without success to figure out how compost can do this. They concluded that the magic came from the whole interplay of compost life, not from any of its parts alone. As compost science progresses, contaminated former industrial sites near the inner cores of most cities can be healed and restored.[23]

Using food scraps to generate electricity also has potential. In Ontario, a company called Eastern Power builds electrical power plants right on top of landfill sites. Pipelines capture underground methane from rotting food, which fires electrical generators. Burning methane rather than letting it escape into the atmosphere reduces its potency as a greenhouse gas by 95 percent. Existing landfills are already leaking enough methane to feed power plants that could supply half a million homes with electricity for a decade, says landfill methane expert Greg Jenish. If the food scraps are used for compost after they've been used to make energy, the benefits double. That's what Canada Composting Ltd. does in Newmarket, Ontario. The company uses a system developed in Germany that separates all organic waste. As the material rots in an airless room, it gives off methane, which powers a six-megawatt electrical power plant. What's left is compost suitable for tree planting. "In two days we go from waste in the front door to two quality products out the back door," says Canada Composting vice-president Paul Blanchard.

The third source of food waste is sewage. We flush and forget, using millions of gallons of water in the process. The toilet is the biggest user of water in Canadian homes. It takes a lot of electricity to clean and pump that water—electricity that comes from coal-fired power plants. This means sewage plants pollute the air as well as the water. Worse still, sewers mix human waste with toxins from dry-cleaners, photo shops and factories. In most cities this toxic stew is dumped directly into water. In Toronto, the sludge has been incinerated. The air pollution from incinerating this sludge is equal to an extra thirty thousand cars on Toronto's streets each day.[24]

Dumping raw sewage on farmland has been suggested as an alternative and beneficial use. This idea is gaining popularity all over North America, but it's dangerous. Although human waste can be an excellent fertilizer,[25] it must be treated first to kill human pathogens (germs that can transfer disease). It must also be free of industrial toxins; otherwise, the soil and crops grown on the farmland will be contaminated.[26]

There are many ways to make sewage safe, clean and useful. Inventor John Todd has developed "living machines," carefully created marshes that can extract nutrients from human waste and neutralize pathogens. Todd has imitated the process nature used to clean waste for billions of years before humans came along. He uses a range of plants, from duckweed to orchids to bulrushes, to do the dirty work. The results are beautiful and odourless water gardens. The space housing the living machine at the Body Shop factory in Toronto has become a natural oasis used for staff lunches and executive meetings. In Bear River, Nova Scotia, the town's living machine grows flowers and food. So many tourists want to see the operation that a gift shop is being built to serve them.

Composting toilets are starting to become popular in cottages and remote locations where water is either scarce or easily contaminated. In Peggy's Cove, Nova Scotia, and at the military base north of Edmonton, Abby Rockefeller's composting toilets save money on water hook-ups and produce a compost that's used for tree planting. In 1995 a home design based on her system for converting waste water and sewage into beautiful gardens won top prize at Canada's Royal Agricultural Winter Fair. The system pipes dish and bath water directly to lawns and gardens instead of into sewage pipes. This "grey water" is rich in nutrients, reducing the need for fertilizer. What fertilizer might be needed comes from human waste, converted into compost by the composting toilet. If such a system ever became widespread, it would revolutionize home building. Costs for sewage hook-ups would be slashed. Homes could be built on land that's rocky or otherwise unsuitable for farming; at present, farmlands are prized for suburban development partly because good soil is easy to dig sewer trenches through.

While you may not be ready to buy a composting toilet today, you can help to cut greenhouse gas emissions in many different ways, by starting a "virtuous circle"—the opposite of a vicious circle—in your community. When you buy goods with minimal or reusable packages, you do more than reduce the pollution caused by the manufacture and transport of disposable packages; you also encourage local producers. In turn, local producers tend to grow a variety of crops for a smaller market rather than one product for a larger market. That leads them to diversification, which leads them to crop rotation and companion planting, which leads them to natural fertilizers and pest controls, free of fossil fuels. When you compost food scraps or use a composting toilet at your cottage or rural home, you do more than reduce the pollution caused by garbage trucks and landfill methane. You bring the end closer to the beginning, to soil conditioned by a life force, not a dead fossil fuel. Food waste is nature's fertilizer. When we learn to use it fully, we can eliminate the $25 billion spent worldwide each year on artificial fertilizers made from fossil fuels.

Capturing the full potential of this transition takes some help from local governments and entrepreneurs—which is good news. This is where the jobs are. Disposing of waste is a high-tech affair, with lots of big trucks, big dumps, big pipes. The money goes into materials, not jobs. Current waste-disposal methods create seven jobs per million dollars spent. The methods we're proposing have the potential to create twenty jobs per million dollars spent.[27]

Some communities are already finding innovative ways to convert food waste into jobs and useful products. In Moose Jaw, Saskatchewan, the local livestock exhibition sponsors a composting program that combines lawn clippings from area homes with the straw and manure from the exhibition's animal stalls. Staff for the project are provided by Moose Jaw Diversified Services, which trains developmentally challenged youth to handle light industrial equipment. The initiative provides useful and paying employment to people who might otherwise be unemployed, while saving city residents 20 percent on the costs of landfilling lawn waste. The project is carried financially through sales of 650 tons a year of finished compost to a local gardening centre.

What we call waste can be a gift, not a curse. When we treat a gift like garbage, we create poison; but when we respect what nature gives us, we become part of creating life.

DEMECHANIZED FARMING

The amount of fuel needed to raise food on an acre of land has gone up eighty times since the turn of the century.[28] There's been a radical shift from agriculture based on biological processes and solar energy to agriculture based on industrial processes and fossil fuel. The challenge for farmers of the future will be to reclaim the skills needed to put biology back at the centre of agriculture. In the process they will reduce the pollution from present-day equipment and develop new methods that use the renewable energy found in human labour and creativity. Below are profiles of two farm families who are ahead of their time.

In Lucknow, Ontario, organic farmers Tony and Fran McQuail have stepped into the future by replacing tractors with horses. They run their farm on the "metabolic" animal energy of six workhorses, all descendants of two Belgian mares they bought in 1976. Horse power makes the same horse sense as any moves to smart production methods, says Tony McQuail. Horses are voice-activated, he notes, just like tomorrow's computers hope to be. Working with them is challenging and fun. Working behind them keeps him fit and spry. Horse methods are also very efficient. McQuail says he can plant seven 500-foot rows of potatoes in forty minutes.

Horses are key players in a farm diversification plan that allows McQuail to make money from several sources. In winter he uses horses to haul logs that have been selectively cut from his wood lot, and to carry delighted children through the snow on Christmas sleighs. In the spring he uses horses to pull old-fashioned seed planters he bought at country auctions for next to nothing. In the summer they eat and clear weeds on lands put to pasture for a season, fertilizing the soil for next year's crop. In the fall they pull harvesting equipment, and then pull families who've come out for a hay ride. Unlike tractors, horses reproduce, and the colts can be sold to other farmers. McQuail figures he got rid of $25,000 worth of debt and expenses per year when he sold his tractor. On the other side of the ledger, the horses earn him an additional $10,000 a year over what he could do with the tractors. Farmers who stick with heavy machines, he figures, are looking a gift horse in the mouth.

Horse power runs on sunlight, says McQuail. The calories horses need come from crops and grasses grown right on the farm. "Agriculture is the art of turning sunshine into something you can sell," he says. "If we as farmers can't generate our own energy, we're part of the problem."

Eric Yoder knows about generating his own energy. He claims to run the smallest farm in Saskatchewan. In a region where two sections (1280 acres) are standard, his farm in Rosthern is just two acres. On that plot he grows thirty varieties of vegetables, which he sells mainly to sixty regular subscribers in Rosthern and Saskatoon who've signed on with his Community Supported Agriculture venture. He calls his company Peasant's Pick, a little dig at President's Choice. For a peasant, he doesn't do too badly. He grosses $16,000 an acre. His expenses are so low, he gets to keep almost all of it.

A lean and muscular fiftysomething, with the trademark beard of this Mennonite community, Yoder's body testifies to the major energy source on his farm: elbow grease. He burns energy at a very efficient rate of 180 calories an hour, he says. "I outdo the Amish," he boasts, a reference to the religious order that refuses to use gas-powered vehicles. "I don't use horses."

A devotee of intensive gardening methods, he plots his land in small squares, each designed for space-efficient use. Every inch is planted. Since he uses no heavy machines, he has no need to waste space on empty rows for them to ride over. His dense planting methods snuff out weeds. To give his plants a head start on the short growing season, and to supply his customers throughout the summer, he starts growing seedlings in his basement and backyard greenhouse in late winter. He can plant outside earlier in the spring than most farmers because he doesn't have to wait for the ground to dry out enough to take the weight of heavy equipment. His heaviest piece of equipment is a $200 hand-operated hoe. He uses it to slice away weeds in the spring before transplanting his seedlings. As a result, he doesn't need chemical sprays to keep the weeds under control.

Some may find Yoder's hours of stooping and hand transplanting oppressive. He loves it. He has no back problems from riding a tractor. No fumes or noises from machines compete with the joys of working in the fresh air and listening to the birds, he says. Unlike other farmers, who have to take a second job in the winter to pay off their machines, he spends six months a year hibernating and reading, mostly on the history of peasant agriculture. He calls farmers who are up to their neck in debt for loans covering machines "technological serfs."

Rating the efficiency of Yoder's farm is tricky. The size and yield are low, but the return on investment is incredibly high—$32,000 a year on a tool that cost $200 years ago plus $100 worth of basement grow-lights. His income is also high when compared with the average net farm income in Saskatchewan, which was $3,400 in 1998 according to the Saskatchewan Department of Agriculture, and dropping. Yoder's yield per acre is high too. "We have this fixation with the efficiency of one lone person operating a huge farm with a pile of machines," he says. "But it's not a one-person operation. From an energy standpoint, it needs the back-up of thousands of people." The alternative, as Yoder's farm demonstrates, is to focus on the energy stored in the soil.

SOIL DEVELOPMENT

Pasta made with the flour of Jerusalem artichokes will turn you into a perennial optimist. The fleshy vegetable with the nutty, crunchy taste—also good in salads, soups and as a side dish replacing potatoes—is a perennial. The more we shift our diet to perennials, the better it is for the soil's ability to store carbon. When soil stores carbon, less carbon gets into the atmosphere to mix with oxygen and form CO_2. That means less global warming.

Perennials—such as fruits, nuts and berries from trees and bushes—keep on growing and growing, year after year. They don't need to be replanted every year like annuals. They hibernate for the winter and pop back up in the spring. Unlike annuals, which mobilize their energy for seed production, perennials store most of the energy needed to renew life in thick mats of roots and underground tubers. That makes them ideal soil mates, better for soil than annuals on two counts. First, their roots hold soil in place better than the roots of annuals do, and protect the soil from wind and water erosion. And second, since the soil doesn't have to be ploughed every year to plant a new crop, the carbon in the soil is less exposed to the air and less likely to be released as carbon dioxide.

The popular stereotype has it that trees are the heroes in the battle against global warming. They draw down carbon dioxide from the atmosphere, breathe out clean oxygen and store the carbon in their fibres. Good corporate citizens get into tree planting because trees can suck up the carbon dioxide released when coal and gas are burned. Fast-growing trees in Costa Rica or Australia can undo the damage of burning coal in Toronto, they say. But this overlooks what's right under our feet here in Canada. While trees and plants do store a great deal of carbon in their fibres, soil can store even more. All the trees and plants in the world hold 560 billion tonnes of carbon. Soil triples that at 1,500 billion tonnes.[29] Trees, with their extensive root systems, play an important role in holding that carbon in the soil, but they are only one among a host of perennials that can do the job. If we make food choices and use farming methods that favour more perennials, we can have the same results from agricultural soil as we have from the soil beneath forests.

Unfortunately, the history of commercial and industrial agriculture is to a large extent a history of suppressing perennials in favour of annuals. Annuals were favoured by early empires for three reasons that still have clout today. Annuals are easier to breed because their seeds can be sorted and selected easily to produce the biggest and most productive plants. Annuals also provide a surplus of seeds, over and above what's needed to guarantee the next crop. These edible seeds, such as grains, store well, and made it possible for the leisured class of priests, soldiers and politicians to live off the surplus cultivated by others. Annuals need a lot of tending, so they encourage a population that stays put and is easily taxed, rather than nomads who live a "hand-to-mouth" existence, eating what nature provides. Little wonder that the ancient upper classes who wrote the first history books identified annuals with the rise of leisure and civilization.[30]

With industrialization, agriculture veered even more sharply towards annuals. The yearly rites of spring ploughing and fall harvesting were a boon for equipment manufacturers. Annuals lend themselves to mechanized farming. One crop, which dominates an entire expanse, is planted and comes to fruition all at once, creating the uniform conditions needed by machines. Perennials, by contrast, tend to crop continuously, like rhubarb, or to bear tender fruit, like raspberries. Both make hand picking necessary. Annuals are also a boon for manufacturers of chemical fertilizers. Annuals pour the earth's energy into seed production, at the expense of roots, stems and leaves that can be left behind to return nutrients to the soil. Over time, the soil becomes depleted and needs artificial fertilizers. Manufacturers of chemical sprays favour annuals as well. The seeds of annuals are high in starch. That means they don't need as much energy from the sun and can afford to be late bloomers. Weeds, by contrast, have little starch, and no choice but to pop up fast in spring. So annuals can't compete with weeds, which creates a need for herbicides. For all these reasons, perennials have been pushed to the side in an industrialized food system.

Canada was "built" by settlers who destroyed perennials. In the east and British Columbia, forests were cleared. In the Prairies, the thick sod of native grasses was broken. As a result of this uprooting, Canadian soils have lost half the carbon they stored a hundred years ago. John Henning, an agricultural economist at McGill University, calls this "the debt nobody wants to talk about." Although the rate of carbon loss has been slowed, this historic destruction of half the carbon in one of the planet's great land masses leaves a lot of ground to make up for. Moving towards perennials can speed repayment of this carbon debt.

It's a treat to put more perennials on the menu. Just consider the familiar list of berries, nuts and fruits. Less familiar now, but once standard fare, are greens such as sorrel, Good King Henry, lovage, salad burnet, sea kale, nine-star broccoli and Turkish rocket.[31] Agricultural scientist Wes Jackson of The Land Institute in Salinas,

Kansas, is working to develop perennial breeds of common food items. Eating perennial grains is already an option. Wild rice, for example, is actually a perennial grain. Using it to supplement conventional rice supports Native peoples who har-vest this perennial crop across northern Ontario, Manitoba and Saskatchewan, and dramatically reduces the transportation required to bring Asian paddy rice to market. The expansion of Asian rice paddies to meet North American demand is a leading source of new methane in the world since paddies, by definition, are deprived of oxygen, and anaerobic rotting produces methane.

And of course there's the Jerusalem artichoke. As well as being good to eat, it's an excellent source of fuel for cars and other motors. Food-alcohol fuel burns cleaner than petroleum, which contains many toxins. Food-alcohol fuel causes less damage if there's a spill, because it breaks down safely and quickly, unlike the oil from the *Exxon Valdez*. And in contrast with fossil fuels, which release carbon stored underground billions of years ago, the carbon released when food-alcohol fuel is burned is from last year's crop, which can be recaptured by this year's growth. Two crops are seen as leading contenders in the trend towards renewable food-alcohol fuels: the Jerusalem artichoke and the wild perennial prairie grasses.[32]

Growing the makings of fuel is just one of the ways farmers can offset global warming. Growing the makings of energy-efficient homes is another.

STRAW BALE CONSTRUCTION

Doing Rumpelstiltskin one better, home builders are now spinning straw into strikingly beautiful and energy-efficient homes. When plastered with stucco, the homes serve as a model of what farming can do to supply the building blocks of a new economy made with home-grown and environmentally friendly materials. Straw bale is a concrete example, without the concrete, of how a new style of farming can actually contribute to reversing global warming.

Straw bale construction promises to turn a farm headache and ecological disaster into walls for as many buildings as will ever be needed. Each year across North America, straw waste is burned off fields. More than sixty tons of global-warming gases, as well as a potential second income, go up in smoke. Finding a use for all that straw would solve the problem. But the idea of straw buildings surprises people who only know about the subject through the story of the three little pigs, where the big bad wolf blows away the lazy piggy's straw home with one huff. That's only a fairy tale. Straw bale construction stacks up against the toughest tests of researchers with the Ottawa-based National Research Council and Central Mortgage and Housing Corporation. They found that straw bale walls could stand up to hurricane-force winds and heavy loads of snow, and were barely scorched by flames raging at 1,800 degrees Fahrenheit.

Though archaeologists have found 10,000-year-old straw bale buildings in Turkey, the first in North America were built by turn-of-the-century settlers in Nebraska. Trees were scarce, so they built their homes from baled straw. Some seventy years later, straw bale came back into vogue among New Mexico and Arizona hippies. Straw bale homes now command the respect of senior building scientists and regulators. In 1995, following an experiment using straw bale to develop low-cost, community-based, environmentally friendly housing on a Navajo reservation, officials with the U.S. federal energy department issued a rave review. The department booklet, *House of Straw: Straw Bale Construction Comes of Age*, says straw bale has the makings of a win-win-win technology, providing "a low-cost, elegant, and energy-efficient living space for the owners, a graceful addition to the community, and a desirable boost to local farm income."[33]

Even more rigorous is the test set out by Sim Van der Ryn and Stuart Cowan in their book *Ecological Design*.[34] They promote five rules for organic architecture that work on natural principles. The first rule is that solutions must grow from place. By its very nature, straw bale acts locally. Straw is plentiful wherever grains are grown. But because straw is so bulky, long-haul transportation isn't really an option. Straw fabrication helps support small rural towns that service farmers.

Straw bale builders have also become quite expert at making buildings that treat local weather as a resource. Thick straw walls "breathe" slowly, serving the same function as mechanical heat-exchangers. On winter days the stone or tile floors commonly used in a straw bale house soak up sunlight heat, which they give off at night. On hot summer days the same "thermal lag" lets floors give off coolness from the night before. Straw, in short, is a "smart" or responsive building material, and helps homes regulate themselves in relationship to local climate.

Cowan and Van der Ryn's second rule is that designers must become environmental bean counters. They must count all the energy "embodied" in a material, from the energy used to make it to the energy used to haul it to a landfill when its life is over. If most building materials were priced to reflect their embodied energy, they would cost a lot more. By contrast, straw bale gives a second life to above-ground agricultural leftovers. The only extra energy costs are baling, delivery and stucco to cover the walls. In a typical home, straw bales replace lumber from forty-two trees. Straw bale insulation has one-thirtieth the embodied energy of wood and fibreglass, a study by the Frank Lloyd Wright School of Architecture shows. And unlike lumber and fibreglass, which get hauled off to the dump when their day is done, straw goes to work one more time, as bedding for animals. The straw and manure can be composted together, producing a better fertilizer that emits less global-warming nitrous oxide than manure left to rot on its own. The return to the soil is belated, but it does return.

Rule number three, Cowan and Van der Ryn say, is to design with living processes rather than inanimate objects. Working in harmony with natural cycles taps into the secrets of how nature cleans air without ventilation equipment, cleans water without chlorine, grows glorious fields without pesticides. Straw bale uses the same insulation strategy as living nature—not cement, not fibreglass, but air. The polar bear stays warm thanks to hollow hairs filled with air that slow the loss of body heat. Likewise, the fur protecting northern caribou has a honeycomb structure that seals in heat with air pockets. The bark in birch trees, the only hardwoods that can survive in the Far North, has cells that trap air for insulation. With enough air to let walls breathe—but not enough to provide oxygen for fire—straw bales in effect put a thick coat of hair on buildings, imitating nature. By contrast, inanimate materials like cement and steel actually conduct cold from the outside, forcing us to counter their impact by throwing fuel on the fire.

Imitating nature pays off for human health too. Straw is non-toxic, unlike many building materials. Because it breathes, again unlike most building materials, moisture and mould don't build up in walls. This homeowners' curse is the result of sudden differences in inside and outside temperatures, which cause warm air to give off moisture. The moisture rots buildings and attracts moulds that contribute to poor indoor air quality.

"Design is far too important to be left solely to designers," Cowan and Van der Ryn say, so their fourth rule makes everyone a designer. Stacking bales requires more social than technical skills, so wall building is typically done by friends who are supervised by one experienced tradesperson. This "sweat equity" shaves about 30 percent off the costs of walls. It also revives the old barn-raising style of neighbourliness, which makes it an exercise in community-building. And it turns home building into a school for general self-reliance and self-confidence. "How can we expect people who have no faith in their ability to make their own house think they could ever figure out how to build an entire economy?" asks David Eisenberg, co-author of *The Straw Bale House*.

Rule five, Cowan and Van der Ryn say, is to make nature visi-ble, so that buildings become a bridge, not a barrier, to the out-doors. This is where straw bale roofs, the trademark of Michel Bergeron's Quebec firm Archibio, go over the top. Bergeron covers a water-proofed roof with bales of straw, then adds a topping of leaves, manure and soil. "Having a living roof is like tending an extra garden," reports Archibio's François Tanquay, who grows tomatoes on his elevated plot. As well as providing superb insulation, this kind of roof lets people see how natural systems can grow on them.

Over and above these five design rules, Cowan and Van der Ryn lay out three principles for environmentally sustainable design: conservation, stewardship and regeneration.

Conservation, the first principle, means using fewer resources. Homes insulated with straw bales stay warm with half the energy of standard homes, according to researchers with California's respected Berkeley Lawrence Laboratory.

Stewardship, the second principle, means we shouldn't kill the goose that lays the golden egg. Straw bales come from a crop that grows every year. By replacing lumber that takes a good forty years to regrow after a forest has been logged, straw bales mean more forests can be left standing.

Cowan and Van der Ryn's third principle is regeneration. This means making up for harm done in the past by giving back to nature. Straw bale roofs are a good example of this. Rather than destroying nature, these roofs create more spaces for nature to flourish. Birds love to dance on them, as in turkey in the straw. In some areas of Europe, goats graze on them.

In this chapter we've come a long way from our starting point—how farming can be transformed into an environmentally responsible activity rather than be the major contributor to global warming that it is today. It's an exhilarating thought that, as we gain more knowledge and wisdom about using farm wastes to replace polluting materials, we can move beyond pollution reduction and make nature's regeneration a reality.

SET THE TABLE FOR THE FUTURE

SET THE TABLE
FOR THE FUTURE

Real Food can go where no diet, recipe or cookbook has gone before. Up to this point we've passed on stories of people who've figured out practical ways to grow, prepare and savour food that brings health, joy, justice and nature to their table. The challenge in this conclusion is a taller order: to outline how Real Food can actually replace the industrial food system as we move into the twenty-first century. We believe the transformative powers of food are up to the challenge, and as Real Food becomes second nature, it will help define the history of the coming century.

Food is too humble for its own good. It's such a routine part of our day that its potential to create change is, as the saying goes, hidden in plain sight. Food has extraordinary qualities as a catalyst of personal and social restoration. It has a unique power—not domination, but power that enables positive change. Consider the following ten unique powers of food that let all of us set the table for the future.

1. Food is powerful because small and easy changes count.

Starting to make these changes is as easy as crumbling some tofu into a spaghetti sauce or adding a clove of garlic to your salad dressing. You don't need to go for retraining, get a licence, form a support group, get on the Internet, buy equipment or give anything up. With food, the passage from desire to decision, decision to action is short and sweet. That's not so with many aspects of life. It's not easy to give up your car or quit your job; but changes in food choices can take place easily and quickly, on your say-so.

Food comes in bite-sized pieces. So too do positive food changes. The menu of opportunities for small but significant improvements is almost endless. There's no need or reason to delay getting started. Many people would smack their lips over a sandwich made with sautéed Swiss chard, onions and crumbled feta cheese on a crusty roll. Organic chard and onions are cheap and easy to find, as is whole wheat bread. For many, that's three significant changes in one serving with very little extra effort. Most people can experiment from among as many as a hundred stress-free, positive options for change every day until they settle into new habits. If you take your coffee regular, you can try cutting back on sugar or switching to organic milk or coffee. Change one serving at a time. Before you know it, change becomes a matter of course, one course at a time. The abrupt make-or-break changes that are the norm for giving up tobacco, alcohol or drugs aren't called for. No reason to bite off more than you can chew. No need to wait for the big day, when conditions are perfect and a comprehensive game plan is in place, before you try oatmeal for breakfast.

The versatility of food combinations makes piecemeal change a piece of cake for individuals. Bureaucratic organizations, on the other hand, can't take advantage of this versatility. Small change is a big problem for them because the economies of scale depend on uniformity, standardization and prefabrication. One-of-a-kinds are not what these organizations do, so delays and stalemates are the norm, in stark contrast with the potential inherent in food for makeshift change and continuous improvement.

We believe that these mass-production, bureaucratic organizations will self-destruct in the twenty-first century. They're organized to suppress diversity so they can create artificial uniformity, but none of the chronic problems of our era—poverty, homelessness, malnutrition, environmental degradation among them—respond to mass-production or bureaucratic methods. Just as computers are locked into choices that can be reduced to an on or off switch, so bureaucratic organizations are locked into too narrow a range of choices to ever work effectively with the subtlety and turbulence that characterize real life. They suffer from hardening of the categories. Immediate, practical solutions fall between the cracks. The art of change in the twenty-first century will be the art of debundling problems and decoupling solutions, which is food's specialty.

Opportunities await companies, community groups and local governments that can work with this. Any restaurant can offer at least one set of menu options for customers who prefer or need vegetarian, vegan or organic fare. Any grocery store can set aside at least one shelf for organic or local foods. Any coffee shop can offer at least one fair-trade choice in coffees and teas. Any city hall can open its plaza to farmers' markets on weekends. And any advocacy group can offer to build support for these initiatives by making their members aware of them, perhaps with a sticker that can be placed on the vendor's window. The world has had enough permanent solutions. Toronto's Environmental Task Force set a blistering pace of continuous improvement when it boiled down "quick start initiatives" from a one-day visioning session with concerned politicians, city staff and a wide range of community activists. There is no need for a master plan that no organization can digest when hundreds of changes can be effected quickly and simply. Quick starts that build momentum are the way to go. "We build the road as we need it" is the slogan of the world-famous Mondragon co-ops of Spain.

Food's power to keep it simple is made to order for local governments. It lets them bolster close relations with citizens instead of being limited by low budgets and weak legislative powers. There are ideas worth considering all over North America. Montreal leads the way in municipal sponsorship of community gardens. Halifax figured out how to banish organic material from the garbage dump and double the life expectancy of its landfill site. Newmarket, near Toronto, is using compost to generate electricity before it's returned to the soil. Fort Saskatchewan, near Edmonton, lets sheep cut the grass in local parks. Peggy's Cove is reclaiming economical and odour-free fertilizer from human waste. Portland, Oregon, and Tucson, Arizona, have passed bylaws to encourage rooftop gardens and straw bale homes. Best practices are in place, and they can be adapted easily. There's no need for lengthy and expensive studies or risky ventures. These municipalities have all put the simple power of food into action. Beware of those who say it's more difficult or complex than that, or that it requires a megaproject. This is not rocket science. It's science the way Einstein defined it: as simple as possible, no simpler.

2. Food is powerful because it unleashes the Power of One.

Food is more subject to individual choice than most decisions. It also makes a personal statement. "One person's meat is another's poison" has a special meaning for those aware of the cruel, polluting and unhealthy practices associated with corporate livestock management. Ethical shopping breaks the biggest food habit of all: the habit of divorcing individual purchasing decisions from their social and ethical consequences. By bringing out the Power of One to make a difference, Real Food will be one of the most potent forces for personal and social renewal in the twenty-first century.

The Power of One will revolutionize major institutions, practices and technologies of the past century. In retrospect, a surprising number of apparent twentieth century advances were built around suppressing the Power of One. Mass solutions became the norm. Compulsory mass vaccination was the answer to contagious disease; compulsory pasteurization was the answer to milk-borne disease; compulsory fluoridation of public drinking water was the answer to tooth decay. When no one makes a choice, no one makes a mistake, the theory goes. But as the century draws to an end, it seems more likely that when no one makes a mistake, the system just might. There's growing concern that pasteurization and chlorination, for example, although solving some problems, also contribute to chronic health problems that can be avoided if we rethink the way we make clean water and healthy milk available.

Technology has evolved along the same impersonal axis as government policy. Mass production was designed to replace the discretion of skilled artisans with more dispensable cogs in a machine. Process or flow technologies—dominant in the energy, chemical, telecommunications and food industries since the 1950s—are automated to take individual human foibles out of the equation. Interconnections are so intricate that various stages are linked by automated switching devices, which don't waste time thinking. Unfortunately, the margin for error, like the margin for individual decisions, is zero. Minor problems in nuclear reactors become runaways. A winter storm leaves a province's fate hanging on one wire.

The twentieth century leaves a curious legacy of individualism. No other century can match the progress in personal, civil and human rights. In many countries, women and racial minorities won recognition for their individual rights and merits. Conformity lost its grip. Governments have renounced their right to keep watch over the bedrooms of a nation, and sexual orientation is now considered a personal choice. Ironically, though, no other century can match the decline in personal autonomy and self-reliance that has been so much a part of the twentieth century. Few people can build their own home or handle even basic repairs. Few can bake their own bread, cook from scratch or make their own clothes. Skills and powers that were once commonplace are now almost lost. We have become dependent on anonymous markets for the basics of life. If a person is totally incapable of looking after himself, the saying goes, he is either in an institution for long-term care or he is a typical North American.

There's no way around the fact that changes in food practices will happen one person at a time. This is cause, not for lament, but for celebration of the power that food endows each of us with.

3. Food is powerful because it brings people together.
Most people enjoy meals more when they have company. Growing and preparing food can be a chore when you're by yourself, but it's fun when you're with others. Food and sociability probably co-evolved because early humans had to cooperate to hunt, gather and prepare food. It's a sterile division of labour that separates sociability from any of the work associated with food.

A surprising number of food problems arise simply because individuals and nuclear families are too isolated. A surprising number of food problems can be solved through cooperation between small, informal groups. If Joe can't handle a garden because he's away in July and Sally can't handle a garden because she's away in August, why can't the two get together and split the harvest? Couples can talk over the activities of the day while cooking something from scratch. In this way, gender equality can go a long way towards eliminating convenience foods. And who made the rule that friends can only be invited over to dinner on formal occasions, when everything is laid on and the whole house is spic and span? There's nothing wrong with a spur-of-the-moment invitation—you bring the salad, we'll make the pasta. Reinventing the kitchen as a centre of sociability, not just a functional work station, can make life easier for everyone but the makers of convenience and fast foods.

The social aspect of food is more than a pleasant bonus; it helps create conditions essential to good health, which can't come from an upset stomach. When we eat and run, or eat on the run, what's known as the "sympathetic" division of the nervous system automatically clicks in, just like in the good old days when a bear chasing a caveman triggered fight-or-flight reactions. "If you eat lunch, you are lunch," is the watchword of the sympathetic nervous system. Your stomach tenses up, your heart races, your mouth goes dry, your back stiffens, your sphincter tightens. We refer to someone in this state as wound up or bristling. What is happening is that your body is working at cross purposes. Mealtime is when you're supposed to switch into "parasympathetic" mode, which does all sorts of laid-back things to your saliva, digestive juices and intestines. We beckon the parasympathetic mode by saying grace, offering a toast or performing some other bread-breaking ritual which establishes that the bear is far away. "People are looking for something harder than this, but you can lose weight and control stress by taking time to eat sociably," says Toronto chiropractor Johanna Carlo. "It doesn't cost anything. You just have to take some time for yourself."

The World Health Organization is making a special study of the Italian town of Campodimele because of the unusually long and healthy lives of its residents. Good food seems to be essential to life in Campodimele. The villagers eat lots of fresh fruit, vegetables, wild mushrooms and snails, and they take their time eating them, hours at a time in public plazas. "If I had to test the ingredients of our elixir," says mayor Paolo Zinella, "I would put in first place the easy temper and calm of the village."[1]

In the twenty-first century, people will also come together around food through what's known as the "third sector," sometimes referred to as the NGO (non-governmental organizations) sector. It's already one of the biggest employers on the continent. It works at the edge, where the line between private and public, formal and informal, planned and unplanned, is blurred. In nature, productivity, diversity and creativity are always highest at the edge, in ocean marshes where salt and fresh waters merge, or where meadows, forests and ponds meet. The same holds true for society. Cities high in creativity and innovation are cities high in edge, rich in places where distinct cultures can meet. With food as one of its pillars, the third sector will blossom in the coming century. It will become what environmentalist Keith Collins calls "the civil service of civil society."

Food allows third-sector organizations such as community and environment groups to trade on their connections to facilitate change. As we've seen in Chapter 3, the World Wildlife Fund introduces farmers to lower cost, lower chemical methods of growing, then links them up with people who can get them a fair price for their effort. Social planning councils in Windsor, Peterborough and the Ottawa Valley launched local labels that help neighbourhood farmers and processors get a foothold in local markets. FoodShare in Toronto provides an incubator kitchen to help new catering companies get started and to give low-income entrepreneurs a leg up. The United Way in Calgary helps community-based food companies find corporate food partners who can help them over the hurdles of distribution.

There are few limits to what these groups can do when food is the lever for change. Most churches already have kitchen facilities. Why not sponsor a hands-on Thanksgiving activity by holding a canning and preserving day at harvest time, or sponsor a community kitchen for new members? Unions have a hard time boosting wages these days, but they could boost purchasing power by coordinating a hundred members who want to buy food from a local Community Supported Agriculture project, or helping members' families organize themselves to buy organic non-perishables in bulk from a natural foods co-op. Conservation groups might sponsor foraging hikes that teach methods of identifying and preparing free wild foods. Let's get creative.

The breakdown of our food system is in some ways a symptom of the breakdown of our ability to link food and sociability. Those without much money are hardest hit by this breakdown, since money is the only currency of an anonymous society. Solving the problem with money alone is an expensive proposition, because the absence of sociability leaves a big hole to fill. Many medical studies confirm that the worst health problems associated with poverty can be traced to the demoralization and disorganization that so often accompany poverty. When low-income groups are cohesive and act together, their resistance to disease increases.[2] Food can be a focal point for restoring pride, esteem and confidence in low-income groups. Community gardens, community kitchens and potluck banquets are the tools of the trade for such initiatives, all of which could do with support from government, but all of which can proceed even when governments turn their backs on the poor.

4. Food is powerful because it creates serendipity—extra benefits that occur naturally.

Food is so central to the operation of nature, society and economics that a tiny pebble of improvement sets off a ripple effect of positive changes. Consider the simple act of planting an apple tree in your backyard and a crab-apple tree in your front yard. Over time, they will provide fresh fruit and the makings of jelly; but that's the least of the benefits. The trees provide habitat for birds and bees, as well as apple blossoms to beautify the street. As they grow, the trees absorb carbon and release oxygen, which helps to offset global warming. In summer the trees shade the house and let you turn down the air-conditioner, reducing the pollution from electrical plants. In winter the trees act as wind-breaks, so that you burn less gas or oil to heat your home, thereby keeping the air cleaner. When it rains, the trees hold water, preventing the overloading of sewage plants with overflow that threatens the quality of drinking water and the usefulness of rivers and lakes as habitat for fish. Simple improvements at any point in the food system generate a host of spin-off benefits.

The popular term for these positive but unintended benefits is *serendipity*. Environmental economists call it *elegance*. You might think that the inherent elegance of food would be encouraged, but that rarely happens. To use the lingo of economists, "the market cannot capture side benefits." In other words, the market has no way to reward the apple-growing homeowner for saving public money on water treatment, air cleaning, global warming or medical care for lung disorders. Governments are organized hierarchically.

There is a water works department, which is not going to pay you money to divert a little rain from the sewers. There is a utility, which is not going to pay you money to save a little power. There is a health ministry, which is not going to pay you money to prevent a visit to the doctor. With governments organized the way they are, it's not too much to say that the very elegance of food is the cause of its political downfall.

Nevertheless, the elegance of food will offer a major opportunity for public policy in the twenty-first century. In all likelihood this challenge will be taken up by the "third sector," the sector with the greatest capacity to form loose partnerships and networks among groups that have mutual interests. Almost every community in Canada has some version of the United Way, which pools donations to a wide variety of social agencies. The United Way has a vested interest in reducing overall costs and freeing up money for new initiatives. This may be where the first meetings between health activists, home and community gardeners, and anti-hunger groups, for example, will take place. When food is recognized as an issue that cuts across and through the traditional boundaries of most issues, Real Food will ride in on a wave of elegance.

5. Food is powerful because it can be used to increase the value of other things.

The value of food so far exceeds its cost that a number of opportunities present themselves to capture that value by increasing access to quality food. Business executives recognize the full value of food when they take clients out for lunch. Meals offer an opportunity to share a pleasant experience, to get to know people in a casual environment, to check out personal qualities that might be significant before a deal is closed. This is why several graduate-level business programs in the United States offer courses on table manners. As soon as governments learned that business lunches oiled business deals, they made them tax-deductible.

However, few companies and government tax policies build on the value of food much beyond the free lunch. Some companies now organize cooking retreats as a way to encourage camaraderie and teamwork, and to develop the emotional intelligence of their operation. Some companies provide free facilities for breast-feeding mothers, saving themselves a bundle on absenteeism costs since breast-fed babies are sick less often. Some companies subsidize healthy meal programs because they more than pay their way in reduced absenteeism and drug-plan costs. We expect that in the twenty-first century company-sponsored healthy food programs will be as common as free coffee is now. Just as today's life insurance plans offer discounts for non-smokers, tomorrow's life, health, workplace disability and drug plans will offer deep discounts for organic eaters.

The health value of good food will become the saviour of medicare in the next century. Canada's cherished medicare program is hitting the financial wall because it finances acute care treatment of chronic illnesses that could be prevented at a fraction of the cost with healthy food. A few months' treatment for cancer or heart disease costs more than a lifetime's supply of foods that can help prevent these diseases. The value of healthy food is undeniable in pre- and post-natal care. Most studies show that a dollar investment in nutrition during these periods pays off three times in short-term medical savings. The Toronto Food Policy Council estimates that it would cost about $106 million to let pregnant women in Ontario charge a select group of low-cost, locally grown bulk foods to their medicare cards. The result would be public savings and improved life chances for newborns.[3]

The same logic applies to school meal programs. The educational value of food and cooking is enormous. It's a way to teach manual dexterity and self-confidence, as well as social skills and basic chemistry. More important, it's a way to give all children the best possible start in school by making sure they have optimum nutrition for learning. We know that a diet high in refined sugars, simple starches and additives contributes to learning and behaviour problems. To pay top dollar for school facilities, equipment and teachers, and then to leave nutrition to chance, is a silly way to prioritize educational financing. Parents also need the support of schools to counter the effects of junk-food ads that target kids. School meal programs offer such educational value for the dollar that they will become a centrepiece of twenty-first-century education.

There are some weird taboos that account for what is free and guaranteed in this society, and what's not. Water, a biological necessity, is free; but food, just as much a biological necessity, isn't. Roads are free, but food isn't. Municipal parks are free, but food isn't. Food is not a commodity with a price that corresponds in any way to its value, yet food is treated as a commodity, as if it had no broader cultural, educational or human importance. The value of food is priceless. In the twenty-first century we will show our respect and recognition for its value by refusing to let money be a barrier to its availability.

6. Food is powerful because it creates employment.

Food takes work. This essential truth about food is good news for job seekers. Because food is essential to life, and work is essential to food production, food provides a sound base for job-rich economic development.

There are several reasons why food production lends itself to a job bonanza. Food production is recession-proof. No matter what, people have to eat, preferably a few times a day, every day. Though there are limits to how much people can and should eat, demand does not fluctuate very much for very long. In a world rocked by economic instability, it makes sense to grow an economy on a stable food foundation.

Food production is labour-intensive, especially when it's done right. Despite Canada's high-tech methods of growing, processing, transporting and preparing food, the food system remains the second-biggest employer in the country. The number of people who work the land has gone down dramatically since 1900, but not the number of people who work on food. Government statistics hide this fact by lumping the people who process food under manufacturing, the people who transport food under transportation, the people who sell food under retail, and so on. But no bag of economic or statistical tricks can deny the fact that food is inherently labour-intensive. Also, farmers today spend as much time working as they did a hundred years ago; they just split their time differently—eight hours on an off-farm job so they can buy the labour-saving farm equipment and chemicals, and then another shift on the farm. The majority of today's farms have someone holding down two jobs. So the progress of labour-saving technology is a bit of a myth. There's no way of getting around the fact that food takes work.

If we accepted that fact and organized our food system to make the best of it, we could proceed to more interesting questions about what kinds of jobs we want to create. We can choose between real farming, done in concert with nature, requiring fewer back-breaking, mind-numbing hours on the tractor and more hours planning, strategizing and selling directly to consumers; or we can choose more factory jobs turning petroleum into a substitute for natural fertilizers, and more trucking jobs hauling food back and forth across the continent. Food can not only create jobs, it can create good jobs.

Food is great for employment because food workers require lots of local services. When a person buys a computer or a yacht, most of that money leaves town that night, because the computers and yachts were made elsewhere. When a person buys food from a local grocer, and the local grocer buys from a local farmer, and the local farmer pays taxes that hire a local teacher, who shops at a local grocery, the money keeps circulating, creating jobs at each pass. This multiplier effect also insulates a local economy from the mood swings of the international marketplace.

Food jobs have few of what economists call "barriers to entry." There's not much use thinking of starting up a steel plant unless you have a few billion dollars to throw around, or getting into software unless you have a national or international distribution system. But individuals and communities can get into food production with a minimum of equipment and steady customers. A Community Supported Agriculture farmer needs about fifty to a hundred customers. Bakers, yogurt makers, and other processors and caterers do well with a few hundred steady customers. A restaurant can make a go of it with seating for sixteen. This is why food jobs are so well suited to small, innovative entrepreneurs.

Food can create jobs through job sharing. If people can take a day off work each week by following the suggestions outlined in Chapter 2, and become more self-sufficient in their own food production and preparation, they create jobs replacing them on their day off. This is one of the most productive strategies for job creation going.

It would be possible to double employment in the food sector if Canada followed a strategy known as food self-reliance. As recently as the 1960s, supermarkets bought 70 percent of their stock within a radius of 120 miles.[4] Canada supplied itself with basic fruits and imported the rest from 28 countries.[5] Today, as we've seen in Chapter 4, the average molecule on any Canadian plate has travelled 1,500 miles, half our basic fruits are imported, and we import from 112 countries.[6] Saskatchewan imports 85 percent of its vegetables.[7] The same holds for Nova Scotia, despite its rich Annapolis Valley. Ontario, with some of the best land in the country, could create at least sixty thousand jobs by substituting domestic production for imports.

Other countries with more severe climates and less fertile land than Canada's have organized food systems based on two concepts: the need for nutritious food and the need to develop food self-reliance. Between 1970 and 1990, Norway increased its consumption of home-grown calories from 39 to 52 percent. Norway's Centre for Ecological Agriculture believes the country can go organic and still be close to nutritional self-sufficiency.[8]

Anthropologists of the future, writing about the twentieth century, will build their careers explaining what overcame a society that regarded a shift to jobs as Wal-Mart greeters and fast-food clerks as progress, that consigned 10 percent of the population to unemployment while importing basic foods, that saw the shift from home-based work to data-entry clerical jobs as liberation, and that sacrificed its health to do all this.

7. Food is powerful because it can be grown anywhere and make good use of resources already paid for.

Food is a great sideline activity. It's perfectly adapted to be grown and prepared in the nooks and crannies of opportunity left over from other activities. The name economists give to these nooks and crannies is "unused capacity." Unused capacity is perhaps the most productive untapped resource in Canada. Making full use of unused capacity for food production is a low-cost strategy for solving problems of hunger, unemployment and environmental degradation in one fell swoop.

The average home is loaded with unused capacity that's already been paid for and that can be put to work to produce food at minimal cost for maximum return. All homes have walls, some of which face the sun. Vines and climbing plants can be encouraged to grow up them, providing food and extra insulation for next to nothing. Many homes have fences. They take up no more space, and look better, if they're converted into living fences of raspberry canes or creeping plants. Most homes have yards, that can be used to grow food. Many homes have roofs that can be converted to rooftop gardens, offering food and extra insulation as well as beauty. Many homes have sunny window sills, where indoor plants and sprouts can flourish. Many homes have porches that, with some renovations, can serve as winter greenhouses. All homeowners take baths or showers and wash their dishes in hot water, and most then discharge the grey water into the sewer. Instead, if environmentally friendly soaps are used, this water could be directed to the garden, with the heat extending the growing season by a couple of months. In these examples, the wall, fence, yard, roof, window-sill, porch and hot water have already been paid for. For a relatively small additional cost they can provide at least one and sometimes two extra functions.

Taking advantage of unused capacity can extend far beyond the home. Most companies have more unused capacity than they know what to do with. Shopping malls have roofs that could provide their restaurants with fresh food. The space allotted to one underground parking spot is all that's needed to have red wriggly worms handle their organic waste, provide soil conditioner for their rooftop garden and save on waste haulage. If the mall has its own power plant, the waste heat, which has already been paid for, could be piped to the roof garden, which could then operate as a greenhouse in winter. In fact Canada could heat every greenhouse that could ever be built to develop food self-reliance entirely with waste heat from electrical plants, which now discharge two-thirds of the heat they generate into rivers, lakes and the air. The same is true for any factory that generates heat for one process and then discharges it into the air. Finding unused capacity in any business—a chance to make or sell additional product with little or no additional fixed costs—is the easiest way to increase profit margins, and it usually improves the quality of the food supply.

Most community organizations have access to unused capacity too. Many churches have kitchens that could be used as community kitchens or for low-income food entrepreneurs on days when parishioners aren't using them. Some organizations have extra office space that can be leased on the cheap to upstart community entrepreneurs.

There's not a community that doesn't have unused capacity in abundance. There's no shortage of low-cost land available for farming—the roofs of and lands around public buildings, vacant land waiting for a developer, damaged or "brownsite" lands that could support container gardens. Perhaps the greatest unused capacity of all is people drawing social assistance when they want to work, and who could be hired by community-sponsored market gardens that displace imported foods for the minimal cost of an income top-up. The math goes like this: If a community-sponsored market garden paid workers $350 a week and the government topped that up to a living wage, the government would save the difference between the top-up and what would have been paid out in social assistance if these workers weren't employed. That's how Churchill Park Co-op in Moose Jaw does it. Our talents for self-reliance are literally hidden under a bushel of imports. When food quality, hunger, unemployment and environmental problems can all be addressed through unused capacity, it's hard for anyone to come up with a good excuse not to give this a try.

To take advantage of unused capacity, agriculture will increasingly move to the city. The compost is there. The scrap lumber for raised beds is there. Most importantly, the customers are there. Today's rural farms will be used for crops and livestock that require large amounts of space or that can make use of marginal grazing land. In the twenty-first century, unused capacity will be the modern way of living off the fat of the land. It will revolutionize our food system, bringing it into line with the needs of efficiency, good employment and respect for the resources of the planet.

8. Food is powerful because it stimulates generosity.

People who would never share their computer, car, home or money will share their food. That's why food is such a logical starting place to bring out the best in people, to increase equality and cooperation. We all eat and there's plenty to go around. The artificiality of our food system is manifest in the fact that it creates scarcity and competition where none exist. This is the dirty secret behind the Canadian and world hunger crisis. There's more effort put into manufacturing scarcity than into managing abundance. Government-sanctioned grading systems keep 20 percent of fruit and vegetables off the market to prevent the collapse of prices. The international trade wars that plague food sales all derive from the fact that most countries have more food than they know what to do with—or more precisely, that the only thing they know to do with food is sell it. Ironically, government and corporate policies to prop up food prices by propping up scarcity are maintained alongside reckless schemes to boost productivity with toxic sprays, factory farms and dangerous biotechnology.

It takes tremendous effort and intervention by governments to create scarcity and prevent prices from collapsing towards zero, because food is life, and it grows wherever life can be sustained and reproduced, which is almost everywhere. Hunger, malnutrition and food banks are a blight on the Canadian landscape, because there is no reason for the scarcity that produces them. Leaving compassion aside, it makes no sense to deny adequate food to people who have no money, and then to pay many times more for their medical care. It makes no sense to demoralize children with hunger, then pay for their demoralization in lifelong social assistance or prison programs that cost many times more than food. Food banks are an insult to our intelligence as well as our conscience. The great majority of food distributed at food banks comes from food wholesalers and retailers who use the food banks to avoid hauling food they can't sell to the dump, and who receive a tax deduction to boot. Food banks are at odds with wise Canadian traditions and represent an Americanization of our social policies. Most of Canada's positive public programs are based on the principle of universality. Everyone, including the well-to-do, enjoys free public education. Everyone, including the rich, receives a pension at age sixty-five. Everyone, including the wealthy, gets medicare. But food is treated differently. It remains a market commodity, even though it lacks the key characteristic of a commodity, scarcity. American-style targeted charity programs for the poor are the result.

In the twenty-first century we will learn how to make food a public good, and how to make it available in the context of universal programs. Community gardens, which give everyone the opportunity to grow food, school meal programs, which provide universal access to quality food for children, and select medicare programs, which make food available to all at risk, are obvious starting points. These programs will honour the generosity inherent in food, generosity that flows from our common humanity and the natural bounty of the good earth. Odd as it seems to imaginations limited by today's food system, this bounteous system goes with the grain of food realities and will require less government effort to maintain than artificial scarcity.

9. Food is powerful because it satisfies both humble biological needs and deeper social and spiritual ones.

We celebrate the major rituals and turning points of life with banquets. We honour great people and causes with special dinners. We mark religious events with feasts. We say a grace or toast before dinner. The great spiritual leader and community organizer Jesus used food as an organizing tool and as a metaphor in many teachings. In the twenty-first century we will revive and enrich these food traditions, and as we learn to appreciate our connections with and dependence on the natural world, we will give food the reverence it deserves.

A positive sign that food is regaining its central role in spiritual life is the incredible popularity of yoga in the 1990s. Yoga is not only a physical exercise program. It's primarily a spiritual exercise for people bent out of shape by materialism. The idea is to align body, mind and soul. In contrast with many religions, yoga treats the body as a temple of the soul. It is not the body, the flesh, that is weak before temptation and prone to sin, but the mind, racing to get on with the business of life and conquer the world. Yoga is a stretch for a culture that sees the mind and rationality as the highest expression of humanity, the tool for *doing*. Yoga tries to discipline and quiet the mind so it can be attuned to *being*.

Not surprisingly, food is as central to yoga practice as stretching and meditation. In Val Morin, Quebec, at the world headquarters of the Sivananda yoga movement, a plaque by the kitchen entrance greets all who volunteer for food preparation. "A kitchen is the best

training ground," wrote yoga teacher Swami Sivananda, "for developing tolerance, endurance, forbearance, mercy, sympathy, love,
adaptability, and the spirit of real service for purifying one's heart
and for realizing the Oneness of Life." The food served is fresh and
whole, as unprocessed as possible. Meals are vegetarian, because
vegetarian meals are good for the heart. They align the heart, or
soul, with the body and mind in the practice of *ahimsa*, the cardi-
nal virtue of yoga. The passive expression of *ahimsa* is avoidance of
injury to others, in this case animals; the active expression of *ahimsa*
is service to others, the generosity of mealtime extended to all.
True to their beliefs, the staff at Val Morin source their food locally and organically whenever possible. They have converted their
parking lot into a garden. Their elegant lodge is of straw bale construction, the largest straw bale building in the world. The next
challenge for yoga, says facility manager Swami Kartikeya, is to
translate its beliefs into active service to the environment, so
human bodies can be aligned with all creation.

There are many ways to turn food into a blessing, not just a commodity. Even the most secular people can find a poem to grace dinner time and a reason to celebrate. Even the most scientific
gardeners can follow the practice of master gardener John Jeavons
and build a gateway that requires them to bend down slightly when
entering hallowed ground. Applying the doctrine of non-cruelty to
other humans or other creatures requires a little reflection and a
few questions to the food store manager about the labour and livestock practices that produced the vegetables, fruit, milk, eggs and
meat in the store. As we learn to use food to reintegrate our lives,
we will develop a food system worthy of what is highest and best
in us. That is a claim that no factory farm or superstore can ever
make.

10. Food is powerful because it has positive energy.
From the loose and stray energy in sun, soil and water, food comes
on with a force strong enough to defy the laws of gravity and grow
upward. Food even defies the strict and relentless laws of thermo-
dynamics, which hold that energy degenerates from high to low
organization; by contrast, food takes dispersed energy and organizes
and concentrates it. It nourishes our health with positive energy

too. Most prescription drugs and most medical procedures rely on negative energy. *Antibiotic*, literally translated, means "against life," while chemotherapy and radiation treatments for cancer inflict poisons on the body. Food, by contrast, provides positive energy to the immune system.

As we learn to appreciate the positive energy in food over the next century, we will stop talking so much about the ways we lack enough power and start doing more about reclaiming the power we give up. We alone have the power to form dinner clubs and buying clubs, community gardens and community kitchens, and to choose to buy from ethical producers.

"Organizing around food," says Herb Barbolet of Vancouver's FarmFolk/CityFolk, one of the most innovative and comprehensive food organizations on the continent, "is about creating opportunities." The opportunities around food defy the most pervasive, dangerous and disempowering myth of our time: TINA, There Is No Alternative. There are plenty of alternatives, all of which rely on the positive energy food generates. Each and every one of us can draw from that positive energy. We have the power of food at our fingertips. The power to make a difference is no further away than that. When we grasp it, we will have Real Food for a change.

DIRECTORY

Annex Organics
c/o Field to Table
200 Eastern Avenue
Toronto, Ontario
M5A 1J1
phone: 416-363-6441

British Columbia Biotechnology Circle
c/o Brewster and Cathleen Kneen
S-6, C-27, R.R. 1
Sorrento, British Columbia
V0E 2W0
phone: 250-675-4866
e-mail: ramshorn@jetstream.net

Canadian Association of Food Banks
530 Lakeshore Blvd. W.
Toronto, Ontario
M5V 1A5
phone: 416-203-9241
Contact person: Julia Bass

Canadian Environmental Law Association (CELA)
401–517 College St.
Toronto, Ontario
M6G 4A2
phone: 416-960-2284
fax: 416-960-9392
e-mail: cela@web.net
Internet: www.web.net/~cela

Canadian Institute for Environmental Law and Policy (CIELAP)
400–517 College St.
Toronto, Ontario
M6G 4A2
phone: 416-923-3529
fax: 416-923-5949
e-mail: cielap@web.net
Internet: www.web.net/~cielap

Canadian Organic Growers
Membership Secretary
Box 6408 Station J
Ottawa, Ontario
K2A 3Y6
phone: 613-231-9047
Internet: www.gks.com/cog

Center for Science in the Public Interest (CSPI)
Box 70373, Station A
Toronto, Ontario
M5W 2X5
phone: 202-332-9110 (Washington, DC)
fax: 202-265-4954
e-mail: cspi@cspinet.org
Internet: www.cspinet.org

City Farmer
Canada's Office of Urban Agriculture
801–318 Homer St.
Vancouver, British Columbia
V6B 2V3
phone: 604-685-5832
fax: 604-685-0431
e-mail: cityfarm@interchange.ubc.ca
Internet: www.cityfarmer.org

Coalition for a Green Economic Recovery
2255B Queen Street East, Suite 127
Toronto, Ontario
M4E 1G3
phone: 416-699-6070

Conservation Council of New Brunswick
180 St. John. St.
Fredericton, New Brunswick
E3B 4A9
phone: 506-458-8747
fax: 506-458-1047
e-mail: ccnbcoon@nbnet.nb.ca
Internet: www.web.net/~ccnb

Ecological Agriculture Projects
Macdonald Campus of McGill University
21,111 Lakeshore
Ste-Anne-de-Bellevue, Quebec
H9X 3V9
phone: 514-398-7771
fax: 514-398-7621
e-mail: info@eap.mcgill.ca
Internet: www.eap.mcgill.ca

Ecological Farmers Association of Ontario
Box 127
Wroxeter, Ontario
N0G 2X0
phone: 519-335-3557
Internet: www.gks.com/efao

EthicScan Canada
Box 54034
Toronto, Ontario
M6A 3B7
phone: 416-783-6776
fax: 416-783-7386
e-mail: Ethic@concentric.net
Internet: www.ethicscan.on.ca

FarmFolk/CityFolk Society
208–2211 W. Fourth Ave.
Vancouver, British Columbia
V6K 4S2
phone: 604-730-0450
toll free in B.C.: 1-888-730-0452
fax: 604-730-0451
e-mail: office@ffcf.bc.ca
Internet: www.ffcf.bc.ca

Action Réseau Consommateurs
1215, Visitation, Bureau 103
Montreal, Quebec
H2L 3B5
phone: 514-521-6820
fax: 514-521-0736

FoodShare Toronto
238 Queen St. W., Lower Level
Toronto, Ontario
M5V 1Z7
phone: 416-392-1628
fax: 416-392-6653
e-mail: fdshare@web.net

International Institute of Concern for Public Health
Suite 710, 264 Queens Quay W.
Toronto, Ontario
M5J 1B5
phone: 416-260-0575
fax: 416-260-3404
e-mail: iicph@compuserve.com

Dan Jason
Salt Spring Seeds
Box 33
Ganges, British Columbia
V0S 1E0
phone: 250-537-5269

LifeCycles
2175 Dowler Place
Victoria, British Columbia
phone: 250-383-5800
fax: 250-386-3449
e-mail: lifecycles@pinc.com

National Farmers Union
250-C Second Ave. S.
Saskatoon, Saskatchewan
S7K 2M1
phone: 306-652-9465

Ontario Natural Food Co-op
70 Fima Crescent
Toronto, Ontario
M8W 4V9
phone: 416-503-1144
fax: 416-503-2848
e-mail: onfc@pathcom.com

Ontario Public Health Association
468 Queen St. E., Suite 202
Toronto, Ontario
M5A 1T7
phone: 416-367-3313
fax: 416-367-2844
e-mail: opha@web.net
Internet: www.web.net/opha

Recycling Council of Ontario
489 College St., Suite 504
Toronto, Ontario
M6G 1A5
phone: 416-960-1025
fax: 416-960-8053
e-mail: rco@rco.on.ca
Internet: www.rco.on.ca

Resource Efficient Agricultural Production (REAP)–Canada
Box 125, Glenaladale House
Ste-Anne-de-Bellevue, Quebec
H9X 3V9
phone: 514-398-7743
fax: 514-398-7972
e-mail: reap@interlink.net

Rural Advancement Foundation International
110 Osborne St., Suite 202
Winnipeg, Manitoba
R3L 1Y5
phone: 204-453-5259
fax: 204-925-8034
e-mail: rafi@rafi.org
Internet: www.rafi.org

Ryerson Centre for Studies in Food Security
Ryerson Polytechnic University
350 Victoria St.
Toronto, Ontario
M5B 2K3
Contact person: Mustafa Koc, Co-Director, Dept. of Sociology
phone: 416-979-5000 ext. 6210
fax: 416-979-5273
e-mail: mkoc@acs.ryerson.ca
Internet: www.ryerson.ca/~foodsec

Toronto Food Policy Council
277 Victoria St., Room 203
Toronto, Ontario
M5B 1W1
phone: 416-392-1107
fax: 416-392-1357
e-mail: tfpc@city.toronto.on.ca
Internet: www.city.toronto.on.ca/public health

Willing Workers on Organic Farms
R.R. 2 Nelson, British Columbia
V1L 5P5
phone: 250-354-4417
e-mail: wwoofcan@insidenet.com
Internet: www.island.net/~awpb/aware/id100.html
Contact person: John Vanden Heuvel

World Wildlife Fund Canada
245 Eglinton Ave. E., Suite 410
Toronto, Ontario
M4P 3B7
phone: 416-489-4567
fax: 416-489-3611
e-mail: panda@wwfcanada.org
Internet: www.wwfcanada.org

ENDNOTES

Unless noted below, the information in this book comes from primary research and interviews.

Introduction

1 There are now some six thousand reports in the scientific literature documenting the relationships between diet and disease. All the major health organizations with chronic diseases as their mission—heart and stroke associations, cancer societies, diabetes associations, etc.—acknowledge the significant role of diet.

2 U.S. Surgeon General, *Report on Nutrition and Health* Washington: U.S. Department of Health and Human Services, Public Health Service, 1988).

3 "Eating less meat can cut risk of cancer, study finds," *Toronto Star,* September 26, 1997.

4 In Canada, amongst incineration emissions, hospital incinerators are second only to municipal waste incinerators for dioxin emissions. This information is taken from a forthcoming report by Environment Canada and the Federal/Provincial Task Force on Dioxins and Furans for the Federal-Provincial Advisory Committee for the Canadian Environmental Protection Act.

5 In Ontario, the Toronto Food Policy Council estimates that less than one-tenth of 1 percent of the health care budget is spent on food and nutrition. (Toronto Food Policy Council, "If the health care system believed you are what you eat ... strategies for integrating our food and health care systems," *Toronto Food Policy Council Discussion Paper*, Series 3, 1997.)

6 Based on research conducted by the Fish and Wildlife Nutrition Project for Health Canada.

7 Many estimates of food waste have been produced, ranging from 20 to 50 percent. This figure is representative of those covering all aspects of the food system, from what's left in the field to what goes bad in your fridge.

8 Hunger kills 7 million children a year, according to the U.N. Children's Fund (reported in the Toronto Star, December 17, 1997). Documents prepared for the 1996 World Food Summit estimated that 840 million people around the world were malnourished (*Globe and Mail*, November 12, 1996). In Canada, 2.5 million people depend on food banks, while in the U.S. some 28 million people go hungry, according to University of British Columbia social work professor Graham Riches (cited in the *Guardian Weekly*, November 24, 1996).

9 The Union of Concerned Scientists in the U.S.A. puts out a quarterly update on new developments in genetic engineering. See their Web site: ***www.ucsusa.org***.

10 This estimate is based on work by John Hendrickson, "Energy use in the U.S. food system: a summary of existing research and analysis," Center for Integrated Agricultural Systems, University of Wisconsin—Madison, 1996.

Chapter 1: **Eat Organic**

1 Organic food cannot be 100 percent free of toxic substances because organic farmers cannot prevent airborne pollutants from landing on their crops. As well, since food is alive, there is always some risk of bacterial contamination. As we outline in later sections, organic production and processing reduces these risks relative to conventional practices, but it cannot eliminate them.

2 The Canadian Food Inspection Agency has primary responsibility for food safety. Its annual budget of less than $400 million amounts to spending less than a cent on every food dollar for food safety. The solution to our food safety problems is not necessarily to spend more public money (effectively a public subsidy to agribusiness), but rather to spend it better, something we address throughout this book.

3 For more on soil management and how it affects food value and taste, see D. Knorr and H. Vogtmann, "Quantity and quality determination of ecologically grown foods," in *Sustainable Food Systems*, ed. D. Knorr (Westport, CT: AVI Publishing, 1983), pp. 352–81; M.C. Linder, "Food quality and its determinants from field to table: growing food, its storage and preparation," in *Nutritional Biochemistry and Metabolism: With Clinical Applications*, ed. M.C. Linder (New York: Elsevier, 1985), pp. 239–54; Alberta Velimirov et al., "The influence of biologically and conventionally cultivated food on the fertility of rats," *Biological Agriculture and Horticulture* 8 (1992):325–37.

4 Many estimates of food waste have been produced, ranging from 20 to 50 percent. This figure is representative of those covering what is left to rot in the field only, due to the inefficiencies of harvesting machinery or difficulties with the harvest.

5 Paul Taylor, "Trans-fatty acids are stealthy health hazard," *Globe and Mail*, May 5, 1998; B. Holub, "Cholesterol-free foods: where's the trans?" *Canadian Medical Association Journal* 144 (1991):330; U. Erasmus, *Fats That Heal, Fats That Kill* (Vancouver: Alive Books, 1993); M. Enig et al., "Isomeric trans fatty acids in the U.S. diet," *Journal of the American College of Nutrition* 9 (1990):471–86; W.C. Willet et al., "Intake of trans fatty acids and risk of coronary heart disease among women," *The Lancet* 341 (1993):581–85.

6 Toronto Food Policy Council, "Cutting out the fat," TFPC *Discussion Paper*, Series 6 (1998).

7 Dan Jason, Greening the Garden: *A Guide to Sustainable Growing* (Gabriola Island, B.C.: New Society, 1991).

8 For more on how older varieties are commonly better adapted to organic farms, see R.J. MacRae et al., "Farm-scale agronomic and economic conversion to sustainable agriculture," *Advances in Agronomy* 43 (1990):155–98.

9 This estimate is based on the volume of processed foods containing canola, soy and corn oils and is put forward by the Campaign to Ban Genetically Engineered Foods.

10 Karen Graham, Food Irradiation: *A Canadian Folly* (Portage la Prairie, Manitoba: Paper Birch Publishing, 1992).

11 Tritsch and Epstein quotes are from Michael Colby, "Nuked meat madness," *Food and Water* (Spring 1998).

12 "Zapping beef with radiation approved in U.S.," *Toronto Star*, December 10, 1997.

13 Environmental Working Group, *Overexposed: Organophosphate Pesticides in Children's Food* (New York: Environmental Working Group, 1998).

14 R. Bertell, *No Immediate Danger: Prognosis for a Radioactive Future* (Toronto: Women's Press, 1985).

15 Theo Colborn et al., *Our Stolen Future: Are We Threatening Our Fertility, Intelligence, and Survival? A Scientific Detective Story* (New York: Dutton, 1996).

16 Taken from discussions with retailers and marketers in the organic food sector. For more on the size of the Canadian organic sector, see A. Macey, "Organic statistics," *Eco-Farm and Garden* (Fall 1998):33.

17 The OECD produces regular reports, titled *Agricultural Policies in OECD Countries: Monitoring and Evaluation*, that rate national subsidies to agriculture. The OECD system rates them by what are called "producer-equivalents." U.S., Canadian and European officials regularly argue about who subsidizes agriculture most heavily. OECD reports are available through their Web site: ***www.oecd.org***

18 *Globe and Mail*, July 22, 1998.

19 D. Pimentel and L. Levitan, "Pesticides: amounts applied and amounts reaching pests," *BioScience* 36 (1986):86–91.

20 One of the earliest to report this result was Robert Van den Bosch, who wrote about it in his book *The Pesticide Conspiracy* (Berkeley, CA: University of California Press, 1989).

21 *World Watch* (March–April 1996).

22 For more on Pirmin Kummer, see Rupert Jannasch, "Pesticide free spuds," *Sustainable Farming* 6, 3 (1996):1–2.

23 For more on the ecological problems of genetically engineered potatoes, see J. Rissler, "Biotechnology and pest control: quick fix vs. sustainable control," *Global Pesticide Campaigner* 1, 2 (1991):1, 6–8; J. Rissler and M. Mellon, *Perils Amidst the Promise: Ecological Risks of Transgenic Crops in a Global Market* (Washington: Union of Concerned Scientists, 1993); Nigel Hawkes, "Ladybirds harmed in transgenic crop test," *The Times* [London], October 22, 1997.

24 Joseph Cummings, an emeritus professor of biochemistry at the University of Western Ontario, is concerned that the B.t. gene might act the same way on the human gut as it does on an insect gut. People with allergies may be in grave danger, he suggests.

25 For more on the history of wheat, see Massimo Montanari, *The Culture of Food* (Oxford: Blackwell, 1994).

26 For more on the multinationals' role in the wheat trade, see two books on Cargill by Brewster Kneen: *Invisible Giant* (Halifax: Fernwood, 1995) and *Trading Up* (Toronto: NC Press, 1990).

27 Patricia Orwen, "Theory fingers cereal fungi as cause of killer diseases," *Toronto Star*, May 21, 1995.

28 A theory put forward by ecological researchers is that excess fertilization with nitrogen creates better growing conditions for weeds,

pests and diseases. Organic farmers have also made this observation, noticing that after conversion to organic methods they had fewer disease problems, which they associate with their more balanced crop fertility programs. For more on this, see M. Altieri, *Agroecology: The Theory and Practice of Alternative Agriculture* (Boulder, CO: Westview Press, 1987).

29 E.F. Schumacher, *Small is Beautiful: Economics as if People Mattered* (New York: Perennial, 1975).

30 Brewster Kneen, "Squeaky curds: a prime example of proximity in practice," *Ram's Horn* 95 (June 1992):3–4.

31 For more on the case against rBGH, see Brewster Kneen, "rBGH ... It's an addictive thing," *Ram's Horn* 119 (October 1994):1–3; Toronto Food Policy Council, "The licensing and use of bovine growth hormone," *Report to the Toronto Board of Health*, July 10, 1991; Toronto Food Policy Council, "The current status of the licensing of bovine growth hormone," *Report to the Toronto Board of Health*, February 21, 1994; Toronto Food Policy Council, "Recombinant bovine growth hormone: how its licensing contradicts existing policies, rules and regulations and sets Canadian agriculture on the wrong course," *Toronto Food Policy Council Discussion Paper*, August 1997.

32 *Rachel's Environment and Health Weekly* 593 (April 9, 1998).

33 Standing Committee on Agriculture and Agri-Food, *Minutes of Proceedings and Evidence*, 35th Parliament, 1st Session, 3:56 (March 7, 1994):1830–35, respecting Consideration of Second Report on the Steering Committee, Pursuant to Standing Order 108(2), consideration of issues relating to the bovine somatotropin hormone (BST).

34 For more on criticisms levelled by Health Canada scientists at their own managers, see Laura Eggertson, "Drug-approval process criticized: some Health Canada managers passed products despite reviewers' concerns, insiders say," *Globe and Mail*, May 28, 1997; "Bureaucrats withholding research data, five Health Canada drug scientists day," *Ottawa Citizen*, July 4, 1997. The scientists' case was deemed without merit from an employee relations standpoint by a tribunal hearing, but the presiding official acknowledged that he could not comment on the scientific merits of the scientists' concerns.

35 Data from the Center for Disease Control, reported in *Nutrition Week*, December 11, 1998.

36 For more on the health problems associated with conventional beef rearing and slaughtering, see Toronto Department of Public Health, "Is food the next public health challenge?" (Toronto: City Clerk's Department, City of Toronto, 1997); Richard Rhodes, *Deadly Feasts: Tracking the Secrets of a Terrifying New Plague* (London: Simon and Shuster, 1997).

37 For more on pasturing poultry, see Peter Bane, "Animal polyculture: the farm of many faces," *Sustainable Farming* (Fall 1995):12–16.

38 Jennifer Scott, "Eating my way across Nova Scotia," *Sustainable Times* (December, 1996).

39 For more on the problems of antibiotic use in agriculture and how they compromise health, see Rod MacRae and Charles Gardner, "What does the research evidence say about ... how antibiotic use in animal production creates antibiotic-resistant bacteria and compromises medical treatment in humans?" *Sustainable Farming* (Winter 1997):4–5; W.D. Black, "The use of antimicrobial drugs in agriculture," *Canadian Journal of Pharmacology* 62 (1984):1044–48; S.D. Holmberg et al., "Animal-to-man transmission of antimicrobial-resistant salmonella: investigations of U.S. outbreaks, 1971–1983," *Science* 225 (1984):833–35; Cornelius Poppe et al., "Drug resistance and biochemical characteristics of salmonella from turkeys," *Canadian Journal of Veterinary Research* 59 (1995):241–48.

40 G.G. Khachatourians, "Agricultural use of antibiotics and the evolution and transfer of antibiotic-resistant bacteria," *Canadian Medical Association Journal* 159 (1998): 1129–36.

41 Andrew Nikiforuk, "The threat of farmyard pharmaceuticals," *Globe and Mail*, March 29, 1997.

42 Rogers' books include *Nature and the Crisis of Modernity*, (Montreal: Black Rose, 1994), *The Oceans Are Emptying: Fish Wars and Sustainability*, (Montreal: Black Rose, 1995) and *Solving History: The Challenge of Environmental Activism*, (Montreal: Black Rose, 1998).

43 William Warner, "The fish killers," in *How Deep is the Ocean? Historical Essays on Canada's Atlantic Fishery*, ed. J. Candow and C. Corbin (Sydney, Nova Scotia: UCCB Press, 1997).

44 Mark Kurlansky, *Cod: A Biography of the Fish That Changed the World* (Toronto: Knopf Canada, 1997).

45 Brian McAndrew, "Fishing for solutions to a growing world crisis," *Toronto Star*, June 14, 1998.

46 Peter Weber, *Net Loss: Fish Jobs and the Marine Environment*, (Washington: World Watch Institute, 1996).

47 Sierra Legal Defense Fund et al., *Containing Disaster: Global Lessons on Salmon Aquaculture* (Vancouver: David Suzuki Foundation, 1997).

48 For more on problems with fish farming, see Anne Platt McGinn, "Blue revolution: the promises and pitfalls of fish farming," *World Watch Magazine* (March/April 1998).

49 David Schardt and Stephen Schmidt, "Seafood on the skids," *Nutrition Action* (June 1998).

50 Numerous studies by the International Joint Commission have confirmed this. For an overview on DDT, see World Wildlife Fund, *Resolving the DDT Dilemma: Protecting Biodiversity and Human Health* (Toronto: WWF-Canada, 1998).

51 According to the U.S.A. Biotechnology Industry Association, about 60 million acres of land—approximately 20 percent of the U.S. acreage—is growing genetically engineered crops. As well, recombinant Bovine Growth Hormone has been on the market in the United States since 1994.

52 Committee on Scientific and Regulatory Issues Underlying Pesticide Use Patterns and Agricultural Innovation, Board on Agriculture, National Academy of Sciences, 1989.

Chapter 2: Eat Smarter

1 R. Douthwaite, *The Growth Illusion: How Economic Growth Has Enriched the Few, Impoverished the Many and Endangered the Planet* (Dublin: Lilliput Press, 1993).

2 Alvin Toffler, *Future Shock* (New York: Mass Market Paperbacks, 1991).

3 *Montreal Gazette*, March 6, 1996.

4 For more on supermarket manipulation, see J. MacClancy, *Consuming Culture: Why You Eat What You Eat* (New York: Henry Holt, 1992); Editors of Rodale Press, *Cut Your Spending in Half Without Settling for Less* (Emmaus, PA: Rodale Press, 1995); P. White, *The Supermarket Tour* (Toronto: Ontario Public Interest Research Group, 1990).

5 *Atlantic Business Magazine* 1 Winter (1998).

6 For more on Warren Buffett, see R. Hagstrom et al., *The Warren Buffett Way: Investment Strategies of the World's Greatest Investor* (New York: John Wiley, 1995).

7 AP Wire Service, September 4, 1996, reporting on an article released that day in the *New England Journal of Medicine*.

8 For more on Alexis Soyer and his recipes, see Helen Morris, *Portrait of a Chef: The Life of Alexis Soyer* (Oxford: Oxford University Press, 1980).

9 *Atlantic Monthly* (September, 1998).

10 Reported in the *Toronto Star* and *Toronto Sun*, February 4, 1998.

11 *Globe and Mail*, October 23 and November 1, 1996.

12 For more on the diet industry in the United States, see Laura Fraser, *Losing It: America's Obsession with Weight and the Industry That Feeds on It* (New York: E.P. Dutton, 1997).

13 *Globe and Mail*, January 8, 1997.

14 W. *Price, Nutrition and Physical Degeneration* (La Mesa, CA: Price-Pottenger Nutrition Foundation, 1945). Price's work has been updated by R.F. Schmid, *Traditional Foods Are Your Best Medicine* (New York: Ballantine, 1987).

15 Barbara Stitt, *Food and Behaviour: A Natural Connection* (Manitowoc, WI: Natural Press, 1997).

16 For more on zinc, see C. Pfeiffer, *Zinc and Other Micro Nutrients* (New Canaan, CT: Pivot, 1978).

17 For more on what pay we really take home when two people in a household are working, see Andy Dappen, *Shattering the Two-Income Myth: Daily Secrets for Living Well on One Income* (Mountlake Terrace, WA: Brier Books, 1997).

18 Jeremy MacClancy, *Consuming Culture: Why You Eat What You Eat* (New York: Henry Holt, 1992).

19 *Guardian Weekly*, September 28, 1997.

20 Thorstein Veblen, *Theory of the Leisure Class* (New York: Penguin Classics, 1994).

21 Lorraine Johnson, *The Ontario Naturalized Garden: The Complete Guide to Using Native Plants* (Vancouver: Whitecap Books, 1995).

22 John Jeavons, *How to Grow More Vegetables Than You Ever Thought Possible on Less Land Than You Can Imagine* (Berkeley, CA: Ten Speed Press, 1995).

23 Mel Bartholomew, *Square Foot Gardening* (Emmaus, PA: Rodale Press, 1981).

24 Duane Newcomb, *Small Space, Big Harvest* (Rockland, CA: Prima Publishing, 1993).

25 Eliot Coleman, *The Four Season Harvest* (White River Junction, VT: Chelsea Green, 1992).

26 Sue Fisher, *Gardener's World: Making the Most of Climbing Plants* (Houston: Parkwest Publications, 1996).

27 For more on energy-efficient landscaping, see A.S. Moffat and M. Schiler, *Energy-Efficient and Environmental Landscaping* (South Newfane, VT: Appropriate Solutions Press, 1994).

28 S. Meyerowitz, *Sprout It!* (Great Barrington, MA: The Sprout House, 1983); Jane Brody, *Jane Brody's Good Foodbook* (New York: Norton, 1985); Christina Bjork and Lena Anderson, *Linnea's Windowsill Garden* (Stockholm: R&S Books, 1978).

29 For more on weeds as food, see A. Szczawinski and N. Turner, *Edible Garden Weeds of Canada* (Markham, Ontario: Fitzhenry and Whiteside, 1988); B.C. Harris, *Eat the Weeds* (Barre, MA: 1969); E. Gibbons, *Stalking the Wild Asparagus* (New York: D. McKay Co., 1962); N. Turner and A. Szczawinski, *Edible Wild Fruit and Nuts of Canada* (Markham, Ontario: Fitzhenry and Whiteside, 1988); D. Jason, *Greening the Garden: A Guide to Sustainable Growing* (Gabriola Island, B.C.: New Society, 1991).

30 *Montreal Gazette*, October 8, 1995.

31 Richard Douthwaite, *Short Circuit: Strengthening Local Economics for Security in an Unstable World* (Dublin: Lilliput Press, 1996).

32 Tapscott's books, published by McGraw-Hill, include *The Digital Economy* (1995), *Opening Digital Markets* (1997), *Growing Up Digital* (1997) and *Blueprint to the Digital Economy* (1998).

33 Michael Hough, *Cities and Natural Process* (London: Routledge, 1995).

34 For an overview of community gardening around the world, see *Productive Open Space Management: Proceedings of an International Conference* (Pretoria, South Africa: Technikon Pretoria and the International Development Research Centre, 1998). For a review of community gardening in Canadian cities, see a chapter in this volume by Sean Cosgrove, "Community gardening in major Canadian cities: Toronto, Montreal and Vancouver compared."

35 *Montreal Gazette*, August 20, 1998.

36 *Toronto Star*, May 14, 1998.

37 *Globe and Mail*, February 9, 1998.

38 *Globe and Mail*, March 26, 1998; *Toronto Star*, March 26 and September 17, 1998.

39 *Canadian HR Reporter*, December 16, 1996.

40 See the special issue on zinc of the *American Journal of Clinical Nutrition* (August 1998).

41 AP Wire Service report on an American National Institutes of Health study, released April 1, 1997.

42 Kilmer McCully, *The Homocysteine Revolution* (New Canaan, CT: Keats Publishing, 1997).

43 Rosabeth Moss Kanter, *When Giants Learn to Dance: Mastering the Challenges of Strategy, Management and Careers in the 1990s* (New York: Simon and Shuster, 1989).

44 *Globe and Mail*, August 25, 1998.

45 *Entrepreneur* (August 1998).

46 *Globe and Mail*, August 1, 1995; *Canadian Press*, August 21, 1995.

47 *Toronto Star*, July 25, 1998.

48 *Canadian Dimension* (January/February 1998).

49 *Washington Post*, October 13, 1996.

50 Julie Suzanne Pollock, "Garlic's peculiar virtues," *In the Hills* (Autumn 1997); Rose Elliot and C. De Paoli, *Kitchen Pharmacy* (New York: Marlowe and Company, 1995); Bill Penny, "Garlic, hence Dracula," *Outreach Connection* (March 5, 1997).

51 "Two garlic heads better than one," *Toronto Star*, March 5, 1997; "Scientist studies garlic's anti-cancer potential," CP Wire Service, January 24, 1997; E. Ernst, "Can allium vegetables prevent cancer?" *Phytomedicine* 4, 1 (1997):79–83; K.R. Melvin and M.A. Chappell, "Cholesterol-lowering effects of garlic powder tablets: a randomized clinical trial," *Lifestyle and Wellness Magazine* (1996).

52 Diane Calabrese, "Tofu: the miracle bean," *Natural Life* 53 (January/February 1997).

53 Agnet, "Wake Forest study shows soy containing a key ingredient is what lowers cholesterol," March 20, 1998 (from a press release); "Soy

phytoestrogens reduce carotid atherosclerosis as much as premarin," March 20, 1998 (from a press release).

54 M. Messina et al. "Soy intake and cancer risk: a review of the in vitro and vivo data," *Nutrition and Cancer* 21 (1994):113–31; A. Cassidy et al., "Biological effects of a diet of soy protein rich in isoflavones on the menstrual cycle of pre-menopausal women," *American Journal of Clinical Nutrition* 60 (1994):333–40; Judith Eaton, "A soy-food a day," *Delicious* (October 1996); "The prostate promise: going for the cancer-preventing diet," *Prevention* (July 1996).

55 R. Elliot and C. de Paoli, *Kitchen Pharmacy* (New York: Marlowe and Company, 1995); Bern Jensen, *Foods That Heal* (Garden City, NY: Avery Publishing, 1993); Jane Brody, *The Good Food Book* (New York: Norton, 1985); Jean Carper, *Food, Your Miracle Medicine* (New York: HarperCollins, 1993); Richard Passwater, *Super Nutrition for Healthy Hearts* (New York: Jove Publications, 1977); Richard Passwater, *The New SuperNutrition* (New York: Pocket Books, 1991); Richard Kunin, *MegaNutrition* (New York: McGraw-Hill, 1981); Kilmer McCully, *The Homocysteine Revolution* (New Canaan, CT: Keats Publishing, 1997); R. Pyatt, *Magic Meals* (West Nyack, NY: Parker Publishing, 1993).

56 W.E. Shute, *Vitamin E Book* (New Canaan, CT: Keats Publishing, 1975).

57 CSPI press release, "Heinz is cheating Canada's babies," September 4, 1996.

58 David Pimentel et al., "Pesticides, insects in foods, and cosmetic standards," *BioScience* 27 (1997):178–85; Gail Feenstra, "Who chooses your food?: a study of the effects of cosmetic standards on the quality of produce" (Los Angeles: California Public Interest Research Group, 1988).

59 Jay Kordich, *The Juiceman's Power of Juicing* (New York: Warner Books, 1993).

60 Gabrielle Palmer is also the author of *The Politics of Breastfeeding*, 2nd edition (London: Pandora, 1993).

61 For more on the emotional security of breast-feeding, see S. Suib Cohen, *The Magic of Touch: Revolutionary Ways to Use Your Most Important Sense* (New York: Clarkson Potter, 1987).

62 *Edmonton Journal*, July 24, 1997.

63 Kelly Oliver, "Nourishing the speaking subject: a psychoanalytic approach to abominable food and women," in *Cooking, Eating, Thinking: Transformative Philosophies of Food*, ed. Deane Curtin and Lisa Heldke (Bloomington: Indiana University Press, 1992), pp. 68–84.

64 *Daedalus* (Spring 1977).

65 For more on breast-feeding workplaces, see Ontario Public Health Association, *Creating a Breastfeeding Friendly Workplace* (Toronto: OPHA, 1996).

Chapter 3: Power Shop

1 For more on corporate concentration in the Canadian food system, see R.J. MacRae et al., "Strategies to overcome barriers to the development of sustainable agriculture in Canada: the role of agribusiness," *Journal of Agricultural and Environmental Ethics* 6 (1993):21–53.

2 Presentation to the City of Toronto Environmental Task Force, September 28, 1998.

3 *Globe and Mail*, August 13, 1998.

4 *Canadian Business*, February 27, 1998.

5 *Globe and Mail*, June 2, 1997, April 29, August 14 and August 15, 1998; *Report on Business Magazine* (July 1998); *Toronto Star*, July 5, 1998.

6 *Globe and Mail*, June 13 and September 29, 1998; *Toronto Star*, May 27, June 13, and June 18, 1998.

7 For more on the WWF apple juice project in the Beaver Valley, see Michael Valpy, "The greening of the apple orchard," *Globe and Mail*, April 11, 1998; B. McAndrew, "Low-pesticide forms yield juicier profits," *Toronto Star*, January 19, 1998.

8 Smithsonian Migratory Bird Center Web site (*www.audubon.org/bird/cafe.html*); John Ryan and A. Durning, *Stuff: The Secret Lives of Everyday Things* (Seattle: Northwest Environment Watch, 1997); *Sustainable Times* (Spring 1997); Michelle Beveridge, "Rainforest Coffee Looks for Home in Canada," Synergy (Spring 1998):26–27; *Full of Beans* [newsletter of Just Us] (Summer 1998).

9 *Toronto Star*, September 5, 1998.

10 *Toronto Star*, May 28 and July 26, 1998; *Globe and Mail*, January 15, 1998.

11 *Toronto Star*, October 27, 1997, May 10, May 11 and September 13, 1998.

12 *Toronto Star*, October 27, 1997, May 10, May 11 and September 13, 1998.

13 *Whole Earth Review* (Spring 1989).

14 *Elm Street* (December 1997).

15 *Edmonton Journal* (July 16, 1997); *Globe and Mail*, September 22, 1997, April 18 and August 8, 1998.

16 *Montreal Gazette*, August 19, 1998.

17 *Financial Post*, January 22, 1992.

18 *Montreal Gazette*, August 25, 1998.

19 *Globe and Mail*, September 15, 1998.

20 *Catholic New Times*, December 1, 1996.

21 For regular updates on biotechnology from a pro-industry perspective, subscribe to Agnet, a University of Guelph listserve on agricultural issues, organized by Dr. Doug Powell, Department of Food Science (dpowell@uoguelph.ca).

22 Reuters, "Gene crop segregation can work—UK's Iceland," April 30, 1998; Nadia Hall, "Stores chief warns of genetic food dangers," *PA News*, March 18, 1998.

23 Ian Elliott, "Genetically modified beans held back from market," *Feedstuffs*, April 20, 1998.

24 Frances Anderson, "Edible bean industry plans to head off biotech backlash," *Ontario Farmer*, October 7, 1997.

25 *Globe and Mail*, January 1, 1998.

26 *Rachel's Environment and Health Weekly*, June 5, 1997.

27 Richard Wolfson, "Shop to avoid biotech foods or Who wants to be a guinea pig?" *Alive* (March, 1997).

28 C. Kneen et al., *A baseline for food policy in British Columbia* (Vancouver: FarmFolk/CityFolk, 1997).

29 B. Kneen, "Feeding the family, trading the leftovers," *Ram's Horn*, 91 (1992):1–4.

30 Lynn Jones and Peggy Patterson, presentation on Local Food Self-reliance, The Third Sudbury Conference on Health, Economy and Environment, 1993.

31 Canadian Auto Workers, *Bounty of Essex County Food Sector Report* (Windsor, Ontario: CAW, 1995).

32 Des Kennedy, "Helping horticulture on a wing and a prayer," *Globe and Mail*, July 18, 1998.

33 Jane Gadd, "Jobs that are driving people sane," *Globe and Mail*, December 31, 1997; Jennifer Bain, "Cooking up new skills," *Toronto Star*, December 28, 1997.

34 For more information, All-A-Board can be reached at (416) 535-2405.

35 *The Official Vermont Maple Cookbook* presents over sixty recipes featuring tree sugar: breads, muffins, cakes, bean casseroles, candied vegetables and shakes. *Simply Maple!* by the Ontario Maple Syrup Producers Association does the same for tarts, creams, glazes, fudges and pies.

36 J. Goldstein, "Sustainable ideas build commercial success," *In Business* (January/February 1997); *Bioinnovations: Newsletter of the Canadian Agricultural New Uses Council* (January 1997).

37 *Toronto Star*, January 8, 1998; Eye, February 10, 1994; Trisse Loxley, "Waiting to Exhale," *Images* (Summer 1996), 61–62; Valerie Worwood, *The Fragrant Pharmacy* (Toronto: Bantam, 1990).

38 For dates on the invention of fire, see J. Livingstone, *Rogue Primate* (Toronto: Key Porter, 1994); *Discover* (June 1997); *NOW*, March 5–11, 1992.

39 *Bioinnovations* (January and March, 1997); *Globe and Mail*, November 17, 1997; *Canadian Press*, November 17, 1997; *Report on Business Magazine* (August 1996); *Marketing*, October 7, 1996; I. Ahmed and D. Morris, *Alcohol Fuels from Whey* (Washington: Institute for Local Self-Reliance, 1991); see also Morris's *The Carbohydrate Economy*, 1992.

40 *Toronto Star*, October 12, 1996.

41 Don Grayton, *The Wheatgrass Mechanism* (Saskatoon: Fifth House, 1990); Janet Abramovitz, *Taking a Stand: Cultivating a New Relationship with the World's Forests*, (Washington: World Watch Institute, 1998); *Bioinnovations* (March 1997).

42 For home-made skin-care recipes, see "Skin So Smooth," *Delicious* (January 1997); J.P. Leblanc, "Summer Skin," *Alive* 164:13–14; Robert Gosselin, *Clinical Toxicology of Commercial Products*, 5th edition. (Baltimore: Williams and Williams, 1984).

43 *Commercial Hemp: The Trade Journal of Our Growing Industry* (Winter 1997); *Toronto Star*, August 6, 1995, March 1, September 2 and October 23, 1997; *Globe and Mail*, October 19, 1996 and June 11, 1998; E. Rosenthal, ed., *Hemp Today* (San Francisco: Quick Americas Archives, 1994).

Chapter 4: Avoid Gassy Foods

1 *Guardian* [London], November 3, 1998.

2 It's common to attribute 15 to 25 percent of global warming emissions to agriculture. The standard breakdown of agriculture emissions looks like this: farming 16 percent, processing 27 percent, wholesale and retail, 10 percent, transportation 10 percent, restaurants 14 percent, home preparation 23 percent. This approach leaves out such obvious items as garbage and human waste, and understates transportation by excluding infrastructure construction. So we feel justified in attributing 25 percent to the food system. Background information and statistics on global warming emissions come from United Nations Environment Program (UNEP), *Report of Working Group 1 to the Intergovernmental Panel on Climate Change* (Nairobi, Kenya, 1996); J. Leggett, ed., *Global Warming: The Greenpeace Report* (Oxford: Oxford University Press, 1990); John Hendrickson, "Energy use in the U.S. food system: a summary of existing research and analysis" (paper presented at the annual meeting of the Agriculture, Food, and Human Values Society, Madison, WI, 1996); Danny Harvey, "Climate change," in *State of the Environment Report for Canada*, ed. P. Bird and D. Rappaport (Ottawa: Canadian Government Publishing Centre, 1991).

3 John Hendrickson, "Energy use in the U.S. food system: a summary of existing research and analysis" (paper presented at the annual meeting of the Agriculture, Food, and Human Values Society, Madison, WI, 1996.

4 Jack Mintz et al., *Report of the Technical Committee on Business Taxation* (Ottawa: Supply and Services, 1998); Jack Mintz, *Taxation of Virgin and Recycled Materials* (Ottawa: Canadian Council of Ministers of the Environment, 1994).

5 Figures and estimates on truck transport and subsidies come from J. Holtzclaw, "America's autos and trucks on welfare: a summary of subsidies," *Mobilizing the Region*, February 3, 1995; Canadians for Responsible and Safe Highways, *Impact on the Highway Infrastructure of Existing and Alternative Vehicle Configurations* (October 1997;) IBI Group, Boon, Jones and Associates, *Full Cost Transportation and Cost-Based Pricing Strategies* (Toronto: IBI Group); Transport 2000, *Information Comparing Auto and Truck Effects*; C. Caccia, M.P., "Climate Change, CO_2 and Subsidies," (1996); *Government of Ontario Public Accounts*. The cost of truck subsidies and cross-subsidies—when road construction and repair, traffic congestion and accidents are included—is at least $3 billion a year.

6 *Economist*, December 13, 1997.

7 John Ryan and A. Durning, Stuff: *The Story of Six Everyday Objects* (Seattle, WA: Northwest Environment Watch, 1997).

8 *Globe and Mail*, June 18, 1998.

9 Brewster Kneen, "Feed the family, trade the leftovers," *Ram's Horn* 91 (1992):1–4.

10 From a report by the World Watch Institute and the world's largest reinsurer company, covered in the *Toronto Star*, November 28, 1998.

11 John Girt, "Common ground: recommendations for policy reform to integrate wildlife habitat, environmental and agricultural objectives on the farm" (Ottawa: Wildlife Habitat Canada, 1990).

12 *Vegetarian Times* (June 1998).

13 *Natural Health* (May/June, 1998).

14 For more on the key to greater "aliveness" and vitality, see S. and L. Kenton, *The New Raw Energy* (London: Vermilion, 1994).

15 For more on vitamin losses, see S. and L. Kenton, *The New Raw Energy* (London: Vermilion, 1994).

16 Claude Lévi-Strauss, *The Raw and the Cooked* (Chicago: University of Chicago Press, 1983).

17 For more on efficient appliances, see David Goldbeck, *The Smart Kitchen* (Woodstock, NY: Ceres Press, 1989).

18 For more on electronic smog, see Mark Pinsky, *The EMF Book: What You Should Know about Electromagnetic Radiation and Your Health* (New York: Time Warner, 1995).

19 Lorna Sass, *Great Vegetarian Cooking Under Pressures* (New York: Hearst Books, 1992).

20 For more on minimizing waste in your kitchen, see Teri Degler and Pollution Probe, *The Kitchen Handbook: An Environmental Guide* (Toronto: McClelland and Stewart, 1992); Jennifer Bain, "A cook's three Rs," *Toronto Star*, June 10, 1998.

21 Landfill and recycling costs picked up by municipalities are another costly gift to fuel-intensive food producers. Worldwide, food packaging is a $380-billion industry (R. Barnet and J. Cavanaugh, *Global Dreams*, New York: Simon and Schuster, 1994) that turns valuable resources and fuel into containers used once. If we assume, conservatively, that food packaging accounts for 10 percent of what's landfilled and 20 percent of what's recycled, we are talking about a yearly Canadian bill for landfilling 1.8 million tonnes of packaging of about $86 per tonne, and yearly losses on recycling 1,240,000 tonnes of recyclable glass, plastic and metal in the range of $265 per tonne. That comes to about $500 million a year, money that could go to developing the reuse infrastructure for local producers as a one-time expenditure. For more on this, see Greg Jenish, *Methane, Climate Change and Waste Management: A Review of Efforts by Toronto, Ontario and Canada to Reduce Waste Related to Emissions of Methane* (Toronto: Canadian Institute for Environmental Law and Policy, 1997).

22 Reuters Wire Service, April 28, 1994; CP Wire Service, March 12, 1993.

23 For more on compost effects on contaminated material, see issues of *Biocycle*, which reports regularly on this issue.

24 M. Cohen et al., "A quantitative estimation of the entry of dioxins, furans and HCB into the Great Lakes from air-borne and water-borne sources" (Flushing, NY: City University of New York, Center for the Biology of Natural Systems, 1995); M. Cohen et al., "Zeroing out dioxin in the Great Lakes: within our reach" (Flushing, NY: City University of New York, Center for the Biology of Natural Systems, 1996).

25 For more on the nutrient value of human manure, see J.C. Jenkins, *The Humanure Handbook* (White River Junction, VT: Chelsea Green, 1996).

26 Joel Bleifus, "Nightmare soil," *In These Times*, September 16, 1995; J. Chisholm, "Precaution is needed for sewage sludge applications to agricultural land" (Toronto: CUPE Local 79, 1998).

27 American Council for an Energy Efficient *Economy, Energy Efficiency and Job Creation* (Washington: American Council for an Energy Efficient Economy, 1992).

28 Vaclav Smil, *General Energetics: Energy in the Biosphere and Civilization* (New York: John Wiley, 1991).

29 Danny Harvey, "Climate change," In *State of the Environment Report for Canada*, ed. P. Bird and D. Rappaport (Ottawa: Canadian Government Publishing Centre, 1991).

30 M. Harris, *Cannibals and Kings* (New York: Random House, 1991).

31 Roger Samson, "Perennial vegetables," *Sustainable Farming* (Fall, 1996).

32 Roger Samson, of REAP-Canada in Montreal, is one of Canada's leading researchers on switchgrass.

33 For more on the technical dimensions of straw bale construction, see A.S. Steen et al., *The Straw Bale House* (White River Junction, VT: Chelsea Green, 1994); National Research Council of Canada studies summarized in *Ontario Eco-Architecture* (April 1996); *In Business* (January/February 1997); *Environmental Building News* (January/February 1996); U.S. Department of Energy, *House of Straw: Straw Bale Construction Comes of Age* (Washington: U.S. Department of Energy); Tom Ponessa, ed. *The Straw Bale Builder* (Tom Ponessa, 259 Park Home Ave., North York, ON, M2R 1A1).

34 Sim Van der Ryn and Stuart Cowan, *Ecological Design* (Washington: Island Press, 1995).

Conclusion: Set the Table for the Future

1 Reuters Wire Service, September 24, 1994.

2 Richard Wilkinson, *Unhealthy Societies and the Afflictions of Inequality* (London: Routledge, 1997).

3 For more on how food can be used to transform health care, including the math on investing in maternal nutrition before birth to avoid low-birth-weight infants, see Toronto Food Policy Council, "If the health care system believed you are what you eat ... strategies to integrate our food and health care systems," *Toronto Food Policy Council Discussion Paper*, Series 3, 1997.

4 Most nations were quite self-reliant in food production until the 1960s. Robert Goodland, "Environmental sustainability in agriculture: diet matters," *Ecological Economics* 23 (1997):189–200.

5 J.W. Warnock, "Canadian grain and the industrial food system" (paper presented at the Learned Societies Conference, Guelph, Ontario, June 1984).

6 Agriculture and Agrifood Canada.

7 Canadian Organic Producers Marketing Cooperative, "Testimony to the Royal Commission on the Economic Union and Development Prospects for Canada" (Saskatoon: Canadian Organic Producers Marketing Cooperative, 1984); D. Waterer, "Production of vegetable crops in Saskatchewan" (summary of presentation to the CSA "Quick Start" Workshop, Fort Qu'Appelle, Saskatchewan, November 1993).

8 Ministry of Agriculture, "On Norwegian nutrition and food policy," *Report #32 to the Storting*, 1975; K. Ringen, "The Norwegian food and nutritional policy," *American Journal of Public Health* 67 (1977):550–51; N. Milio, "An analysis of the implementation of Norwegian nutrition policy, 1981–87," report prepared for the World Health Organization 1990 Conference on Food and Nutrition Policy (Chapel Hill: University of North Carolina, 1988); *New Farmer and Grower* 46 (Spring 1995):8.

INDEX

ABOUT THE AUTHORS

Wayne Roberts chairs the Coalition for A Green Economic Recovery and teaches Green Entrepreneurship in the graduate program of York University's Faculty of Environmental Studies. He has a Ph.D. in Canadian social and economic history, and has written six books, including the bestselling *Get A Life! How to Make a Good Buck, Dance Around the Dinosaurs, and Save the World While You're At It*. He is a member of Toronto's Environmental Task Force, and speaks regularly about green economics.

Rod MacRae coordinates Toronto's Food Policy Council, and consults regularly with environmental organizations, including the World Wildlife Fund and Ecological Agriculture Projects of McGill University. He has a Ph.D. in sustainable food and agriculture policy, and speaks to groups across the country about how to improve the food system.

Lori Stahlbrand is a former broadcaster with CBC Radio who has hosted major news and current affairs shows across the country and produced several documentaries on environmental issues. She holds a Masters degree from York University's Faculty of Environmental Studies where she teaches part-time in the graduate programme. She is a consultant to public health, environment and community groups on media and related issues.